TEXTBOOK OF OPERATIONAL MANAGEMENT

TEXTBOOK OF OPERATIONAL MANAGEMENT

By
Shashi Kant Yadav

DISCOVERY PUBLISHING HOUSE PVT. LTD.
NEW DELHI-110 002

Published by:
Tilak Wasan

DISCOVERY PUBLISHING HOUSE PVT. LTD.
4831/24, Ansari Road, Prahlad Street
Darya Ganj, New Delhi-110002 (India)
Phone: +91-11-23279245, 43764432
Fax: +91-11-23253475
E-mail: parul.wasan@gmail.com
info@discoverypublishinggroup.com
discoverypublishinghouse@gmail.com
web: www.discoverypublishinggroup.com

***First Edition:* 2011**
ISBN: 978-81-8356-845-6

Textbook of Operational Management

Printed at:
Mehra Offset Press
Delhi

Preface

This book on operational management has been specially written to meet the requirements of the M.Sc., M.Com., and M.B.A., students for all Indian Universities.

The subject matter has been discussed in such a simple way that the students will find no difficulty to understand it. The proof of various theorems and examples has been given with minute details. Each chapter of this book contain complete theory and fairly large number of solved examples, sufficient problems have also been selected from various universities examination paper.

In the preparation of this book large number of books and research papers have been consulted so no authenticity unclaimed.

The author has express gratitude to Mr. Tilak Wasan and staff of M/s Discovery Publishing House Pvt. Ltd., for their whole hearted cooperation in the publications of this book.

The author tried hard to accurate and up-to-date in statement and realises the impressibility of completely avoiding errors. Therefore the author will greatly appropriate having his authentic called to any questionable statement.

Author

Contents

1

Some Concept of Simplex Method

INTRODUCTION

This chapter contains a rigorous discussion on the mathematical method called the *simplex method* developed by G.B. Dantzig in 1947 for solving linear programming problems. The simplex method is an *iterative procedure* and refers to the idea of moving from one extreme (corner) point to another of the solution space or feasible region (convex polyhedron) that is formed by the constraints and non-negativity conditions of the linear programming problem. Since the number of extreme points (corners or vertices) of a solution space is finite, the method leads to the optimal extreme point (optimal solution) in a finite number of steps or indicates that there exist an unbounded solution.

In what quantities and by which press or processes. In this connection. Allured Marshal point out that the businessman always studies his production function and his input price, then substitutes one point for another till has costs become minimum possible. Since each assignment problem can be formulated as a 0 or 1 integer linear programming problem, such a problem can also be solved by the simplex method. As can be seen in the general mathematical formulation of the assignment problem, there are n × n decision variables and n + n or In equalities. In particular, for a problem involving 5 workers/jobs, there will be 25 decision variables and 10 equalities. It is, again, difficult to solve manually. L.V. Kentrovich, was the first who was interested in the application of mathematical models to solve such business problems. It was observed in the graphical approach to the solution of L.P.P. that in a given situation the set of constraints determines the feasible region and objective function gives the optimal point, the one that minimizes or maximizes, as the case may be. But the graphical method suffers from a great limitation that it can handle problems involving only two decision variables

Formulated model by Canter roved is termed as Linear Programming" which is a decision-making technique uncle given constraints on the assumption that the relation ships amongst the variables representing phenomenon happen to be linear Because of its relative simplicity. Linear Programming was the first area of constrained optimization which attract mathematicians. The *"Simplex Method"* was the first numerical technique developed to solve linear programming problems. It was developed by George B. Dentition in the late summer of 1947. With the help of econometrics Leonid Heroics and T.C. Koopmans, Dantzin finally developed the algorithm which was mistakenly rejected earlier as being very inefficient. The importance of simplex method was much more recognized when in 1947 J. Don Neumann developed the concept of duality. This concept opened many research areas in linear programming and further enhanced its usefulness and problem-solving ability.

During 1950's, contributions have been made by E.M.L. Belle, C.E. Lemke, W. Orchard-Hays, P. Wolfe and others. Together with Dantzing, Philip Wolfe proposed in 1959 a decomposition algorithm, where by large-scale linear programming models can be decomposed into smaller parts that can be optimized independently. A revolutionary break through in solving complex linear programming problems has recently been achieved by Narender Karmarker, an Indian mathematician. His suppositional *Karmarkar algorithm* has stunned the computer and O.R. communities of the globe. This algorithm is far more effective and efficient than the simplex method. It can handle 10^{10} lakh variables at a time, whereas the simplex method could handle only up to 10^{1000} variables, and that too hemonsuming more computer time. Karmarkar's method enables computers to track, in a fraction of time, a greater combinational of tasks than ever before.

BASIC SOLUTION VARIALBLES (B.S.)

Consider a system A x = b of m equations in n unknowns (n > m) and r (A) = r (Ab) = m *i.e.,* none of the equations is redundant.

A solution obtained by setting any (n – m) variables to zero is called a basic solution, provided the determinant of the coefficient of the remaining m variables is not zero. Such m variables (any of them may be zero) are called basic variables and remaining (n – m) zero valued variables are called non-basic variables.

Thus for a solution to be basic, at least n – m variables must be zero. Here we note that the matrix formed by the coefficients of the m basic variables, or say formed by the vectors associated to the basic variables is non-singular as its determinant does not vanish. Hence the vectors associated to the basic variables are L.I.

Thus *a solution in which the vectors associated to m variables are L.I. and remaining n – m variables are zero is called a basic solution.*

Hence a basic solution can be constructed by selecting the m L. I. vectors out of n and setting the variables associated to the remaining (n – m) columns to zero. If B is the matrix of m L.I. vectors of A and x_B is the vector of the corresponding variables (basic variables), then the basic solution is given by

$$Bx_B = b$$

or

$$x_B = B^{-1}b.$$

The number of basic solutions thus obtained will be at the most $^nC_m = \frac{n!}{m!(n-m)!}$ since m vectors out of n can be selected in ^nC_m ways. Note that a B. S. corresponds to some basis. Basic solution are of two types: Non-degenerate basic solution and degenerate basic solutions.

If any of the basic variables vanishes, the solution is called degenerate basic solution. On the other hand, *if none of the basic variables vanishes, the solution is called non-degenerate basic solution.*

Thus a non-degenerate basic solution constant exactly m non-zero and (n – m) zero variables.

Theorem:

A necessary and sufficient condition for the existence and non-degeneracy of all the basic solutions of Ax = b is that every set of m columns of the augmented matrix Ab = [A, b] is L.I.

Proof:

The condition is necessary. Suppose all the basic solution of the system Ax = b exist and are non-degenerate. Therefore, every set of m-column vectors of A is L.I.

Let $\alpha_1, \alpha_2, \ldots, \alpha_m$ be one set of m-column vectors of A, then the given system gives

$$\alpha_1 x_1 + \alpha_2 x_2 + \ldots + \alpha_m x_m = b.$$

Now since each solution is non-degenerate, $x_1 \neq 0$ and hence by replacement theorem vector b can replace α_1 in the basis $\alpha_1, \alpha_2, \ldots \alpha_m$. Thus vectors b, $\alpha_2, \alpha_3, \ldots, \alpha_m$ also from a basis and hence they are L.I. Similarly b can replace α_2 as x_2 is also non-zero. Hence α_1, b, $\alpha_3, \ldots, \alpha_m$ are also L.I. In a similar way we can show that b with any (m – 1) vectors of A forms a L.I. set. Hence every set of m columns of the augmented matrix Ab = [A, b] is L.I. *The condition is sufficient.* Suppose every set of m column vectors of Ab = [A, b] is L.I. Then obviously every set of m-column vectors of A is also L.I. and hence all the basic solutions exist.

Now consider any m-column vectors $\alpha_1, \alpha_2, ..., \alpha_m$ of A which are L.I. and let $x_1, x_2, ..., x_m$ be the corresponding basic solution. Then

$$x_1 \alpha_1 + x_2 \alpha_2 + ... + x_m \alpha_m = b$$

or
$$-1.b + x_1 \alpha_1 + x_2 \alpha_2 + ... + x_m \alpha_m = 0.$$

Now if $x_1 = 0$, then we have

$$-1.b + x_2 a_2 + ... + x_m \alpha_m = 0,$$

which shows that the vectors $b, \alpha_2, ..., \alpha_m$ are L.D.

But this is a contradiction as we have already assumed that m vectors of [A, b] are L.I. Hence $x_1 \neq 0$.

Similarly, we can show that $x_2, ... x_m$ are also different from zero *i.e.*, the solution is non-degenerate.

In this way, it can be shown that all the basic solution are non-degenerate.

Cor. 1. *The necessary and sufficient condition for any given basic solution $x_B = B^{-1}b$ to be non-degenerate is the linear independence of b and every (m – 1) columns from B.*

Proof:

The condition is necessary. We know that if a solution is non-degenerate ($x_i \neq 0$, j = 1, 2, ... ,m), b can replace any column of B and still a basis is maintained. Hence b and any (m – 1) columns of B are L.I.

The condition is sufficient. Let b and any (m – 1) columns of B be L.I. Any column of B can be replaced by b and still a basis is maintained. Hence $x_1, ..., x_m$ are all non-zero.

Basis Feasible Solution. A.B.F.S. is a basic solution which also satisfies the non-negativity restrictions.

Thus in B.F.S. all basic variables are $\neq 0$ *i.e.*, all basic variables are non-negative.

Optimum Basic Feasible Solution. A basic feasible solution is said to be optimum, if it also optimizes (max. or min.) the objective function.

EQUALITY OF TWO MATRICES

Definition : *Two matrices $A = [a_{ij}]$ and $B = [b_{ij}]$ are said to be equal if*

(i) *they are of the same size, and*

(ii) *the elements in the corresponding places of the two matrices are the same i.e., $a_{ij} = b_{ij}$ for each pair of subscripts i and j.*

ADDITION OF MATRICES

Definition: *Let A and B be two matrices of the same type m × n. Then their sum (to be denoted by A + B) is defined to be the matrix of the type m × n obtained by adding the corresponding elements of A and B. Thus if* $A = [a_{ij}]_{m\times n}$ and $B = [b_{ij}]_{m\times n}$, then $A + B = [a_{ij} + b_{ij}]_{m\times n}$.

Note that A + B is also a matrix of the type m × n.

For example, if

$$A = \begin{bmatrix} 3 & 2 & -1 \\ 4 & -3 & 1 \end{bmatrix}_{2\times 3} \text{ and } B = \begin{bmatrix} 1 & -2 & 7 \\ 3 & 2 & -1 \end{bmatrix}_{2\times 3},$$

$$\text{then } A + B = \begin{bmatrix} 3+1 & 2-2 & -1+7 \\ 4+3 & -3+2 & 1-1 \end{bmatrix} = \begin{bmatrix} 4 & 0 & 6 \\ 7 & -1 & 0 \end{bmatrix}_{2\times 3}.$$

Note: It should be noted that addition is defined only for matrices which are of the same size. If two matrices A and B are of the same size, they are said to be conformable for *addition.* It the matrices A and B are not of the same size, we cannot find their sum.

MATRIX ADDITION PROPERTIES

(i) *Matrix addition is commutative. If A and B be two m × n matrices, then A + B = B + A.*

(ii) *Matrix addition is associative. If A, B, C be three matrices each of the type m × n then (A + B) + C = A + (B + C).*

(iii) *Existence of additive identify. If 0 be the m × n matrix each of whose elements is zero, then A + 0 = A = 0 + A for every m × n matrix A.*

(iv) *Existence of the additive inverse.*

Negative of a Matrix

Definition : *Let* $A = [a_{ij}]_{m\times n}$. *Then the negative of the matrix A is defined as the matrix* $[-a_{ij}]_{m\times n}$ *and is denoted by – A.*

The matrix – A is the additive inverse of the matrix A. Obviously, – A + A = O = A + (– A).

Here O is the null matrix of the type m × n. It is identity element for matrix addition.

Subtraction of Two Matrices

Definition : *If A and B are two m × n matrices, then we define A – B = A + (– B).*

Thus, the difference A – B is obtained subtracting from each element of A the corresponding element of B.

(v) *Cancellation laws hold good in the case of addition of matrices i.e.,* if A, B, C are *three* $m \times n$ *matrices, then*

$$A + B = A + C \Rightarrow B = C$$

and $B + A = C + A \Rightarrow B = C.$

(vi) *The equation* $A + X = O$ *has a unique solution* $X = -A$ *in the set of all* $m \times n$ *matrices.*

SINGULAR MATRICES

Definition : *A square matrix A is said to be non-singular or singular according as* $|A| \neq 0$ *or* $|A| = 0$.

TRANSPOSE OF A MATRIX

Definition : *Let* $A = [a_{ij}]_{m\times n}$. *Then the* $n \times m$ *matrix obtained from A by changing its rows into columns and its columns into rows is called the transpose of A and is denoted by the symbol 'A' or* A^T.

The operation of interchanging rows with columns is called transposition. Symbolically, if

$$A = [a_{ij}]_{m\times n},$$

then $A' = [b_{ji}]_{n\times m}$,

where $b_{ji} = a_{ij}$,

i.e., the $(j, i)^{th}$ element of A' is the $(i, j)^{th}$ element of A.

For example, the transpose of the 3×4 matrix

$$A = \begin{bmatrix} 1 & 2 & 3 & 4 \\ 2 & 3 & 4 & 1 \\ 3 & 4 & 2 & 1 \end{bmatrix}_{3\times 4} \text{ is the } 4 \times 3 \text{ matrix}$$

$$A' = \begin{bmatrix} 1 & 2 & 3 \\ 2 & 3 & 4 \\ 3 & 4 & 2 \\ 4 & 1 & 1 \end{bmatrix}_{4\times 3}$$

The first row of A is the first column of A'. The second row of A is the second column of A'.

The third row of A is the third column of A'.

Theorems: *If A' and B' be the transposes of A and B respectively, then*

(i) $(A')' = A;$

(ii) *$(A + B)' = A' + B'$, A and B being of the same size.*

(iii) *$(kA)' = kA'$, k being any complex number.*

(iv) *$(AB)' = B'A'$, A and B being conformable to multiplication.*

The above law (iv) is called the reversal law for transposes *i.e., the transpose of the product is the product of the transposes taken in the reverse order.*

ADJOINT OR ADJUGATE OF A SQUARE MATRIX

Definition : *Let $A = [a_{ij}]_{n \times n}$ be any $n \times n$ matrix. The transpose B' of the matrix $B = [A_{ij}]_{n \times n}$, where Aij denotes the cofactor of the element a_{ij} in the determinant $|A|$, is called the adjoint of the matrix A and is denoted by the symbol adj A.*

Thus the adjoint of a matrix A is the transpose of the matrix formed by the cofactors of A *i.e.,* if

$$A = \begin{bmatrix} a_{11} & a_{12} & \cdots & a_{1n} \\ a_{21} & a_{22} & \cdots & a_{2n} \\ \cdots & \cdots & \cdots & \cdots \\ a_{n1} & a_{n2} & \cdots & a_{nn} \end{bmatrix},$$

then Adj A = the transpose of the matrix $\begin{bmatrix} A_{11} & A_{12} & \cdots & A_{1n} \\ A_{21} & A_{22} & \cdots & A_{2n} \\ \cdots & \cdots & \cdots & \cdots \\ A_{n1} & A_{n2} & \cdots & A_{nn} \end{bmatrix}$

$$= \text{the matrix} \begin{bmatrix} A_{11} & A_{21} & \cdots & A_{n1} \\ A_{12} & A_{22} & \cdots & A_{n2} \\ \cdots & \cdots & \cdots & \cdots \\ A_{1n} & A_{2n} & \cdots & A_{nn} \end{bmatrix}.$$

Note: Sometimes the adjoint of a matrix is also called the adjudged of that matrix.

Theorem: *If A is any square matrix of order n, then A (adj A) = $|A|$ In = (adj A) A.*

INVERTIBLE MATRICES: INVERSE OR RECIPROCAL OF A MATRIX

Definition : *Let A be any n-rowed square matrix. Then a matrix B, if it exists, such that*

$$AB = BA = I_n$$

is called inverse of A.

Note: For the products AB, BA to be both defined and be equal, it is necessary that A and B are both square matrices of the same order. Thus, *non-square matrices cannot possess inverse.*

Existence of the Inverse

Theorem: *The necessary and sufficient condition for a square matrix A to possess the inverse is that* $|A| \neq 0$.

Note : If A be an invertible matrix, then the inverse of A is $1/|A|$ Adj. A. It is usual to denote the inverse of A by A^{-1}.

Thus, $A^{-1} = \frac{1}{|A|}$ Adj. A, provided $|A| \neq 0$.

Thus the necessary and sufficient condition for a matrix to be invertible is that it is non-singular.

Theorem 1: *If A, B be two n-rowed non-singular matrices, then AB is also non-singular and* $(AB)^{-1} = B^{-1} A^{-1}$,

i.e., the inverse of a product is the product of the inverses taken in he reverse order.

Theorem 2: *If A be an* $n \times n$ *non-singular matrix, then* $(A')^{-1} = (A^{-1})'$ *i.e., the operations of transposing and inverting are commutative.*

VECTORS

Definition : *Any ordered n-tuple of numbers is called an n-vector.* By an ordered n-tuple we mean a set consisting of numbers in which the place of each number is fixed. If $x_1, x_2, \ldots x_n$ be any n numbers, then the ordered n-tuple $\mathbf{X} = (x_1, x_2, \ldots, x_n)$ is called an n-vector. The ordered triad (x_1, x_2, x_3) is called a 3-vector. Similarly (1, 0, 1, – 1) and (1, 8, – 5, 7) are 4-vectors. The n numbers $x_1, x_2, \ldots$,mn are called components of the n-vector $\mathbf{X} = (x_1, x_2, \ldots, x_n)$.

A vector may be written either as a row vector or as a column vector. If A be a matrix of the type $m \times n$, then each row of A will be an n-vector and each column of A will be an m-vector. A vector whose components are all zero is called a zero vector and will be denoted by O. If k be any number and X be any vector, then relative to the vector X. k is called a scalar.

Algebra of Vectors

Since an n-vector is nothing but a row matrix or a column matrix. Therefore we can develop an algebra of vectors in the same manner as the algebra of matrices.

Equality of Two Vectors

Two n-vectors X and Y where $X = (x_1, x_2, \ldots x_n)$ and $Y = (y_1, y_2, \ldots y_n)$ are said to be equal if and only if their corresponding components are equal i.e., if $x_i = y_i$, for all i = 1, 2, ... ,n.

For example if,

$$X = (1, 4, 7)$$

and Y = (1, 4, 7), then X = Y.

MULTIPLICATION OF A VECTOR BY A SCALAR (NUMBER)

If k be any number and

$$X = (x_1, x_2, \ldots x_n),$$

then by definition

$$k\,X = (kx_1, kx_2, \ldots, kx_n).$$

The vector k X is called the scalar multiple of the vector X by the scalar k.

Properties of Addition and Scalar Multiplication of Vectors

If X, Y, Z be any three n-vectors and p, q be any two numbers, then obviously

(i) X + Y = Y + X.

(ii) X + (Y + Z) = (X + Y) + Z.

(iii) p (X + Y) = pX + pY.

(iv) (p + q) X = pX – qX.

(v) p (qX) = (pq) X.

A VECTOR AS A LINEAR COMBINATION OF VECTORS

Definition : *A vector X which can be expressed in the form*

$$X = k_1 X_1 + k_2 X_2 + \ldots + k_r X_r$$

is said to be a linear combination of the set of vectors

$$X_1, X_2, \ldots, X_r$$

Here $k_1, k_2, \ldots, k_r$ are any numbers.

The following two results are quite obvious:

(i) *If a set of vector is linearly dependent, then at least one member of the set can be expressed as a linear combination of the remaining members.*

(ii) *If a set of vectors is linearly independent then no member of the set can be expressed as a linear combination of the remaining members.*

LINEAR DEPENDENCE AND LINEAR INDEPENDENCE OF VECTORS

Linearly Dependent Det of Vectors

Definition : *A set r n-vectors $X_1, X_2, \dots X_r$ is said to be linearly dependent if there exist r scalars (numbers) $k_1, k_2, \dots k_r$ not all zero, such that*

$$k_1 X_1 + k_2 X_2 + \dots + k_r X_r = O,$$

where, O, denotes the n-vector whose components are all zero.

Linearly Independent Set of Vectors

Definition : *A set r n-vectors $X_1, X_2, \dots X_r$ is said to be linearly independent if every relation of the type*

$$k_1 X_1 + k_2 X_2 + \dots + d_r X_r = O$$

implies $k_1 = k_2 = k_3 = \dots = k_r = 0.$

SYSTEMS OF LINEAR NON-HOMOGENEOUS EQUATIONS

Sometimes we think that we can solve every two simultaneous of the type

$$\left.\begin{aligned} a_1x + b_1y = c_1 \\ a_2x + b_2y = c_2 \end{aligned}\right\}.$$

But it is not so. For example, consider the simultaneous equations

$$\left.\begin{aligned} 3x + 4y = 5 \\ 6x + 8y = 13 \end{aligned}\right\}.$$

There is no set of values of x and y which satisfies both these equations. Such equations are said to be *inconsistent.*

Let us take another example. Consider the simultaneous equations

$$\left.\begin{aligned} 3x + 4y = 5 \\ 6x + 8y = 10 \end{aligned}\right\}.$$

These equations are consistent since there exist values of x and y which satisfy both of these equation. We see that $x = -\frac{4}{3}c + \frac{5}{3}$, $y = c$ constitute a solution of these equation, where c is arbitrary. Thus these equations possess an infinite number of solution.

Now we shall discuss the nature of solution of a system of non-homogeneous linear equations.

Let
$$\left.\begin{array}{l} a_{11}x_1 + a_{12}x_2 + \ldots + a_{1n}x_n = b_1 \\ a_{21}x_1 + a_{22}x_2 + \ldots + a_{2n}x_n = b2 \\ \ldots \ldots \ldots \ldots \ldots \ldots \ldots \ldots \ldots \ldots \\ \ldots \ldots \ldots \ldots \ldots \ldots \ldots \ldots \ldots \ldots \\ a_{m1}x_1 + a_{m2}x_2 + \ldots + a_{mn}x_n = b_m \end{array}\right\}$$

be a system of m non-homogeneous equations in n unknowns $x_1, x_2, \ldots, x_n$.

If we write

$$A = \begin{bmatrix} a_{11} & a_{12} & \ldots & a_{1n} \\ a_{21} & a_{22} & \ldots & a_{2n} \\ \ldots & \ldots & \ldots & \ldots \\ a_{m1} & a_{m2} & \ldots & a_{mn} \end{bmatrix}_{m\times n}, \quad X = \begin{bmatrix} x_1 \\ x_2 \\ \ldots \\ x_n \end{bmatrix}_{n\times 1},$$

$$B = \begin{bmatrix} b_1 \\ b_2 \\ \ldots \\ b_m \end{bmatrix}_{m\times 1}$$

where A, X, B are $m \times n$, $n \times 1$ and $m \times 1$ matrices respectively, the above equations can be written in the form of a single matrix equation $AX = B$.

Any set of values of $x_1, x_2, \ldots x_n$ which simultaneously satisfy all these equations is called a solution of the system (1). When the system of equations has one or more solutions, the equations are said to be *consistent*, otherwise they are said to be inconsistent.

The matrix $[A\ B] = \begin{bmatrix} a_{11} & a_{12} & \ldots & a_{1n} & b_1 \\ a_{21} & a_{22} & \ldots & a_{2n} & b_2 \\ \ldots & \ldots & \ldots & \ldots & \ldots \\ a_{m1} & a_{m2} & \ldots & a_{mn} & b_m \end{bmatrix}$

is called the augmented matrix of the given system of equations.

CONDITION FOR A SYSTEM OF N EQUATIONS IN N UNKNOWNS TO HAVE A UNIQUE SOLUTION

Theorem:

If A be an n-rowed non-singular matrix, X be an $n \times 1$ matrix, B be an $n \times 1$ matrix, the system of equation $AX = B$ has a unique solution.

Proof:

If A be an n-rowed non-singular matrix, the ranks of the matrices A and [A B] are both n. Therefore the system of equations $AX = B$ is consistent *i.e.,* possesses a solution.

Pre-multiplying both sides of $AX = B$ by A^{-1}, we have

$$A^{-1} AX = A^{-1} B$$

i.e., $IX = A^{-1} B$

i.e., $X = A^{-1} B$

is a solution of the equation $AX = B$.

To show that the solution is unique, let us suppose that X_1 and X_2 be two solution of $AX = B$.

Then $\quad Ax_1 = B, AX_2 = B$

$\Rightarrow \quad AX_1 = AX_2$

$\Rightarrow \quad A^{-1}AX_1 = A^{-1}AX_2$

$\Rightarrow \quad IX_1 = IX_2$

$\Rightarrow \quad X_1 = X_2.$

Hence the solution is unique.

WORKING RULE FOR FINDING THE SOLUTION OF THE EQUATION AX = B

Suppose the coefficient matrix A is of the type $m \times n$, *i.e.,* we have m equations in n unknowns.

Write the augmented matrix [A B] and reduce it to a Echelon form by applying only E-row transformations on it. This Echelon form will enable us to know the ranks of the augmented matrix [A B] and the coefficient matrix A. Then the following different cases arise:

Case I. Rank A < Rank [A B].

In this case the equations $AX = B$ are inconsistent *i.e.,* they have no solution.

Case II. Rank A = Rank [A B] = r (say).

In this the equations $AX = B$ are consistent *i.e.,* they possess a solution. If $r < m$, then in the process of reducing the matrix [A B] to Echelon form, $(m - r)$ equations will be eliminated. The given system of m equations will then be placed by an equivalent system of r equations. From these r equations we shall be able to express the values of some r unknowns in terms of the remaining $n - r$ unknowns which can be given any arbitrarily chosen values.

If $r = n$, then $n - r = 0$, so that no variable is to be assigned arbitrary values and therefore in this case there will be a unique solution.

If $r < n$, then $n - r$ variables can be assigned arbitrary values. So in this case there will be an infinite number of solution. Only $n - r + 1$ solutions will be linearly independent and the rest of the solutions will be linear combinations of them.

If $m < n$, then $r \leq m < n$. Thus in this case $n - r > 0$. Therefore when the number of equations is less than the number of unknowns, the equations will always have an infinite number of solutions, provided they are consistent.

USEFUL RESULTS OF LINEAR ALGEBRA

1. *Basic.* A subset S of E^n is said to be the basis of E^n if
   (i) S is linearly independent
   (ii) S generates E^n *i.e.,* $E^n = L(S)$.
2. *Generating Set.* A set of vectors $\alpha_1, \alpha_2, \ldots, \alpha_k \in E^n$ is said to generate E^n if every vector belonging to E^n can be expressed as a linear combination of $\alpha_1, \alpha_2, \ldots \alpha_k$.
3. Any two bases of E^n have same number of elements.
4. Each set of $n + 1$ or more vectors of E^n is L.D.
5. If a set n vectors of E^n spans E^n then S is a basis of E^n
6. If S is a basis of E^n then every vector $\alpha \in E^n$ can be uniquely expressed as a linear combination of vectors of S.

MATHEMATICAL DESCRIPTION OF A GENERAL LINEAR PROGRAMMING PROBLEM

A general linear programming problem can be stated as:

Find $x_1, x_2, \ldots x_n$ which optimize the linear function

$$Z = c_1 x_1 + c_2 x_2 + \ldots + c_n x_n \quad \ldots(1)$$

subject to the constraints

$$\left.\begin{array}{l} a_{11}x_1 + a_{12}x_2 \ldots + a_{1n}x_n (\leq = \geq) b_1 \\ a_{21}x_1 + a_{22}x_2 + \ldots + a_{2n}x_n (\leq = \geq) b_2 \\ \ldots \ldots \ldots \ldots \ldots \ldots \ldots \ldots \ldots \ldots \ldots \\ \ldots \ldots \ldots \ldots \ldots \ldots \ldots \ldots \ldots \ldots \ldots \\ a_{m1}x_1 + a_{m2}x_2 + \ldots + a_{mn}x_n (\leq = \geq) b_m \end{array}\right\} \quad \ldots(2)$$

and the non-negative restrictions $x_1, x_2, \ldots, x_n \geq 0$,

where a_{ll} $a_{11}, a_{12}, \ldots, a_n, b_1, b_2, \ldots, b_m, c_1, c_2, \ldots, c_n$ are constants and $x_1, x_2, \ldots x_n$ are variables.

The function Z given in (1) is called the *objective function,* the conditions given in (2) are called the linear constraints and the conditions given in (3) are called the non-negative restrictions of the linear programming problem.

This linear programming problem may be stated in matrix form as follows:

Find $x_1, x_2, \dots, x_n$, so as to optimize

$$Z = c\,x$$

subject to $A\,x\ (\leq = \geq)\ b$

and $x \geq 0$,

where $A = [a_{ij}]_{m\times n}$ is called the coefficient matrix.

$c = [c_1, c_2, \dots, c_n]$ is a row matrix known as price vector,

$$b = \begin{bmatrix} b_1 \\ b_2 \\ \dots \\ \dots \\ b_m \end{bmatrix}$$ is a column matrix called the requirement vector,

$$x = \begin{bmatrix} x_1 \\ x_2 \\ \dots \\ \dots \\ x_n \end{bmatrix}$$ is a column matrix of variables

and 0 is a null matrix of the type $n \times 1$.

TWO MATRICES MULTIPLICATION

Definition : *Let $A = [a_{ij}]_{m\times n}$ and $B = [b_{jk}]_{m\times n}$ be two matrices such that the number of columns in A is equal to the number of rows in B. Then the $m \times p$ matrix $C = [c_{ik}]_{m\times p}$ such that*

$$c_{ik} = \sum_{j=1}^{n} a_{ij} b_{jk}$$ *[Note that the summation is with respect to the repeated suffix j]*

is called the product of the matrices A and B in that order and we write C = AB.

The product AB of two matrices A and B exists if and only if the number of columns in A is equal to the number of rows in B. Two such matrices are said to be conformable for multiplication.

The rule of multiplication is row-by-column multiplication.

For example, if $A = \begin{bmatrix} a_{11} & a_{12} \\ a_{21} & a_{22} \\ a_{31} & a_{32} \end{bmatrix}_{3\times 2}$, $B = \begin{bmatrix} b_{11} & b_{12} \\ b_{21} & b_{22} \end{bmatrix}_{2\times 2}$

$$then AB = \begin{bmatrix} a_{11}b_{11} + a_{12}b_{21} & a_{11}b_{12} + a_{12}b_{22} \\ a_{21}b_{11} + a_{22}b_{21} & a_{21}b_{12} + a_{22}\, b_{22} \\ a_{31}b_{11} + a_{31}b_{21} & a_{31}b_{12} + a_{32}b_{22} \end{bmatrix}_{3\times 2}$$

Note: If the product AB exists, then it is not necessary that the product BA will also exist. For example if A is a 4 × 5 matrix and B is a 5 × 3 matrix, then the product AB exists while the product BA does not exist.

LINEAR PROGRAMMING PROBLEM AN L.P.

Linear Programming : Linear programming is an important optimization (maximization or minimization) technique used in decision making in business and every-day life for obtaining the maximum or minimum values as required of a linear expression subject to satisfying certain number of given linear restrictions.

Linear Programming Problem (L.P.P.) : The linear programming problem is general calls for optimizing (maximizing/minimizing) a linear function of variables called the objective function subject to a set of linear equations and/ or linear inquisitions called the constraints or restrictions.

The term linear means that all the relations governing the problem are linear and the term *Programming* refers to the process of determining a particular programme or plan of action.

Constraints : The system of linear inquisition (or equations) under which the objective function is to be optimized is called constraints.

Objective Function : The function which is to be optimized (maximized or minimized) is called an objective function.

BASIC REQUIREMENTS OF A LINEAR PROGRAMMING PROBLEM (L.P.P.)

(i) *Linearity:* A primary requirement of a L.P.P. is that both the objective function and all the constraints must be expressed in terms of linear equations and inequalities.

Linearity implies that the products of variables such as xy, x^2y etc., powers of variables such as x^2, x^3 etc., and combinations of variables of the type ax + b log y etc. are not allowed.

(ii) *Additivity:* Additivity means that if it takes x minutes on machine A to make product P and Y minutes to make product Q, then the total time on machine A devotes to this production is x + y, provided the time required to change the machine from product P to product Q is negligible.

(iii) *Multiplicativity:* Multiplicativity means that if the cost of production of 1 unit of an item is Rs. 10, then cost of production of x units of the same item is Rs. 10x. In terms of profit we can say that the profit from selling a given number of units is the profit per unit multiplied by the number of units sold.

(iv) *Divisibility:* Divisibility means that the fractional levels of variables must be permissible besides integral values.

(v) *Finite Number of Constraints:* The number of activities involved in a problem should be finite, thus leading to a finite number of constraints in the problem.

(vi) *Well-defined Objective Function:* The objective function of the L.P.P. should be clear and well-defined. The objective may be either to maximize the profit by utilizing the available resources or it may be to minimize the cost by using limited amount of various resources required for production.

(vii) *Quantitative Measurement of Elements:* It is necessary that each element may be capability being measured quantitatively. Numerical data must be given so that the relationships among the elements may be considered.

(viii) *Presence of Constraints and Restrictions:* The available resources which are to be allocated among various competing activities should be limited.

(ix) *Alternate Lines of Action:* There must be different lines of actions available to perform the job.

(x) *Non-negative Restrictions:* All the variables considered for making decisions assume non-negative values.

FORMULATION AS A LINEAR PROGRAMMING PROBLEMS

Step 1. We study the situation to find the day decision to be made and in this connection loading for variables helps considerable.

Step 2. Select symbols for variable quantities identified in step I.

Let the number units of the products A, B and C manufactured daily be designated by x_1, x_2 and x_3 respectively.

Step 3. Express feasible alternatives mathematical in terms of the variables. These feasible alternatives are those which are physically, economically and financially possible. Since it is not possible to manufacture any negative quantities, it is quite obvious that in the present situation feasible alternatives are sets of values of x_1, x_2 and x_3 satisfying $x_1 \geq 0$, $x_2 \geq 0$, $x_3 \geq 0$.

Step 4. Identify the objective quantitatively and express it as a linear function of variables. The objective here is to maximize the profit. In view of the assumption that all the units produced are consumed in the market, it is given by the linear function

$z = 3x_1 + 2x_2 + 4x_3.$

Step 5. Express in words the influencing factors or constraints (or restrictions) which occur generally because of the constraints on availability (resources) or requirements (demands). Express these restrictions also as linear equalities/inequalities in terms of the variables. Here in order to produce x_1 units of product A, x_2 units of product B and x_3 units of product C, the total times needed on machines P and Q are given by

$$4x_1 + 3x_2 + 5x_3 \text{ and } 2x_1 + 2x_2 + 4x_3$$

respectively. Since the manufacturer does not have more than 2,000 minutes available on machine P and 2,500 minutes available on machine Q, we must have

$$4x_1 + 3x_2 + 5x_3 \leq 2{,}000$$

and $2x_1 + 2x_2 + 4x_3 \leq 2{,}000.$

Also, the manufacturer has to satisfy the following given additional restrictions:

$$x_1 \leq 150,\ x_1 \geq 100;$$
$$x_2 \geq 200 \text{ and } x_3 \geq 50.$$

Hence the manufacturer's problem can be put in the following mathematical form:

Determine three non-negative real numbers x_1, x_2 and x_3 such that

(i) $4x_1 + 3x_2 + 5x_3 \leq 2{,}000$

(ii) $2x_1 + 2x_2 + 4x_3 \leq 2{,}500$

(iii) $100 \leq x \leq 150,\ x_2 \leq 250,\ x_3 \leq 50$

and for which the expression (objective function)

$z = 3x_1 + 2x_2 + 4x_3$

may be a maximum (greatest).

This problem is called linear programming problem since a linear function of three variable x_1, x_2 and x_3 defined by

$$z = 3x_1 + 2x_2 + 4x_3$$
$$x_1 + x_2 \leq 24. \qquad \text{...(4)}$$

Also the number of necklaces and bracelets manufactured can never be negative, therefore

$$x_1 \geq 0, x_2 \geq 0.$$

Hence, the linear programming problem formulated from the given problem is as follows:

Maximize $Z = 100x_1 + 300x_2$

subject to the constraints

$$x_1 + 2x_2 \leq 32$$

$$x_1 + x_2 \leq 24$$

and the non-negative restrictions $x_1 \geq 0, x_2 \geq 0$.

LINEAR PROGRAMMING REQUIREMENTS

Any organization, big or small, has at its disposal men, machines, money and materials, the supply of which may be limited. Supply of resources bring limited, the management must find the best allocation of its resources in order to maximize the profit or minimize the loss or utilize the production capacity to the maximum extent. However, this involves a number of problems which can be overcome by quantitative methods, particularly the linear programming.

In general, linear programming can be used for optimization problems if the following conditions are satisfied:

(i) There must be a well-defined objective function (profit, cost or quantities produced) which is to be either maximized or minimized and which can be expressed as a linear function of decision variables.

(ii) There must be restrictions on the amount or extent of attainment of the objective and these restrictions must be capable of being expressed as linear qualities or inequalities in terms of variables.

(iii) There must be alternative courses of action. For example, a given product may be processed by two different machines and the problem may be as to how much of the product to allocate to which machine.

(iv) Another necessary requirement is that decision variables should be interrelated and non-negative. The non-negativity condition shows that linear programming deals with real-leaf situations for which negative quantities are generally illogical.

(v) As stated earlier, the resources must be in limited supply. For example, if a firm starts producing getter number of a particular product, it must make smaller number of other products as the total production capacity is limited.

SOME DEFINITIONS AND RESULTS

Graphical Solution of a LPP. The solution of a LPP obtained by graphical method i.e., by drawing the graphs corresponding to the constraints and the non-negative restrictions is called the graphical solution of a LPP.

Unbounded Solution. If the value of objective function can be increased or deceased indefinitely, such solutions are called unbounded solutions.

Fundamental Extreme Point Theorem. An optimum solution of a LPP, if it exists, occurs at one of the extreme points (i.e., corner points) of the convex of the set of all feasible solutions.

Solution of a LPP. A set of values of the variables x_1, x_2, ... ,n satisfying the constraints of a LPP is called a solution of the LPP.,

Feasible Solution of a Linear Programming Problems. A set of values of the variables x_1, x_2, ... ,xn satisfying the constraints and non-negative restrictions of a linear programming problems is called feasible solution of the linear programming problems.

Optimal Solution of a LPP. A feasible solution of a linear programming problems is said to be optimal (or optimum) if it also optimizes (i.e., maximizes or minimizes as the case may be) the objective function of the problem.

SIMULTANEOUS SOLUTION OF LINEAR INEQUATIONS

The graph of the solution set of a system of simultaneous inquisitions is the region containing the point (x, y) which satisfy all the inquisitions of given system simultaneously.

To draw the graph of the simultaneous linear inquisitions *i.e.,* to find the solution set of the simultaneous linear inquisitions, we find the region of the xy-plane, common to all the portions comprising the solution sets of the given inquisitions. If there is no region common to all the solutions of the given inquisitions, we say that the solution set of the system of inquisition is empty. It should be noted that the solution set of simultaneous linear inquisition may be an empty set or it may be the region bounded by the straight lines corresponding to given linear inquisitions or it may be an unbounded region with straight line boundaries.

LINEAR PROGRAMMING PROBLEM

There are two techniques of solving a linear programming problems by graphical method:

(i) Corner-Point Method and

(ii) ISO-Profit or ISO-Cost Method:

CORNER-POINT METHOD

This method of solving linear programming problems graphically is based on the principle of extreme point theorem.

While solving a linear programming problems graphically y this method, we first obtain the region in the xy-plane containing all points that simultaneously satisfy all constraints including non-negative restrictions. This polygonal region so obtained is called the cover polygon of the set of all feasible solutions of the linear programming problems. It is also called the feasible region or the permissible region.

We determine the vertices (or corner points) of this convex polygon. These vertices are called the extreme points or corner points of the set of all feasible solution of the linear programming problems. After obtaining the extreme points, we cheek the objective function at these points to get the optimum value. The point where the objective function attains its optimum value gives the optimal solution of the given linear programming problems.

If two vertices of the convex polygon give the optimal value of the objective function, then all points on the line joining these two vertices give the optimal value of the objective function and LPP is said to have infinite number of optimal solutions.

If the convex polygon is an empty set, then the linear programming problems has no solution.

Procedure to solve a LPP graphically by corner-point method :

1. Consider each constraint as an equation.
2. Plot each equation on graph, as each one will geometrically a straight line.
3. The common region thus obtained satisfying all the constraints and the non-negative restrictions is called the feasible region. It is a convex polygon.
4. Determine the vertices (corner points) of the convex polygon. These vertices are known as the extreme points or corners of the feasible region.
5. Find the values of the objective function at each of the extreme points. The point at which the value of the objective function is optimum (maximum or minimum) is the optimal solution of the given linear programming problems.

ISO-PROFIT OR ISO-COST METHOD

While solving a linear programming problems graphically by this method, we first sketch the region in the xy-plane containing all points that simultaneously satisfy all constraints including non-negative restrictions to obtain the feasible region.

We determine the vertices (or corner points) of the feasible region and then draw a straight line in the feasible region corresponding to the equation obtained by giving some convenient value k to the objective function Z. This line is called an iso-profit or iso-cost line, since every point on this line well yield the same profit or loss of Rs. k, as the case may be.

Now if the objective function is of maximization type, then we draw lines, parallel to the line Z = k, over the feasible region in the increasing direction away from the origin till it passes through a vertex of the polygon and its increasing direction away from the origin becomes maximum. *The co-ordinates of this vertex well give the maximum value of the objective function.* This line is yet another iso-profit line whose every point well yield the same maximum profit.

If the objective function is of minimization type, then we draw lines, parallel to the line Z = k, over the feasible region in the decreasing direction towards the origin till it passes through a vertex of the polygon and its distance from the origin is minimum. *The co-ordinates of this vertex will give the minimum value of the objective function.* This line is an iso-cost line whose every point will yield the same minimum cost.

Procedure to solve a LPP graphically y ISO-profit or ISO-cost method:

1. Consider each constraint as an equation.
2. Plot each equation on graph as each one will geometrically represent a straight line.
3. The polygonal region so obtained, satisfying all the constraints and the non-negative restrictions is the convex set of all feasible solution of the given LPP, which is also known as feasible region.
4. Determine the extreme points of the feasible region.
5. Give some convenient value k to the objective function Z and draw the corresponding straight line in the xy-plane.
6. If the problem is of maximization, then draw lines parallel to the line Z = k and obtain a line which is farthest from the origin and has at least one point common to the feasible region.

   If the problem is of minimization, then draw lines parallel to the line Z = k and obtain a line which is nearest to the origin and has at least one point common to the feasible region.
7. The common points so obtained is the optimal solution of the given LPP.

Formulation as a Linear Programming Problem

Step 1. The key decision to be made is to determine the number of acres to be devoted to the three crops at each of the three farms.

Step 2. Let x_j j = 1, 2, ... ,9, represent these nine quantities identified in Step 1. Let us demonstrate these variables as follows:

(Allocation in acres)

Farm	crop 1	2	3
A	x_1	x_2	x_3
B	x_4	x_5	x_6
C	x_7	x_8	x_9

Step 3. Feasible alternatives are the sets of values of x_1, x_2 and x_3 satisfying $x_1, x_2, x_3 \geq 0$, since negative acreages are meaningless.

Step 4. The objective is to maximize the total net profit (in rupees) of the organization, i.e., to maximize

$$z = 4000\,(x_1 + x_2 + x_3) + 3000(x_4 + x_5 + x_6) + 1000(x_7 + x_8 + x_9).$$

Step 5. Constraints are the availability of usable land, water for irrigation, requirement of minimum acreage and social equality of percentage of the usable acreage planted for each farm. These are

1. *Land:*

$$x_1 + x_4 + x_7 \leq 400$$
$$x_2 + x_5 + x_8 \leq 600$$
$$x_3 + x_6 + x_9 \leq 300$$

2. *Water:*

$$5x_1 + 4x_4 + 3x_7 \leq 1500$$
$$5x_2 + 4x_5 + 3x_8 \leq 2000$$
$$5x_3 + 4x_6 + 3x_9 \leq 900$$

3. *Crop requirement:*

$$x_1 + x_2 + x_3 \leq 700$$
$$x_4 + x_5 + x_6 \leq 800$$
$$x_7 + x_8 + x_9 \leq 300$$

4. *Social equality:*

$$\frac{x_1 + x_4 + x_7}{400} = \frac{x_2 + x_5 + x_8}{600}$$

$$\frac{x_2 + x_5 + x_8}{600} = \frac{x_3 + x_6 + x_9}{300}$$

$$\frac{x_1 + x_2 + x_3}{3} = \frac{x_1 + x_4 + x_7}{400}$$

i.e., $3(x_1 + x_4 + x_7) - 2(x_2 + x_5 + x_8) = 0$

$x_2 + x_5 + x_8 - 2(x_3 + x_6 + x_9) = 0$

$4(x_3 + x_6 + x_9) - 3(x_1 + x_4 + x_7) = 0$

This complete the formulation.

$2x_1 + 3x_2 \leq 20$

$2x_2 + 5x_3 \leq 25$

$3x_1 + 2x_2 + 4x_3 \leq 30$

and the non-negative restrictions

$x_1 \geq 0, x_2 \geq 0, x_3 \geq 0.$

Working Rule for Marking Feasible Region

Consider the constraint $ax + by \leq c$, where $c > 0$.

First draw the straight line $ax + by = c$ by joining any two points on it. For this find two convenient points satisfying this equation.

This straight line divides the xy-plane in two parts. The inequation $ax + by \leq c$ will represent that part of the xy-plane which lies to that side of the line $ax + y = c$ in which the origin lies.

Again consider the constraint $ax + y \geq c$, where $c > 0$.

Draw the straight line $ax + y = c$ y joining any two point on it.

This straight line divides the xy-plane in two parts. The inequation $ax + by \geq c$ will represent that part of the xy-plane which lies to that side of the line $ax + by = c$ in which the origin does not lie.

Mathematical Formation of a Linear Programming Problems

To make use of the linear programming technique it is important to recognize a problem which can be handled by linear programming and then to formulate its mathematical model.

WORKING RULE TO FORM A LINEAR PROGRAMMING PROBLEM

The following steps are helpful in the formulation of a linear programming problem:

1. Identify the variables in LPP and denote them by x_1, x_2, x_3 etc.

2. Identify the objective function and express it as a linear function of the variables x_1, x_2, x_3 etc.
3. Find the type of the objective function. It may be in the form of maximizing profits or minimizing costs.
4. Identify all the constrains and express them as linear inquisitions or equations.

SLACK AND SURPLUS VARIABLES

1. *Slack Variables:* If a constraint has a sign $\leq$, then in order to make it an equality we have to add some thing positive to the left hand side.

The positive variables which are added to L.H. sides of the constraints to convert them into equalities are called the slack variables.

For example, consider the linear programming problem

Max. $Z = 2x_1 + 3x_2 + 4x_3$

s.t. $x_1 + x_2 = x_3 \leq b_1$

$2x_1 + 4x_2 - x_3 \leq b_2$ ...(1)

$x_1, x_2, x_3 \geq 0.$

In order to convert constraints (1) into equalities (equations) we add x_4 and x_5 on L.H.S. of (1), them we have

$$x_1 + x_2 + x_3 + x_4 = b_1$$

and $2x_1 + 4x_2 - x_3 + x_5 = b_2$.

Hence x_4 and x_5 are called the slack variables.

2. *Surplus Variables:* If a constant has a sign $\geq$, them in order to make it an equality we have to subtract something positive from its L.H.S. The positive which are subtracted from the L.H. sides of the constants to convert them into equalities are called the surplus variables.

For example, consider the linear programming problem

Max. $Z = 2x_1 + 4x_2 + 4x_3$

s.t. $x_1 + x_2 + 2x_3 \leq b_1$

$2x_1 + 4x_2 + 6x_3 \geq b_2$ ...(2)

$x_1 - 2x_2 + 4x_3 \geq b_3$

The constraints (2) are inequalities. In order to convert them into equalities we have to add something in the L.H.S. of first and subtract something from the L.H. sides of the second and the third inequalities of (2), *i.e.*, we have following equalities

$$x_1 + x_2 + 2x_3 + x_4 = b_1,\ 2x_1 + 4x_2 + 6x_3 - x_5 = b_2$$
$$x_1 - 2x_2 + 4x_3 - x_6 = b_3$$

Here, x_4 is the slack variables while x_5 and x_6 are the surplus variables.

LINEAR PROGRAMMING SCOPE

Despite the restriction that relationship must be approximately linear, linear programming, as an OR technique, has been recognized and widely used in industry as an effective tool for business problems, during the last three decades.

The first application of linear programming technique was made in 1947 in the U.S. Air Force. After the Second World War, it became necessary to concentrate on the development of a model that would define the optimal and efficient coordination of a nation's energies in the event of a total war. The Air Force officially named this task as *Project SCOOP* (Scientific Computation of Optimum Programmes) and it was in 1947 that George Dantzing and his associates found out a technique for solving military planning problems while working on this project.

This technique consisted of representing the various activities of an organization as a *linear programming modern* and arriving at the optimal programme by minimizing a linear objective function. Dantzing developed the 'Simplex Method' for deriving an optimal feasible solution which solved the project SCOOP. Since then, the military has been building linear programming models for crew training, for scheduling of routine maintenance activities, for personnel assignments and for contract bidding, etc. The use of linear programming in business and industry has been tremendous since 1951. The first and the most widely used industrial applications have been in all phases of the petroleum industry, viz., exploration, production, refining, distribution and pollution control.

Here an oil refinery has a choice of buying crude oil from several different sources with different products like aviation fuel, diesel fuel and gasoline with varying quantities. The constraints may be the restrictions an quantity of the caned oil available at a particular source, the capacity of the refinery to produce a particular product etc. The second must eater user of linear programming is the food processing industry. Metal worrying industries use linear programming for loop loading and for determining the cleric between the producing all buying a particular pat.

LIMITATIONS OF THE GRAPHICAL METHOD

This method can be applied to problems involving only two variables while most of the practical situations do involve more than two variables.

Therefore it is not a powerful tool of L.P.

TECHNIQUE APPLICATIONS OF THE LINEAR PROGRAMMING

In this section we discuss some important applications of linear programming in our life.

1. Agricultural applications. Linear programming can be applied in agricultural planning for allocating the available limited resources such as acreage, labour, water supply and working capital to the various carps so that the total net revenue may be maximum.
2. Military applications. Linear programming technique may be applied in selecting an air weapon system against grilles so as to keep them pinned down utilizing the minimum amount of aviation gasoline; in maximizing the total tonnage of bombs dropped on the enemy's targets; in determining the transportation schedule of the essential items such as weapons, medicines etc. in least time; in determining schedule of the essential items such as weapons, medicines etc. in least time; in determining the number of defence units used in the attack in order to provide the required level of protection at the lowest possible cost.
3. Blending problem. Such problems arise when a new product is to be prepared by mixing the certain other things, maintaining some economical blend of the new product. By using the L.P. technique, we can determine the most economical blend of the new product subject to the availability of the raw materials and the minimum or maximum limitation to the constituents. Such problems occur frequently in the petroleum, paint and steel industries etc.
4. Feed mix. The problem of finding the best diet *i.e.,* the combination of food that can be supplied at minimum cost, satisfying the daily requirement of the nutrients is also a L.P.P.
5. Personnel assignment problem. Linear programming technique can be used to allocate the available man power to various jobs in the best way (which minimizes the total cost or maximizes the total profit).
6. Transportation problem. This type of problem occurs very frequently in practical life or say matches with many real situations. In general transportation problems are concerned with the distribution of a certain product from several sources to number of localities at minimum cost.
7. Problem management. Linear programming can be applied in production management for determining product mix, product smoothing and assembly time balancing.

8. Trim loss problems. If an item is made in a particular size by cutting it from a sheet of standard size, the optimum combination of requirements can be determined so that trim loss may be minimum.
8. Efficiencing on operation of system of dame. In this problem we determine
10. Markcting management. Linear programming helps in analyzing the effectiveness of advertising complain and time based on the available advertising media. It also helps travelling salesman in finding the shortest route for his tour.variations in water storage of dams which generate power so as to maximize the energy obtained from the entire system. The physical limitations of storage appear as inequalities.

LIMITATIONS OF LINEAR PROGRAMMING

In spite of wide area of applications, in practical situations, the linear programming technique has certain limitations as follows:

1. The effect of time and uncertainty is not considered in linear programming model. Thus the model should be defined in such a way that any change due to internal as well as external factors can be incorporated.
2. Parameters appearing in the model are assumed to be constant while in real life situations they are neither constant nor deterministic.
3. Linear programming deals with only single objective whereas in real life situations problems occur with multi-objectives.
4. All practical L.P.P. involve extensive calculations and hence computer facility is required. In many situations the computations become tedious even on large digital computers.
5. The L.P. technique is applicable to that class of problems in which the objective function and the constraints both are linear. But in many practical problems, it is not possible to express both the objective function and the constraints in linear form.
6. There is no guarantee of having integral valued solutions. For cxample, in finding out how many men and machines would be required to perform a particular job, rounding off the solution to the nearest integer will not give an optimal solution.

ADVANTAGES OF LINEAR PROGRAMMING

It indicates how the available resources can be used in the best way. It improves the quality of decisions. Thus it helps in attaining the optimum use of productive resources and manpower. It also reflects the drawbacks of the production process. The modification in mathematical solution is also possible by using linear programming method.

MATRICAL AND LINEAR ALGEBRA

Consider the system of linear equations

$$3_x + 4_y - 3_z = 5,$$
$$6_x + 8_y - 3_z = 1,$$
$$4_x - 2_y + z = 2.$$

Here x, y and z are unknowns and their coefficient are all numbers arranging the coefficients in the order in which they occur in the equations and enclosing them in square brackets. We obtain a rectangular array of the form

$$\begin{bmatrix} 2 & 9 & 7 \\ 3 & 4 & -3 \\ 6 & 8 & -3 \\ 4 & -2 & 1 \end{bmatrix}.$$

This rectangular array is an example of a *matrix*. The horizontal lines (→) are called rows or *row vectors*, and vertical lines (↓) are called *columns* or *column vectors* of the matrix. There are 4 rows and 3 column in this matrix. Therefore it is a matrix of the type 4 × 3. The numbers 3, 4, – 3, 2 etc., constituting this matrix are called its *elements*. The difference between a matrix and a number should be clearly understood. A matrix is not a number. It has goes got no numerical value.

It is a new thing formed with the help of numbers. It is just an ordered collection of number arranged in the form of a rectangular area. Simply 7 is a number. But in our notation of matrices [7] is a matrix of the type 1 × 1 and we cannot have 7 = [7]. We cannot have a relation of equality between a matrix and a number.

We shall use capital letters (in bold type or in italic type) to denote matrices.

$$\text{Thus } A = \begin{bmatrix} 5 & 0 & 1 \\ 6 & 1 & 7 \end{bmatrix}_{2\times 3} \text{ and } B = \begin{bmatrix} 0 & 0 & 0 \\ 0 & 0 & 0 \\ 0 & 0 & 0 \end{bmatrix}_{3\times 3}$$

are both matrices. They are of the type 2 × 3 and 3 × 3 respectively.

Sometimes we also use the brackets ( ) or the double bars, || ||, in place of the square brackets [ ] to denote matrices.

$$\text{Thus } A = \begin{pmatrix} 2 & 2 \\ 2 & 2 \end{pmatrix}, B = \begin{pmatrix} 3+5i & 9 \\ -4 & 3-5i \end{pmatrix}, C = \begin{Vmatrix} 7 & 7 \\ 7 & 7 \end{Vmatrix},$$

are all matrices each of the type 2 × 2.

MATRIX

Definition : *Asset of mn numbers (real or complex) arranged in the form of a rectangular array having m rows and n columns is called an m × n matrix [to be read as 'm by n' matrix].*

An m × n matrix is usually written as

$$A = \begin{bmatrix} a_{11} & a_{12} & \ldots a_{1n} \\ a_{21} & a_{22} & \ldots a_{2n} \\ a_{31} & a_{32} & \ldots a_{3n} \\ \ldots & \ldots & \ldots \\ \ldots & \ldots & \ldots \\ a_{m1} & a_{m2} & \ldots a_{mn} \end{bmatrix}.$$

In a compact form the above matrix is represented by $A = [a_{ij}]$, i = 1, 2, ... ,m, j = 1, 2, ... n or simply by $[a_{ij}]_{m \times n}$. We write the general element of the matrix and enclose it in brackets of the type [ ] or of the type ( ).

The numbers a_{11}, a_{12} etc. of this rectangular array are called the *elements* of the matrix. The element a_{ij} belongs to the jth row and the jth column and is sometimes called the $(i, j)^{th}$ element of second suffix j, the number of the column in which the element occurs. In a matrix, the number of rows and the columns need not be equal.

SUB-MATRICES OF A MATRIX

Definition : *Any matrix obtained by omitting some rows and columns from a given (m × n) matrix A is called a submatrix of A.*

The matrix A itself is a sub-matrix or A as it can be obtained from A by omitting no rows or columns. A squares submatrix of a square matrix A is called a *principal submatrix,* if its diagonal elements are also the diagonal elements of the matrix A. Principal submatrices are obtained only by omitting corresponding rows and columns.

MULTIPLICATION OF A MATRIX BY A SCALAR

Definition : *Let A be any m × n matrix and k any complex number called scalar. The m × n matrix obtained by multiplying every element of the matrix A by k is called scalar multiple of A by k and is denoted by kA or Ak. Symbolically, if* $A = [a_{ij}]_{m \times n}$, *then* $kA = Ak = [ka_{ij}]_{m \times n}$.

For example, if k = 2 and $A = \begin{bmatrix} 3 & 2 & -1 \\ 4 & -3 & 1 \end{bmatrix}_{2 \times 3}$,

then $2A = \begin{bmatrix} 2 \times 3 & 2 \times 2 & 2 \times -1 \\ 2 \times 4 & 2 \times -3 & 2 \times 1 \end{bmatrix}$

$$= \begin{bmatrix} 6 & 4 & -2 \\ 8 & -6 & 2 \end{bmatrix}_{2\times 3}.$$

PROPERTIES OF MULTIPLICATION OF A MATRIX BY A SCALAR

Theorem 1: *If A and B are two matrices each of the type $m \times n$, then $k(A + B) = kA + kB$ i.e., scalar multiplication of matrices distributes over the addition of matrices.*

Theorem 2: *If p and q are two scalars and A is any $m \times n$ matrix, then $(p + q) A = pA + qA$.*

Theorem 3: *If p and q are two scalars and A is any $m \times n$ matrix, then $p(qA) = (pq) A$.*

Theorem 4: *If A be any $m \times n$ matrix and k be any scalar, then*

$(-k) A = -(kA) = k(-A)$.

Theorem 5: *If A be any $m \times n$ matrix, then*

(i) $1\, A = A$,

(ii) $(-1) A = -A$.

Theorem 6: *If A and B are two $m \times n$ matrices, then*

$$-(A + B) = -A - B.$$

PROPERTIES OF MATRIX MULTIPLICATION

(i) *Matrix multiplication is associative, if convertibility is assured; i.e., $A(BC) = (AB)C$ if A, B, C are $m \times n$, $n \times p$, $p \times q$ matrices respectively.*

(ii) *Multiplication of matrices is distributive with respect to addition of matrices i.e.,*

$$A(B + C) = AB + AC,$$

where A, B, C are any three, $m \times n$, $n \times p$, $n \times p$ matrices respectively.

(iii) *The multiplication of matrices is not always commutative.*

Whenever $AB = BA$, the matrices A and B are said to commute.

If $AB = -BA$ the matrices A and B are said to anti-commute.

(iv) *If A be any $m \times n$ matrix and $O_{n,p}$ be an $n \times p$ null matrix, then $AO_{n,p} = 0_{m,p}$ where $O_{m,p}$ is an $m \times p$ null matrix.*

Similarly, if $O_{m,n}$ be an $m \times n$ null matrix and A be any $n \times p$ matrix, $O_{m,n} A = O_{m,p}$.

If A be any n-rowed square matrix and O be an -rowed null matrix, then AO = OA = O.

(v) *The equation $AB = O$ does not necessarily imply that at least one of the matrices A and B must be a zero matrix. Or*

The product of two matrices can be a zero matrix while neither of them is a zero matrix.

(vi) *In the case matrix multiplication if $AB = O$, then it does not necessarily imply that $BA = O$.*

(vii) *If A be an $m \times n$ matrix, I_n denotes the n-rowed unit matrix, it can be easily seen that, $AI_n = A = I_m A$.*

DETERMINANT OF A SQUARE MATRIX

Let A be any square matrix. The determinant formed by the elements of A is said to be the determinant of matrix A. This is denoted by |A| or det A. Since in a determinant the number of tows is equal to the number of columns, therefore only square matrices can have determinants.

Hence, if $A = \begin{bmatrix} 12 & 0 & 13 \\ 15 & 12 & 11 \\ 13 & 11 & 14 \end{bmatrix}$, then $\det A = |A| = \begin{bmatrix} 12 & 0 & 13 \\ 15 & 12 & 11 \\ 13 & 11 & 14 \end{bmatrix}$.

DIFFERENCE BETWEEN A MATRIX AND A DETERMINANT

(i) A matrix "A" cannot be reduced to a number whereas the determinant can be reduced to a number.

(ii) The number of rows may or may not be equal to number of columns in a matrix while in a determinant the number of rows is equal to the number of columns.

(iii) Interchanging the rows and column, a different matrix is formed while in a determinant, an interchange of rows and columns does not change the value of the determinant.

SPECIAL TYPES OF MATRICES

(a) Square Matrix

Definition : *An $m \times n$ matrix for which for which $m = n$ (i.e., the number of rows is equal to the number of columns) is called a square matrix of order n.* It is also called an n-rowed square matrix. The elements a_{11}, a_{22}, a_{33}, ... ,a_{nn} are called the diagonal elements and the line along which they lie is called the principal diagonal of the matrix. For example the matrix

$$A = \begin{bmatrix} 0 & 1 & 2 & 3 \\ 2 & 3 & 1 & 0 \\ 5 & 0 & 1 & 0 \\ 0 & 0 & 1 & 2 \end{bmatrix}_{4 \times 4}$$

is a square matrix of order 4. The elements 0, 3, 1, 2 constitute the principal diagonal of this matrix.

(b) Unit Matrix or Identity Matrix

Definition : *A square matrix each of whose diagonal elements is 1 and each of whose non-diagonal elements is equal to zero is called a unit matrix or an identity matrix and is denoted by I. In will denote a unit matrix of order n. Thus a sure matrix* $A = [a_{ij}]$ *is a unit matrix if* $a_{ij} = 1$ *when* $i = j$ *and* $a_{ij} = 0$ *when* $i \neq j$.

(c) Null Matrix of Zero Matrix

Definition : *The m × n matrix whose elements are all 0 is called the null matrix (or zero matrix) of the type m × n. It is usually denoted by 0 or more clearly by* $0_{m,n}$. *Often a null matrix is simply denoted by the symbol 0 read as 'zero'.*

(d) Row Matrices and Column Matrices

Definition : *Any 1 × n matrix which has only one row and n columns is called a row matrix or row vector. Similarly any m × 1 matrix which has m rows and only column is a column matrix or column vector.*

For example, $\mathbf{X} = [2\ 7\ {-8}\ 5\ 11]_{1\times5}$ is a row matrix of the type 1 × 5 while

$$Y = \begin{bmatrix} 2 \\ -9 \\ 11 \end{bmatrix}_{3\times1}$$ is a column matrix of the type 3 × 1.

SOLVED EXAMPLES

Example 1:

A manufacturer produces three models (I, II and III) of a certain product. He uses two types of raw materials (A and B) of which 4000 and 6000 units respectively are available. The raw material requirements per unit of the three models are given below:

Raw Material	*Requirement per unit of given model*		
	I	II	II
A	2	3	5
B	4	2	7

The labour time for each unit of model I is twice that of model II and three times that of model. III. The entire labour force of the factory can produce the equivalent of 2500 units of model I. A market survey indicates that the minimum demand of the three models are 500, 500 and 375 units

respectively. However, the ratio of the number of units produced must be equal to 3:2:5. Assume that the profits per unit of models I, II and III are rupees 60, 40 and 100 respectively. Formulate the problem as a L.P.P. in order to determine the number of units of each product which will maximize profit.

Solution:

Let the manufacturer produce x_1, x_2, x_3 units of models I, II and III respectively. Since the profit per unit on model I, II and III is Rs. 40 and Rs. 100 respectively, the objective function is to maximize the profit:

$$Z = 60x_1 + 40x_2 + 100x_3 \qquad ...(1)$$

The raw materials used and available give rise to the following constraints respectively:

$$2x_1 + 3x_2 + 5x_3 \pounds 4000 \qquad ...(2)$$

$$4x_1 + 2x_2 + 7x_3 \leq 6000 \qquad ...(3)$$

Now if t be the labour time required for one unit of model I, then the time required for one unit of model II will be $\frac{1}{2}t$ and that for the model III will be $\frac{1}{3}t$. As the factory can produce 2500 units of model I, so the restriction on the production time will be

$$tx_1 + \frac{1}{2}tx_2 + \frac{1}{3}tx_3 \leq 25000t \text{ i.e., } x_1 + \frac{1}{2}x_2 + \frac{1}{3}x_3 \leq 2500. \qquad ...(4)$$

Now according to the market demand, we must have

$$x_1 \leq 500,\ x_2 \leq 500,\ x_3 \leq 375. \qquad ...(5)$$

Further the ratio of the number of different types of models is 3:2:5 *i.e.,* $x_1 = 3k$, $x_2 = 2k$, $x_3 = 5k$.

These give rise to the constraint

$$\frac{1}{3}x_1 = \frac{1}{2}x_2 \text{ and } \frac{1}{2}x_2 = \frac{1}{5}x_3 \qquad ...(6)$$

Thus, the linear programming problem is as follows:

Maximize $Z = 60x_1 + 40x_2 + 100x_3$

subject of the conditions:

$$2x_1 + 3x_2 + 5x_3 \leq 4000$$

$$4x_1 + 2x_2 + 7x_3 \leq 6000$$

$$x_1 + \frac{1}{2}x_2 + \frac{1}{2}x_2 \leq 2500$$

$$\frac{1}{3}x_1 = \frac{1}{2}x_2, \frac{1}{2}x_2 = \frac{1}{5}x_3$$

and $x_1 \geq 500$, $x_2 \geq 500$, $x_3 \geq 375$.

Example 2:

A complete unit of a certain product consists of four units of component A and three units of component B. The two components (A and B) are manufactured from two different raw materials of which 100 units and 200 units respectively are available. Three departments are engaged in the production process wit each department using a different method for manufacturing the components.

The following table gives the raw material requirements per production run and the resulting of each component. The objective is to determine the number of production runs for each department which will maximize the total number of component units of the final product:

Department	*Input per run (units) Raw material*		*Output per run (units) Component*	
	I	II	A	B
A	7	5	6	4
B	4	8	5	8
C	2	7	7	3

Formulate a linear programming model to the above problem.

Solution:

Let x_1, x_2, x_3 be the number of production runs for the departments A, B, C respectively.

The raw materials available give the restrictions

$$7x_1 + 4x_2 + 2x_3 \leq 100 \quad ...(1)$$

$$5x_1 + 8x_2 + 7x_3 \leq 200 \quad ...(2)$$

The total numbers of units produced by three departments:

$6x_1 + 5x_2 + 7x_3$ (component A) and $dx_1 + 8x_2 + 3x_3$ (component B).

Now final product requires 4 units of component A and 3 units of component B. So the maximum number of units of the final product cannot exceed the smaller value of

$$\frac{1}{4}(6x_1 + 5x_2 + 7x_3) \text{ and } \frac{1}{3}(4x_1 + 8x_2 + 3x_3).$$

Thus the objective function becomes

$$\text{Max. } Z = \sin\left[\frac{1}{4}(6x_1 + 5x_2 + 7x_3), \frac{1}{3}(4x_1 + 8x_2 + 3x_3)\right].$$

Since the objective function is not linear, a suitable transformation can be used to convert this into a L.P.P.

$$\text{Let, min. } \left[\frac{1}{4}(6x_1 + 5x_2 + 7x_3), \frac{1}{3}(4x_1 + 8x_2 + 3x_3)\right] = v.$$

$$\text{Then } \frac{1}{4}(6x_1 + 5x_2 + 7x_3) \geq v \text{ and } \frac{1}{3}(4x_1 + 8x_{12} + 3x_3) \geq v.$$

Thus we get the L.P.P. as follow:

Maximize $\quad Z = v.$

subject to the constraints:

$6x_1 + 5x_2 + 7x_3 - 4v \geq 0$

$4x_1 + 8x_2 + 3x_3 - 3v \geq 0$

$7x_1 + 4x_2 + 2x_3 \leq 100$

$5x_1 + 8x_2 + 7x_3 \leq 200$

and the non-negativity restrictions $x_1, x_2, x_3, v \geq 0$.

Example 3:

Draw the diagram of the solution set of the system of linear inequations:

$2x + 3y \leq 6$, $x + 4y \leq 4$, $x \geq 0$, $y = 0$.

Solution:

Changing the given inequations into equations, we get

$2x + 3y = 6$,

$x + 4y \leq 4$, $x \geq 0$, $y \geq 0$.

Region represented by $2x + 3y \leq 6$. The line $2x + 3y = 6$ meets x-axis at (3, 0) and (0, 2). Join the points (3, 0) and (0, 2) by a thick line to obtain the graph of the line $2x + 3y = 6$. Since the point (0, 0) satisfies the inequation $2x + 3y \leq 6$, therefore the portion of the xy-plane divided by the line $2x + 3y = 6$ containing the origin along with the line represents the solution set of the inequation $2x + 3y \leq 6$.

Region represented by $x + 4y \leq 4$. The line $x + 4y = 4$ meets x-axis at (4, 0) and y-axis at (0, 1). Join the points (4, 0) and (0, 1) by a thick line to obtain the graph of the line $x + 4y = 4$. The point (0, 0) does not lie on the line $x + 4y = 4$. Since (0, 0) satisfies the inequation $x + 4y \leq 4$, therefore the portion of the xy-plane divided by the line $x + 4y = 4$ containing the origin along with the line represents the solution set of the inequation $x + 4y \leq 4$.

Region represented by $x \geq 0$. The inequation x ³ 0 represents the region lying on the right hand side of the y-axis including y-axis.

Region represented by $y \geq 0$. The inequation $y \geq 0$ represents the region lying above the x-axis including x-axis.

The coming region (shaded region in the figure) of the above four regions represents the solution set of the given system of inequations.

Example 4:

A goldsmith manufactures necklaces and bracelets. The total number of necklaces and bracelets that he can handle per day is at most 24. It takes one hour to make a bracelet and half an hour to make a necklace. It is assumed that he can work for a maximum of 16 hours a day. Further the profit an a bracelet is Rs. 300 and the profit on a necklace is Rs. 100. Formulate this problem as a linear programming problem so as to maximize the profit.

Solution:

Suppose the goldsmith manufactures x_1 necklaces and x_2 bracelets per day.

Since the profit an a necklace is Rs. 100 and profit on a bracelet is Rs. 300, therefore the total profit Z in Rs. is given by

$$Z = 100x_1 + 300x_2 \qquad ...(1)$$

Since it takes half an hour to make one necklace, so the time required to make x_1 necklaces = (1/2) x; hours.

Again it takes one hour to make one bracelet, so the time required to make x_2 bracelets = 1. x_2 hours = x_2 hours.

Therefore, total time required to make x_1 necklaces and x_2 bracelets

$$= \left(\frac{x_1}{2} + x2\right) \text{ hours.} \qquad ...(2)$$

Since total time available per day is 16 hours, therefore

$$\frac{x_1}{2} + x_2 \leq 16 \text{ or } x_1 + 2x_2 \leq 32. \qquad ...(3)$$

The total number of necklaces and bracelets that the goldsmith can manufacture in a day is almost 24, so we have

Example 5:

A goldsmith manufactures necklaces and bracelets. The total number of necklaces and lets that he can handle per day is at most 24. It takes one hour a bracelet and half hour to make a necklace. It is assumed that he can work for a maximum of 16 hours a day. Further the profit on a bracelet is Rs. 300 and the profit on a necklace is Rs. 100. Find how many of each should be produced daily to maximize the profit.

Solution:

The mathematical form of the given problem is:

Maximize $Z = 100x + 300y$

subject to the constraints $x + 2y \leq 32$; $x + y \leq 24$

and the non-negative restrictions $x \geq 0$, $y \geq 0$.

Solving simultaneously the inequations of all the constraints and the non-negative restrictions by graphical method, the feasible region consists of the shaded region. Thus the shaded region POST is the set of all points which simultaneously satisfy all the constraints and the non-negative restrictions. Solving simultaneously the equations of the corresponding intersecting lines, we get the co-ordinates of the vertices of the shaded region as P(0, 16), O(0, 0), S(24, 0), T(16, 8). Now the values of the objective function at these corner points are as given in the tale below:

Point (x, y)	*Value of the objective function* $Z = 100x + 300y$
P(0, 16)	$100 \times 0 + 300 \times 16 = 4800$
O(0, 0)	$100 \times 0 + 300 \times 0 = 0$
S(24, 0)	$100 \times 24 + 300 \times 0 = 2400$
T(16, 8)	$100 \times 16 + 300 \times 8 = 4000$

Clearly, Z is maximum at P(0, 16). Hence , $x = 0$, $y = 16$ is the optimal solution of the given problem and the optimal value of Z is 4800 *i.e.*, the goldsmith earns maximum profit when he makes 16 bracelets and 0 necklace a day and that his maximum profit in this case is Rs. 4800.

Example 6:

Exhibit graphically the solution set of the following system of linear inequations:

$x + y \geq 1$, $-3x - 4y \geq -12$,

$-x + 2y \geq -2$, $x \geq 0$, $y \geq 0$.

Solution:

Region represented by $x + y \geq 1$. The straight line $x + y = 1$ meets x-axis at (1, 0) and y-axis at (0, 1). We join the points (1, 0) and (0, 1), by a thick line. Since the origin (0, 0) does not satisfy the inequation $x + y \geq 1$, therefore the portion of the xy-plane divided by the line $x + y = 1$ which does not contain the origin along with the line represents the solution set of the inequation $x + y \geq 1$.

Region represented $y - 3x - 4y \geq - 12$ i.e., by $3x + 4y \leq 12$. The straight line $3x + 4y - 12$ meets x-axis at (4, 0) and y-axis at (0, 3). We join the points (4, 0) and (0, 3) by a thick line. Since the point (0, 0) satisfies the inequation $3x + 4y \leq 12$, therefore the portion of the xy-plane divided by the line $3x + 4y = 12$ which contains the origin along with the line represents the inequation $- 3x - 4y \geq - 12$.

Region represented by $- x + 2y \geq -2$. The straight line $-x + 2y = -2$ meets x-axis at (2, 0) and y-axis at (0, – 1). We join the points (2, 0) and (0, –1) and y-axis by a thick line. Since the origin (0, 0) satisfies the inequation $- x + 2y \geq - 2$, therefore the portion of the xy-plane divided y the line $-x + 2y = - 2$ which contains the origin along with the line represents the inequation $- x + 2y \geq - 2$.

Region represented by $x \geq 0$. The inequation $x \geq 0$ represents the region lying on the right hand side of the y-axis including y-axis.

Region represented by $y \geq 0$. The inequation $y \geq 0$ represents the region lying above the x-axis including x-axis.

Hence, the shaded region *i.e.,* the region common to the given five inequations, represents the solution set of the given system of inequations.

Example 7:

A toy company manufactures two types of dolls; a basic version-doll A and a deluxe version-doll B. Each doll of type B takes twice as long to produce as one of type A, and the company would have time to make a maximum 2000 per day if it produces only the basic version. The supply of plastic is sufficient to produce 1500 dolls per day (both A and B combined). The deluxe version requires a fancy dress of which there are only 600 pieces per day available. If the company makes a profit of Rs. 3 and Rs. 5 per doll respectively, on dolls A and B, how many of each should be produced per day in order to maximize profit?

Solution:

Formulation of the linear programming problem.

Let x dolls of type A and y dolls of type B be produced per day.

If Z be the total profit A requires of time so that a doll of type B requires 2t units of time. The total time required to produce x dolls of type A and y dolls of type B = (x + 2y)t units. But the company has time sufficient to produce a maximum 2000 dolls per if it produces only the dolls of type A.

$\therefore \quad (x + 2y)t \le 2000t \Rightarrow x + 2y \le 2000.$

Since plastic is available to produce 1500 dolls per day only, therefore

$x + y \le 1500.$

Also fancy dress is available per day only for 600 dolls of type B.

$\therefore \quad y \le 600.$

Since the number of dolls produced, whether of type A or of type B, cannot be negative, therefore $x \ge 0$ and $y \ge 0$.

Hence the linear programming problem is as follows:

Maximize $Z = 3x + 5y$

subject to the constraints

$x + 2y \le 2000$

$x + y \le 1500$; $y \le 600$

and the non-negative restrictions $x \ge 0$, $y \ge 0$.

Solution of the problem.

First of the problem.

First consider the constraints as the equalities

$x + 2y = 2000$;

$x + y = 1500$

$y = 600$.

We draw these straight lines in the xy-plane.

The feasible region of the problem *i.e.*, the region consisting of those points (x, y) in the xy-plane which satisfy all the constraints and the non-negative restrictions is the shaded region OPQRS.

To find the maximum value of the objective function Z.

Solution by using corner point method. Solving simultaneously the equations of the corresponding intersecting lines of the feasible region, we get the coordinates of the corner points of the feasible region as

O(0, 0), P(1500, 0), Q(1000, 500), R(800, 600) and S(0, 600).

The values of the objective function Z at these corner points are as given below:

Point (x, y)	*Value of the objective function* $Z = 3x + 5y$
O(0, 0)	$3 \times 0 + 5 \times 0 = 0$
P(1500,0)	$3 \times 0 + 5 \times 0 = 0$
Q(100,500)	$3 \times 1000 + 5 \times 500 = 5500$
R(800,600)	$3 \times 800 + 5 \times 600 = 5400$
S(0, 600)	$3 \times 0 + 5 \times 600 = 3000$

Thus, Z is maximum at the corner point Q *i.e.,* for x = 1000 and y = 500 and the maximum value of Z is 5500. The optimal solution of the problem is x = 1000, y = 500.

Hence, 1000 dolls of type A and 500 dolls of type B should be produced per day to maximum the profit and the maximum profit per day is Rs. 5500.

The optimal solution may also be found by the following alternative method.

Alternative Solution by Iso-profit Line Method

To find the maximum value of the objective function Z, we give some particular value to Z, say 1500 and draw the line 3x + 5y = 1500, represented by AB, passing through the feasible region. It is an iso-profit line as the value of Z at each of its points is the same.

We now move this line parallel to itself away from the origin so that its distance from the origin becomes maximum yet it has at least one point in the feasible region. We see that in this position this line pales through only one point Q (1000, 500) of the feasible region. This line is an iso-profit line having only one point viz. Q in the feasible region which will yield the maximum value of Z.

Hence, Z is maximum for x = 1000 and y = 500 and the maximum value of Z is

$$3 \times 1000 + 5 \times 500 = 5500.$$

Example 8(a):

Minimize $Z = 5x_1 + 6x_2$

subject to the constraints

$$x_1 + x_2 \geq 50,$$

$$x + 2x_2 \leq 3x_1 + 4x_2 \leq 100$$

and the non-negative restrictions $x_1 \geq 0$ *and* $x_2 \geq 0$.

Solution:

Solving simultaneously the inequations of the constraints and the non-negative restrictions by graphical method, we see that there exist no values of x_1 and x_2 that simultaneously satisfy all the constraints and the non-negative restrictions.

Hence, the given problem does not have any feasible solution.

Example 8(b):

Using Iso-profit line method, compute the maximum value of the expression $2x + 3y$ subject to the conditions:

$$2x + y \leq 5$$

$$x - y \leq 1$$

$$y \leq 2$$

and the non-negative restrictions $x \geq 0$, $y \geq 0$.

Verify the maximum value by computing the values at the boundary points of the polygon.

Solution:

Solving simultaneously the inequations of all the conditions and the non-negative restrictions by graphical method, the feasible region (the set of the points satisfying all the conditions and the non-negative restrictions) consists of the shaded region OSTML.

Here, we are to maximize the objective function

$$Z = 2x + 3y.$$

To find the maximum value of the objective function Z, we give some particular value to Z, say 5 and draw the line $2x + 3y = 5$, represented by AQ, passing through the feasible region. It is an iso-profit line as the value of Z at each of its points is the same. We now move this line parallel to itself away from the origin so that it passes through only one point $\left[\text{here the corner po int } M\left(\frac{3}{2}, 2\right)\right]$ of the feasible region. This line is an iso-profit line having only one point viz. M in the feasible region which will yield the maximum value of Z.

Hence, Z is maximum for $x = \frac{3}{2}$ and $y = 2$ and the maximum value of Z is

$$2 \times \frac{3}{2} + 3 \times 2 = 9.$$

Verification. Solving simultaneously the equations of the corresponding intersecting lines of the feasible region, we get the co-ordinates of the vertices of the shaded region as O(0, 0), S(1, 0), T(2, 1), M $\left(\frac{3}{2}, 2\right)$ and L(0, 2). The values of the objective function at these corner points are as given below:

Point (x, y)	*Value of the objective function* $Z = 2x + 3y$
O(0, 0)	$2 \times 0 + 3 \times 0 = 0$
S(1, 0)	$2 \times 1 + 3 \times 0 = 2$
T(2, 1)	$2 \times 2 + 3 \times 1 = 7$
M $\left(\frac{3}{2}, 2\right)$	$2 \times \frac{3}{2} + 3 \times 2 = 9$
L(0, 2)	$2 \times 0 + 3 \times 2 = 6$

Thus, the maximum value of 2x + 3y is 9 and is attained when x = 3/2, y = 2.

Example 8(c):

A firm is engaged in breeding hens. In view of the need to ensure certain nutrients (say x_1, x_2, x_3), it is necessary to buy two types of food, say A and B. One unit of food A contains 36 units of x_1, 3 units of x_2 and 20 units of x_3. One units of food B contains 6 units of x_1, 12 units of x_2 and 10 units of x_3. The minimum daily requirement of x_1, x_2 and x_3 is 108, 36 and 100 units respectively. The cost of food A is Rs. 20 per units whereas food B costs Rs. 40 per unit. Find the minimum food cost so as to meet the minimum daily requirement of nutrients.

Solution:

Let x units of food A and y units of food B be bought to fulfil the minimum requirement of the nutrients x_1, x_2, x_3 and to minimize the cost.

If Z be the cost in Rs. of the two types of food bought, then

$$Z = 20x + 40y.$$

According to the minimum daily requirements of x_1, x_2, x_3, we have

$$36x + 6y \geq 108$$

$$3x + 12y \geq 36$$

$$20x + 10y \geq 100$$

Also, since the quantity of each type of food bought be negative, therefore $x \geq 0$, $y \geq 0$.

Thus the LPP formulated from the given problem is:

Minimize $Z = 20x + 40y$

subject to the constraints

$36x + 6y > 108$

$3x + 12y \geq 36$

$20x + 10y \geq 100$

and the non-negative restrictions $x \geq 0$, $y \geq 0$.

Solving simultaneously the inequations of all the constraints and the non-negative restrictions by graphical method, the feasible region (the set of all points satisfying all the constraints and the non-negative restrictions) consists of the shaded region LSTP.

To find the minimum value of Z, we give some particular value to Z, say, 320 and draw the line $20x + 40y = 320$, represented by AB, passing through the feasible region. It is an iso-cost line as the value of Z at each of its points is the same. We now move this line parallel to itself towards the origin so that it passes through only one point [here the corner point T(4, 2)] of the feasible region. This line is an iso-cost line having only one point viz. T in the feasible region which will give the minimum value of Z.

Therefore, Z is minimum for $x = 4$ and $y = 2$ and the minimum value of Z is

$$20 \times 4 + 40 \times 2 = 160.$$

Hence, 4 units of food A and 2 units of food B should be ought to fulfill the minimum requirements of x_1, x_2, x_3 at a minimum cost of Rs. 160.

Example 9(a):

Exhibit the solution set of the linear inequations

$3x + 2y \geq 6,$

$x \geq 1, y \geq 1.$

Solution:

Consider the equation

$$3x + 2y = 6,$$

$$x = 1, y = 1.$$

To find the solution set of the given system of inequation, we first find the solution sets of the given distinct inequations separately.

Region represented by $3x + 2y \geq 6$. The straight line $3x + 2y = 6$ meets x-axis at (2, 0) and y-axis at (0, 3). Since the given inequality is not strict, we join these points by a thick line. Clearly, the point (0, 0) not lying on the line $3x + 2y = 6$ does not satisfy the inequation $3x + 2y \geq 6$.

Region represented by $x \geq 1$. Clearly, the line $x = 1$ is parallel to y-axis at a distance of 1 unit from the origin lying to the right hand side of y-axis. Since the given inequality is not strict, we draw this line as a thick line. The point (0, 0) not lying on the line $x = 1$ does not satisfy the inequation $x \geq 1$, therefore, out of the two portions of the xy-plane divided by this line, the portion not containing the origin along with the line represents the solution set to the inequation $x \geq 1$.

Region represented by $y \geq 1$. Clearly, the line $y = 1$ is parallel to x-axis at a distance of 1 unit from the origin lying above x-axis. Since the given inequality is not strict, we draw this line as a thick line. The point (0, 0) not lying on the line $y = 1$ does not satisfy the inequation $y \geq 1$, therefore out of the two portions of the xy-plane divided by this line, the portion not containing the origin along with the line represents the solution set of the inequation $y \geq 1$. Here the shaded region command to the given three inequation represents the solution set of the given system of inequations. We serve that solution set of the given system of linear inequations is an unbounded region.

Example 9(b):

A firm manufactures A, B veld. The profit per unit soled of each product of Rs. 3, Rs. 2 and Rs. 4 respectively. The time required to manufacture one unit of each of the three products and the daily capacity of the two machines P and Q is given 24 the total below.

Machine	*Time per unit (minutes)*			*Machine capacity*
	A	*B*	*C*	*(Minutes day)*
P	*4*	*3*	*5*	*2000*
2	*2*	*2*	*4*	*2500.*

It is required to determine the daily number of unit to be manufactured for each product so as to maximize two profity. How are the firm must manufacture at least to A's, 200 B's and 50 C's but move then 150 A's. It is assumed that all the amounts produced are connected in the martlet.

Example 9(c):

Find all the basic solution of the following system:

$$x_1 + 2x_2 + x_3 = 4$$
$$2x_1 + x_2 + 5x_3 = 5$$

and prove that they are non-degenerate.

Solution:

The given system of equations can be expressed in matrix form as $Ax = b$ where $A = (\alpha_1, \alpha_2, \alpha_3)$

$$\alpha_1 = \begin{bmatrix} 1 \\ 2 \end{bmatrix}, \alpha_2 = \begin{bmatrix} 2 \\ 1 \end{bmatrix},$$

$$\alpha_3 = \begin{bmatrix} 1 \\ 5 \end{bmatrix}, x = \begin{bmatrix} x_1 \\ x_2 \\ x_3 \end{bmatrix},$$

$$b = \begin{bmatrix} 4 \\ 5 \end{bmatrix}.$$

Here n = number of variables = 3 and m = number of equation = 2. Hence there can be almost ${}^3C_2 = 3$ basic solution.

Three sets of two vectors out of a_1, a_2, a_3 are as follows:

$$B_1 = [\alpha_1, \alpha_2] = \begin{bmatrix} 1 & 2 \\ 2 & 1 \end{bmatrix},$$

$$B_2 = [\alpha_1, \alpha_3] = \begin{bmatrix} 1 & 1 \\ 2 & 5 \end{bmatrix},$$

$$B_3 = [\alpha_2, \alpha_3] = \begin{bmatrix} 2 & 1 \\ 1 & 5 \end{bmatrix}.$$

We have $|B_1| = -3 \neq 0$. $|B_2| = 3 \neq 0$. $|B_3| = 9 \neq 0$.

If follows that every set of two vectors of A is L.I. Hence all the three basic solutions exist. If x_{B1}, x_{B2}, x_{B3} are the vectors of corresponding basic variables, then

$$x_{B1} = {}_{B1}^{-1}b = -\frac{1}{2}\begin{bmatrix} 1 & -2 \\ -2 & 1 \end{bmatrix}\begin{bmatrix} 4 \\ 5 \end{bmatrix} = \begin{bmatrix} 2 \\ 1 \end{bmatrix}$$

$$x_{B2} = B_2^{-1}b = \frac{1}{3}\begin{bmatrix} 5 & -1 \\ -2 & 1 \end{bmatrix}\begin{bmatrix} 4 \\ 5 \end{bmatrix} = \begin{bmatrix} 5 \\ -1 \end{bmatrix}$$

$$x_{B3} = B_3^{-1}b = \frac{1}{9}\begin{bmatrix} 5 & -1 \\ -1 & 2 \end{bmatrix}\begin{bmatrix} 4 \\ 5 \end{bmatrix} = \begin{bmatrix} 5/3 \\ 2/3 \end{bmatrix}.$$

To find all the basic solution. In basis B_1, basis vectors are α_1, $\alpha 2$. Σo

$$x_{B1} = \begin{bmatrix} x_1 \\ x_2 \end{bmatrix} = \begin{bmatrix} 2 \\ 1 \end{bmatrix} \Rightarrow x_1 = 2, x_2 = 1.$$

These two variables are the basic variables and the remaining variables x3 is non-basic. It will have value zero. Thus the basic solution associated to the basis B_1 is given by (2, 1, 0). Similarly other basic solutions are (5, 0, –1) and (0, 5/3, 2/3).

In all the three basic solution none of the basic variables is zero, hence they are all non-degenerate.

Example 10:

According to the medical experts it is necessary for an adult to consume at least 75 gms of proteins, 85 gms of fats and 300 gms of carbohydrates daily. The following table gives the analysis of the food items readily available in he market with their respective costs.

Food	*Food value (in gm.) per 100 gms*			*Cost in*
Type	*Proteins*	*Fats*	*Carbohydrates*	*Rs. per kg*
A	18.0	15.0	–	3.0
B	16.0	4.0	7.0	4.0
C	4.0	20.0	2.5	2.0
D	5.0	8.0	40.0	1.5
Minimum daily requirement	75.0	85.0	300.0	

Formulate a linear programming problem for an optimum diet.

Solution:

Let the daily diet consist of x_1 kg of food A, x_2 kg of food B, x_3 kg of food C and x_4 kg of food D.

Then the total cost per day in Rs. is

$$Z = 3x_1 + 4x_2 + 2x_3 + 1.5x_4. \quad ...(1)$$

Total amount of proteins in the daily diet is

$$(180x_1 + 160x_2 + 40x_3 + 50x_4).$$

Since the minimum daily requirement of proteins is 75 gms, therefore we have

$$180x_1 + 160x_2 + 40x_3 + 50x_4 \geq 75. \quad ...(2)$$

Similarly, considering the total amounts of fats and carbohydrates in the diet, we have

$$150x_1 + 40x_2 + 200x_3 + 80x_4 \geq 85 \quad ...(3)$$

and $70x_2 + 25x_3 + 400x_4 \geq 300.$ ...(4)

Since, the daily diet cannot contain quantities with negative values of any food item, therefore

$$x_1 \geq 0,\ x_2 \geq 0,$$
$$x_3 \geq 0,\ x_4 \geq 0.$$

Hence, the linear programming problem formulated for the given diet problem is:

Minimize $Z = 3x_1 + 4x_2 + 2x_3 + 1.5x_4$

subject to the constraints

$$18x_1 + 160x_2 + 40x_3 + 50x_4 \geq 75$$
$$150x_1 + 40x_2 + 200x_3 + 80x_4 \geq 85$$
$$70x_2 + 25x_3 + 400x_4 \geq 300$$

and the non-negative restrictions

$$x_1 \geq 0,\ x_2 \geq 0,\ x_3 \geq 0$$

and $x_4 \geq 0$.

Example 11:

Show that the feasible solution $x_1 = 1$, $x_2 = 0$, $x_3 = 1$ and $Z = 6$ to the system of equations

$$x_1 + x_2 + x_3 = 2$$
$$x_1 - x_2 + x_3 = 2,$$
$$x_i \geq 0$$

which minimizes $Z = 2x_1 + 3x_2 + 4x_3$ is not basic.

Solution:

In the given F.S. there are only two non-zero variables namely x_1 and x_3. If vectors associated to these variables be a1 and a_3 then the determinant of column vectors corresponding to variables x_1, x_3 is $\begin{vmatrix} 1 & 1 \\ 1 & 1 \end{vmatrix} = 1 - 1 = 0.$

$\therefore$ the vectors α_1, α_3 are L.D.

Hence the solution is not a basic solution.

Example 12(a):

A dietician mixes two types of food in such a way that the vitamin contents of the mixture contain at least 8 units of vitamin A and 10 units of vitamin C. Food X contains 2 units/kg of vitamin A and 1 unit/kg of vitamin C while food Y contains 1 unit/kg of vitamin A and 2 units/kg of vitamin C.

One kg of food X costs Rs. 5 whereas one kg of food Y costs Rs. 7 Determine the minimum cost of such a mixture.

Solution:

Let the dietician mix x kg of food X and y kg of food Y. Then

$$x \geq 0,\ y \geq 0.$$

Since the minimum requirement of vitamin A is 8 units, therefore

$$2x + y \geq 8.$$

Similarly, since the minimum requirement of vitamin C is 10 units, therefore

$$x + 2y \geq 10.$$

The total cost Z in Rs. of purchasing x kg of food X and y kg of food Y is

$$Z = 5x + 7y.$$

Hence the mathematical form of the LPP of the given problem is

Minimize $Z = 5x + 7y$

subject to the constraints $2x + y \geq 8$

$x + 2y \geq 10$

and the non-negative restrictions

$$x \geq 0,\ y \geq 0.$$

Solving simultaneously the inequations of all the constraints and the non-negative restrictions by graphical method, the feasible region consists of the shaded region shown in the figure. The co-ordinates of the corner points of this region are P(0, 8), T(2, 4) and S(10, 0). Now the values of the objective function at these corner points are as given in the table below:

Point (x, y)	*Value of the objective function* $Z = 5x + 7y$
P(0, 8)	$5 \times 0 + 7 \times 8 = 56$
T(2, 4)	$5 \times 2 + 7 \times 4 = 38$
S(10, 0)	$5 \times 10 + 7 \times 0 = 50$

Clearly, Z is minimum at T(2, 4). Hence x = 2 and y = 4 is the optimal solution of the given problem and the optimal value is Z = 38.

Hence, the dietician should mix 2 kg of food X and 4 kg of food Y to make the required mixture at minimum cost. The minimum cost in this case is Rs. 38.

ISO-Cost Method

To find the minimum value of Z, we give some particular value to Z, say 70 and draw the line $5x + 7y = 70$, represented by AB, passing through the feasible region. It is an iso-cost line, as the cost of making the mixture is the same at each of its points. We now move this line parallel to itself towards the origin so that it passes through only one point [here the corner point T(2, 4)] of the feasible region. This line is an iso-cost line having only one point viz. T in the feasible region which gives the minimum value of Z.

Hence, Z is minimum for $x = 2$ and $y = 4$ and the minimum value of Z is

$$5 \times 2 + 7 \times 4 = 38.$$

Thus, the dietician should mix 2 kg of food X and 4 kg of food Y to make the required mixture at minimum cost. In this case minimum cost will be Rs. 38.

Example 12(b):

Which of the following vectors $x = [x_1, x_2, x_3, x_4, x_5, x_6, x_7]$ is a B.F.S. of the system

$$x_1 + 2x_2 + x_3 + 3x_4 + x_5 = 9$$

$$2x_1 + x_2 + 3x_4 + x_6 = 9$$

$$-x_1 + x_2 + x_3 + x_7 = 0,$$

$$x_1, x_2, \ldots, x_7 \geq 0.$$

(i) $x_1 = [2, 2, 0, 1, 0, 0, 0]$

(ii) $x_2 = [0, 0, 9, 0, 0, 9, -9]$

(iii) $x_3 = [3, 3, 0, 0, 0, 0, 0]$

(iv) $x_4 = [0, 0, 0, 0, 9, 9, 0]$

(v) $x_5 = [1, 0, 0, 0, 8, 7, 1]$

(vi) $x_6 = [0, 0, 0, 3, 0, 0, 0]$.

Solution:

We have denoted the column vector by symbol [ ].

(i) The vectors associated to non-zero variables are

$$\alpha_1 = [1, 2, -1],$$

$$\alpha_2 = [2, 1, 1],$$

$\alpha_4 = [3, 3, 0]$.

Obviously there exist scalars 1, 1 and – 1 such that

$$1.\alpha_1 + 1.\alpha_2 - 1.\alpha_4 = [0, 0, 0] = 0.$$

$\therefore$ vectors a_1, a_2, a_4 associated to non-zero variables are L.D.

Hence x is not a B.F.S.

(ii) The vectors associated to non-zero variables are

$$\alpha_3 = [1, 0, 1], \alpha_6 = [0, 1, 0], \alpha_7 = [0, 0, 1].$$

$$\text{Now } |\alpha_3\ \alpha_6\ \alpha_7| = \begin{vmatrix} 1 & 0 & 0 \\ 0 & 1 & 0 \\ 1 & 0 & 1 \end{vmatrix} = 1 \neq 0$$

$\therefore$ vectors α_3, α_6, α_7 are L.I.

Hence x_2 is a basic solution but not a basic feasible solution as x_7 is negative.

(iii) This solution contains 5 zero variables. So it may be a B.F.S. Now vectors associated to non-zero variables are

$\alpha_1 = [1, 2, -1]$, $\alpha_2 = [2, 1, 1]$.

Now these vectors together with the vector $\alpha_5 = [1, 0, 0]$ are L.I. as

$$|\alpha_1\ \alpha_2\ \alpha_5| = \begin{vmatrix} 1 & 2 & 1 \\ 2 & 1 & 0 \\ -1 & 1 & 0 \end{vmatrix} = 3 \neq 0.$$

Hence x_3 is B.F.S. with x_1, x_2, x_5 as basic variables.

Since one of the basic variables namely x_5 vanishes, so this is a degenerate B.F.S.

(iv) This solution contains 5 zero variables. So it may be a B.F.S. Now vectors associated to non-zero variables are $a_5 = [1, 0, 0]$, $a_6 = [0, 1, 0]$. Obviously these vectors together with $a_7 = [0, 0, 1]$ are L.I. Hence x_4 is a B.F.S. with x_5, x_6, x_7 as basic variables. Since one of the basic variables namely x_7 vanishes, so this is degenerate B.F.S.

(v) This solution does not contain alteast 7 – 3 = 4 variables zero or it contains more than 3 (no. of equations) non-zero variables, so it is not a B.F.S.

(vi) This solution contains one non-zero variable. The vector associated to this variable is $a_4 = [3, 3, 0]$.

$$\text{We have } |\alpha_4\ \alpha_6\ \alpha_7| = \begin{vmatrix} 3 & 0 & 0 \\ 3 & 1 & 0 \\ 0 & 0 & 1 \end{vmatrix} = 3 \neq 0$$

∴ vectors α_4, α_6, α_7 are L.I.

Hence x_6 is a B.F.S. with x_4, x_6, x_7 basic variables. Since basic variables x_6, x_7 also vanish, so it is a degenerate B.F.S.

Example 12(c):

Solve by graphical method, the linear programming problem:

Minimize $Z = 20x + 10y$

subject to the constraints, $x + 2y \leq 40$

$3x + y \geq 30$

$4x + 3y \geq 60$

and the non-negative restrictions $x, y \geq 0$.

Solution:

The feasible region consisting of all points whose co-ordinates simultaneously satisfy all constraints including non-negative restrictions of the given LPP.

Thus the shaded region PRST is the set of all feasible solution. Solving simultaneously the equations of the corresponding intersecting lines, we get co-ordinates of the vertices of the shaded region as: P(40, 0), R(15, 0), S(6, 12) and T(4, 18).

Now the value of the objective function at these corner points is as given in the table below:

Point (x, y)	*Value of the objective function:* $Z = 20x + 10y$
P(40, 0)	$20 \times 40 + 10 \times 0 = 800$
R(15, 0)	$20 \times 15 + 10 \times 0 = 300$
S(6, 12)	$20 \times 6 + 10 \times 12 = 240$
T(4, 18)	$20 \times 4 + 10 \times 18 = 260$

Clearly, Z is minimum at S(6, 12). Hence, x = 6, y = 12 is the optimal solution of the given and the optimal value of Z is 240.

Example 12(d):

A manufacture of patent medicines is proposed to prepare a production plan for medicines A and B. There are sufficient ingredients available to make 20, 000 bottle of medicine A and 40,000 bottles of medicine B, but there are only 45,000 bottles into which either of the medicines can be filled. Further, it takes three hours to prepare enough material to fill 1000 bottles of medicine

A and one hour to prepare enough material to fill 1000 bottles of medicine B and there are 66 hours available for this operation. The profit is Rs. 8 per bottle for medicine A and Rs. 7 per bottle for medicine B. Formulate this problem as a L.P.P.

Solution:

Suppose the manufacturer produces x_1 thousand bottles of medicine A and x_2 thousand bottles of medicine B.

Since there are only 45,000 bottles available for filling the medicine A and B, therefore we have $x_1 + x_2 \leq 45$.

It takes three hours to prepare enough material to fill 1000 bottles of medicines A. Therefore the time required to fill x_1 thousand bottles of medicine A is $3x_1$ hours.

Similarly, the time required to fill x_2 thousand bottles of medicine B is x_2 hours.

Thus, the total time required to fill x_1 thousand bottles of medicines A and x_2 thousand bottles of medicine B is $(3x_1 + x_2)$ hours.

The total time available for this operation is 66 hours. So, we have $3x_1 + x_2 \leq 66$.

There are sufficient ingredients available to make 20 thousand bottles of medicine A and 40 thousand bottles of medicine B, therefore we have $x_1 \leq 20$, $x_2 \leq 40$.

Since the number of bottles cannot be negative, therefore we have $x_1 \geq 0$, $x_2 \geq 0$.

The profit per bottle for medicine A is Rs. 8 and for medicine B is Rs. 7. So, the total profit in Rs. on x_1 thousand bottles of medicine A and x_2 thousand bottles of medicines B is given by

$$Z = 8 \times 1000x_1 + 7 \times 1000x_2 = 8000x_1 + 7000x_2.$$

Hence, the linear programming problem formulated for the given problem is

Maximize $Z = 8000x_1 + 7000x_2$,

subject to the constraints:

$x_1 + x_2 \leq 45$

$3x_1 + x_2 \leq 66$

$x_1 \leq 20$

$x_2 \leq 40$

and the non-negative restrictions $x_1 \geq 0$, $x_2 \leq 0$.

Example 13:

The manager of a courier company wishes to hire extra helpers during the Christmas season, because of a large increase in the volume of mail handling and delivery. Keeping in view the limited office space and the budgetary conditions, the number of temporary helpers must not exceed 10. According to past experience, a man can handle 300 letters and 80 packages per day, and a woman can handle 400 letters and 50 packages per day. It is believed that the daily volume of extra mail and packages will be no less than 3400 and 680 respectively. A man receives Rs. 25 a day and a woman receives Rs. 22 a day. How many men and women helper should be hired to keep the pay-roll at a minimum?

Solution:

Let x men and y women by hired by the company to keep the pay-roll at a minimum.

If Z be the daily pay-roll in Rs. of the extra helpers, then

$$Z = 25x + 22y.$$

Since the maximum number of helpers can be only 10, therefore

$$x + y \leq 10.$$

Given that a man can handle 300 letters daily and a woman can handle 400 letters daily and that the number of extra letters expected daily is not less than 3400, we must have

$$300x + 400y \geq 3400.$$

Similarly $80x + 50y \geq 680$.

Since the number of men and women hired cannot be negative, we have

Thus the LPP formulated for the given problem can be stated as:

Minimize $Z = 25x + 22y$

subject to the constraints $x + y \leq 10$

$$300x + 400y \geq 3400; \; 80x + 50y \geq 680$$

and the non-negative restriction $x \geq 0, \; y \geq 0$.

Solving simultaneously the inequations of all the constraints and the non-negative restrictions by graphical method, the feasible region {the set of all points satisfying all the constraints and the non-negative restrictions} consists of the point G(6, 4) only.

Therefore the optimal solution is x = 6 and y = 4, and the optimal value of

$$Z = 25 \times 6 + 22 \times 4 = 239.$$

Hence 6 men and 4 women helpers should be hired by the courier company to meet its seasonal requirements and keep the pay-roll at a minimum of Rs. 238.

Example 14:

A firm manufactures two types of products A and B and sells them at a profit of Rs. 2 on type A and Rs. 3 on type B. Each product is processed on two machines E and F. Type A requires one minute of processing time on E and two minutes on F, type B requires one minute on E and one minute on F. The machine E is available for not more then 6 hours 40 minutes while machine F is available for 10 hours during any working day. Formulate the problem as a linear programming problem.

Solution:

Let the manufacturer produce x_1 units of the product of type A and x_2 units of the product of type B.

The given information can be systematically arranged in the form of the following table:

Machine	*Time of processing (minutes per unit)*		*Time available*
	Type A (x_1 units)	*Type B (x_2 units)*	*(minutes)*
E	1	1	400
F	2	1	600
Profit per unit	Rs. 2		Rs. 3

Since the machine E takes 1 minute time for processing a unit of type A and 1 minute time of processing a unit of type B, therefore the total time required on machine E is $(x_1 + x_2)$ minutes.

But the machine E is available for not more than 6 hours and 40 minutes = 400 minutes, therefore we have

$$x_1 + x_2 \leq 400.$$

Similarly, the total time (in minutes) required on machine F is $2x_1 + x_2$.

Since the machine F is available for not more than 10 hours = 600 minutes, therefore we have

$$2x_1 + x_2 \leq 600.$$

Since it is not possible to produce negative quantities, so we have

$$x_1 \geq 0, x_2 \geq 0.$$

The profit on type A is Rs. 2 per unit so the profit on selling x_1 units of type A will be Rs. $2x_1$. Similarly, the profit on selling x_2 units of type B will be Rs. $3x_2$.

Therefore, the total profit (in Rs.) on selling x_1 units of type A and x_2 units of type B is

$$Z = 2x_1 + 3x_2.$$

Hence the required linear programming problem formulated for the given problem is

Maximize

$$Z = 2x_1 + 3x_2$$

subject to the conditions

$$x_1 + x_2 \leq 400$$
$$2x_1 + x_2 \leq 600$$
$$x_1 \geq 0, x_2 \geq 0.$$

Example 15(a):

Solve by graphical method, the Linear Programming Problem.

Max. $Z = -3x_1 + 2x_2$

s.t. $x_1 \leq 3,\ x_1 - x_2 \leq 0$

and $x_1,\ x_2 \geq 0.$

Solution:

It has been seen in the last example that as Z increases both the variables can be made arbitrarily large. But in this example we observe that an unbounded solution does not necessarily imply that all the variables can be made arbitrarily large as Z approaches infinity.

Example 15(b):

A certain farming organization operates three farms of comparable productivity. The output each farm is limited both by the usable acreage and by the amount of water available for irrigation. The data for the up coming season are the following:

Farm	*Usable acreage*	*Water available in acre metre*
1	*400*	*150*
2	*600*	*200*
3	*300*	*90*

The organization is considering three crops for planting which differ primarily in their expected profit per acre and in their consumption of water. Furthermore, the total acreage that can be devoted to each of the crops is limited by the amount of appropriate harvesting equipment available:

Crop	*Maximum*	*Water consumption acreage per acre*	*Expected profit in acre metre*
A	*700*	*0'5*	*Rs. 4,000*
B	*800*	*0'4*	*Rs. 3,000*
C	*300*	*0'3*	*Rs. 1,000*

In order to maintain a uniform workload among the farms, it is the policy of the organization that the percentage of the usable acreage planted must be the same at each farm. However, any combination of the crops may be grown at any of the farms. The organization wishes to know how much of each crop should be planted at the respective farms in order to maximize expected profit. Formulate this as a linear programming problem.

Example 15(c):

A manufacture of patent medicines is proposed to prepare a production plan for medicines A and B. There are sufficient ingredients available to make 20, 000 bottle of medicine A and 40,000 bottles of medicine B, but there are only 45,000 bottles into which either of the medicines can be filled. Further, it takes three hours to prepare enough material to fill 1000 bottles of medicine A and one hour to prepare enough material to fill 1000 bottles of medicine B and there are 66 hours available for this operation. The profit is Rs. 8 per bottle for medicine A and Rs. 7 per bottle for medicine B. Formulate this problem as a L.P.P.

Solution:

Suppose the manufacturer produces x_1 thousand bottles of medicine A and x_2 thousand bottles of medicine B.

Since there are only 45,000 bottles available for filling the medicine A and B, therefore we have $x_1 + x_2 \leq 45$.

It takes three hours to prepare enough material to fill 1000 bottles of medicines A. Therefore the time required to fill x_1 thousand bottles of medicine A is $3x_1$ hours.

Similarly, the time required to fill x_2 thousand bottles of medicine B is x_2 hours.

Thus, the total time required to fill x_1 thousand bottles of medicines A and x_2 thousand bottles of medicine B is $(3x_1 + x_2)$ hours.

The total time available for this operation is 66 hours. So, we have $3x_1 + x_2 \leq 66$.

There are sufficient ingredients available to make 20 thousand bottles of medicine A and 40 thousand bottles of medicine B, therefore we have $x_1 \leq 20$, $x_2 \leq 40$.

Since the number of bottles cannot be negative, therefore we have $x_1 \geq 0$, $x_2 \geq 0$.

The profit per bottle for medicine A is Rs. 8 and for medicine B is Rs. 7. So, the total profit in Rs. on x_1 thousand bottles of medicine A and x_2 thousand bottles of medicines B is given by

$$Z = 8 \times 1000x_1 + 7 \times 1000x_2 = 8000x_1 + 7000x_2.$$

Hence, the linear programming problem formulated for the given problem is

Maximize $Z = 8000x_1 + 7000x_2$,

subject to the constraints:

$$x_1 + x_2 \leq 45$$
$$3x_1 + x_2 \leq 66$$
$$x_1 \leq 20$$
$$x_2 \leq 40$$

and the non-negative restrictions $x_1 \geq 0$, $x_2 \leq 0$.

Example 16:

Old hens can be bought at Rs. 2 each and young ones at Rs. 5 each. The old hens lay 3 eggs per week and the young ones lay 5 eggs per week, each egg being worth 30 praise. A hen (young or old) costs Re. 1 per week to feed. I have only Rs. 80 to spend for hens. How many of each kind should I buy to give me a maximum profit, assuming that I cannot house more than 20 hens?

Solution:

Suppose I buy x old hens and y young hens.

Since old hens lay 3 eggs per week and the young ones lay 5 eggs per week, the total number of eggs I have per week is 3x + 5y. Consequently, each egg being worth 30 paise, my total income per week is Rs. 0.3 (3x + 5y).

Also, the expenses for feeding (x + y) hens, at the rate of Re. 1 per hen per week

$= \text{Rs. } (x + y).$

Thus, the total profit Z in Rs. earned per week is given as

$$Z = 0.3\ (3x + 5y) - (x + y) = 0.5y - 0.1x.$$

Since the cost of one old hen is Rs. 2 and that of one found hen is Rs. 5 and I have only Rs. 80 to spend for hens, therefore

$$2x + 5y \leq 80.$$

Since I cannot house more than 20 hens, therefore

$$x + y \leq 20.$$

Again, the number of hens purchased, whether old ones or young ones, be negative.

Therefore, $x \geq 0$ and $y \geq 0$.

Thus the LPP formulated for the given problem is:

Maximize $Z = 0.5y - 0.1x$

subject to the constraints $2x + 5y \leq 80$

$x + y \geq 20$

and the non-negative restrictions $x \geq 0$ and $y \geq 0$.

Solving simultaneously the inequations of all the constraints and the non-negative restrictions by graphical method, the feasible region (the set of all points satisfying all the constraints and the non-negative restrictions) consists of the shaded region OBEC.

To find the maximum value of the objective function $Z = 0.5y - 0.1x$, we give some particular value to Z, say 1 and draw the line $0.5y - 0.1x = 1$, represented by PQ, passing through the feasible region. It is an iso-profit line as the value of Z at each of its is the same.

We now move this line parallel to itself away from the origin so that it passes through only one point [here the corner point B(0, 16)] of the feasible region. This line is an iso-profit line having only one point viz. B in the feasible region which will yield the maximum value of Z.

Thus, Z is maximum for x = 0 and y = 16 and the maximum value of Z

$= 0.5 \times 16 - 0.1 \times 0 = 8.$

Hence, I should buy only 16 young hens and no old hen in order to get the maximum profit of Rs. 8 per week.

Remark : The point giving the maximum value of the objective function may also be located by finding the values of the objective function at all the different corner points of the feasible region.

Solving simultaneously the equations of the corresponding lines of the feasible region, we get the co-ordinates of the vertices of the feasible region as O(0, 0), B(0, 16), E $\left(\frac{20}{3}, \frac{40}{3}\right)$ and C(20, 0). The values of the objective function at these corner points are as given below:

Point (x, y)	*Value of the objective function* $Z = 0.5y - 0.1x$
O(0, 0)	$0.5 \times 0 - 0.1 \times 0 = 0$
B(0, 16)	$0.5 \times 16 - 0.1 \times 0 = 8$
E $\left(\frac{20}{3}, \frac{40}{3}\right)$	$0.5 \frac{40}{3} - 0.1 \times \frac{20}{3} = 6$
C(20, 0)	$0.5 \times 0 - 0.1 \times 20 = -2$

Thus, the maximum value of Z is 8 and is attained when $x = 0$ and $y = 16$.

Example 17(a):

The objective of a diet problem is to ascertain the quantities of certain foods that should be eaten to meet certain nutritional requirement at a minimum cost. The consideration is limited to mild, green vegetables and eggs, and to vitamins A, B, C. The number of milligrams of each of these vitamins contained within a unit of each food and their daily minimum requirement along with the cost of each food is given in the table below:

Vitamin	*Litre of Milk*	*Kg. of Vegetables*	*Dozen of Eggs*	*Minimum Daily Requirement*
A	1	1	10	1 mg.
B	100	10	10	50 mg.
C	10	100	10	10 mg.
Cost in Rs.	20	10	8	

Formulate a linear programming problem for this diet problem.

Solution:

Let the daily diet consist of x_1 litres of milk, x_2 kgs. of vegetables and x_3 dozens of eggs.

Then total cost Z per day in Rs. is given by

$$Z = 20x_1 + 10x_2 + 8x_3. \quad ...(1)$$

Total amount of vitamin A in the daily diet is

$(x_1 + x_2 + 10x_3)$ mg.,

which should be at least equal to 1 mg., therefore

$$x_1 + x_2 + 10x_3 \geq 1. \quad ...(2)$$

Similarly, considering the total amounts of vitamins B and C in the daily diet, we have

$$100x_1 + 10x_2 + 10x_3 \geq 50 \quad ...(3)$$

and $10x_1 + 100x_2 + 10x_3 \geq 10$ ...(4)

Since the quantities of different food items to be consumed cannot be negative, therefore we have

$$x_1 \geq 0, x_2 \geq 0, x_3 \geq 0.$$

Hence, the linear programming problem formulated from the given diet problem is:

Minimize $Z = 20x_1 + 10x_2 + 8x_3$,

subject to the constricts

$$x_1 + x_2 + 10x_3 \geq 1$$
$$100x_1 + 10x_2 + 10x_3 \geq 50$$
$$10x_1 + 100x_2 + 10x_3 \geq 10$$

and the non-negative restrictions $x_1 \geq 0, x_2 \geq 0, x_3 \geq 0$.

Example 17(b):

The owner of the Metro Sports wishes to determine how many advertisements to place in the selected three monthly magazines A, B and C. His objective is to advertise in such a way that total exposure to principal buyers of expensive sports good is maximized. Percentages of readers for each magazine are known. Exposure in any particular magazine is the number of advertisements placed multiplied by the number of principal buyers. The following data may be used:

Exposure Category	*Magazines*		
	A	B	C
Readers (in Lacks)	1	0.6	0.4
Principal Buyers	10%	15%	7%
Cost per advertisement (in Rs.)	5000	4500	4250

The budgeted amount is at most Rs. 1 take for the advertisements. The owner has already decided that magazine A should have no more than 6 advertisements and that B and C, each have at last two advertisements, formulate a LP model for the problem.

Solution:

Let x_1, x_2, x_3 be the number of insertions in magazines A, B and C respectively.

Then the LP formulation will be as follows:

Maximize Z = (10% of 100000) x_1 + (15% of 60000) x_2 + (7% of 40000) x_3

or Maximize $Z = 10000x_1 + 90000x_2 + 2800x_3$

subject to the constitutive restrictions $x_1, x_2, x_3 \geq 0$.

Example 18:

A tyre factory produces three types of tyre T_1, T_2, T_3. Three different types of chemicals say C_1, C_2, C_3 are required for production. One T_1 tyre needs 2 units of C_1, 3 units of C_3; one T2 tyre needs 3 units 3 units of C_1, 2 units of C_2 and 2 units of C_3; and one T3 tyre needs 5 units of C_2 and 4 units of C_3. The factory has only a stock of 20 units of C_1, 25 units of C_2 and 30 units of C_3. Further the profit from the sale of one tyre T_1 is Rs. 6, one tyre T_2 is Rs. 10 and of one tyre T_3 is Rs. 8. Assuming that the factory can sell all that it produces, formulate a linear programming problem to maximize its profits.

Solution:

Let the factory produce x_1 tyres of type T_1, x_2 tyres of type T_2 and x_3 tyres of type T_3.

The given information can be put in a tabular form as given below:

	Tyre T_1	*Tyre T_2*	*Tyre T_3*	*Total chemical available*
Chemical C_1	2	3	0	20
Chemical C_2	0	2	5	25
Chemical C_3	3	2	4	30
Profit in Rs. (per tyre)	6	10	8	

The total profit Z in Rs. is given as

$$Z = 6x_1 + 10x_2 + 8x_3. \quad ...(1)$$

The total quantity of chemical C_1 required = $(2x_1 + 3x_2)$ units.

Since the factory has a stock of 20 units of chemical C_1, therefore we have

$$2x_1 + 3x_2 \le 20 \quad ...(2)$$

Similarly, considering the total quantity of the chemicals C_2 and C_3 required, we have

$$2x_2 + 5x_3 \le 25 \quad ...(3)$$

and $3x_1 + 2x_2 + 4x_3 \le 30.$ ...(4)

Also we have

$$x_1 \ge 0,\ x_2 \ge 0,\ x_3 \ge 0, \quad ...(5)$$

since the factory cannot produce negative quantities.

Hence, the linear programming problem formulated from the given problem is as follows:

Maximize $Z = 6x_1 + 10x_2 + 8x_3$

subject to the constraints

Example 19:

Solve by graphical method, the L.P.P.

Max. $Z = 3x_1 + 2x_2$

s.t. $x_1 - x_2 \le 1,\ x_1 + x_2 \ge 3$

and $x_1,\ x_2 \ge 0.$

Solution:

From this figure it is clear that the line representing the objective function can be moved far even parallel to itself in the direction of Z increasing and still have some points in the feasible region.

Hence Z can be made arbitrarily large and the problem has no finite maximum value of Z. Such problem are said to have unbounded solution.

Example 20:

A manufacturer of biscuits is considering four types of gift packs containing three types of buckets: orange cream (OC), chocolate cream (CC), and wafers (W). Market research conducted recently to assess the preferences of the consumers shows the following types of assortments to be in good demand:

Assortments	*Contents*	*Selling price per kg (Rs.)*
A	*Not less than 40% of OC*	20
	Not more than 20% of CC	
	Any quantity of W	
B	*Not less than 20% of OC*	25
	Not more than 40% of CC	

Assortments	*Contents*	*Selling price per kg (Rs.)*
	Any quantity of W	
C	*Not lass than 50% of OC*	22
	Not more than 10% of CC	
	Any quantity of W	
D	*Not restrictions*	12

For the biscuits, the manufacturing capacity and costs are given below:

Biscuits variety	*OC*	*CC*	*W*
Plant capacity (kg/day)	200	200	150
Manufacturing cost (Rs/kg.)	8	9	7

Formulate a linear programming model to find the production schedule which maximizes the profit assuming that there are no market restrictions.

Solution:

Let x_{ij} kg. be the quantity used in ith assortment of the jth type of biscuits, where i = A, B, C, D and j = OC, CC, W (number 1, 2, 3 respectively).

Then in assortment A, x_{A1}, x_{A2}, x_{A3} denote the quantity in kg. of OC, CC and W type of biscuits respectively. Similarly we can interpret for other assortments.

Now the given data can be put in the form of L.P.P. as follows:

Maximize $Z = 20\ (x_{A1} + x_{A2} + x_{A3}) + 25\ (x_{B1} + x_{B2} + x_{B3}) + 22\ (x_{C1} + x_{C2} + x_{C3}) + 12\ (x_{D1} + x_{D2} + x_{D3}) - 8\ (x_{A1} + x_{B1} + x_{C1} + x_{D1}) - 9\ (x_{A2} + x_{B2} + x_{C2} + x_{D2}) - 7\ (x_{A3} + x_{B3} + x_{C3} + x_{D3}$

or Maximize $Z = 12x_{A1} + 11x_{A2} + 13x_{A3} + 17x_{B1} + 16x_{B2} + 18x_{B3} + 14x_{C1} + 13x_{C2} + 15x_{C3} + 4x_{D1} + 3x_{D2} + 5x_{D3}$

subject to the constraints:

$x_{A1} \geq 0.40 (x_{A1} + x_{A2} + x_{A3})$

$x_{A2} \leq 0.20 (x_{A1} + x_{A2} + x_{A3})$ gift pack A

$x_{B1} \geq 0.20 (x_{B1} + x_{B2} + x_{B3})$

$x_{B2} \leq 0.40 (x_{B1} + x_{B2} + x_{B3})$ gift pack B

$x_{C1} \geq 0.50 (x_{C1} + x_{C2} + x_{C3})$

$x_{C2} \leq 0.10 (x_{C1} + x_{C2} + x_{C3})$ gift pack C

Plant capacity constraints are: $x_{A1} + x_{B1} + x_{C1} + x_{D1} \leq 200$

$x_{A2} + x_{B2} + x_{C2} + x_{D2} \leq 200$

$x_{A3} + x_{B3} + x_{C3} + x_{D3} \leq 150$

and non-negativity restrictions are $x_{ij} \geq 0$ (i = A, B, C, D; j = 1, 2, 3).

Example 21:

A company has two grades of inspectors, I and II, who are to be assigned for a quality control inspection. It is required that at least 2000 pieces be inspected per 8 hour day. Grade I inspectors can check pieces at the rate of 50% hour with the accuracy of 97%. Grade II inspectors can check pieces at the rate of 40% hour with the accuracy of 95%.

The wage rate of Grade I inspector is Rs. 4.50% hour and that of Grade II is Rs. 2.50/hour. Each time an error is made by an inspector, the cost to the company is one rupee. The company has available for the inspection job, 10 grade I and 5 grade II inspectors. Formulate the problem to minimize the total cost of inspection.

Solution:

Let the no. of inspectors of grade I and II be x_1 and x_2 respectively. They will inspect (8 × 50) x1 + (8 × 40) x_2 pieces daily. As the company requires attest 2000 items to be inspected daily, of the constraint is

$(8 \times 50) x_1 + (8 \times 40) x_2 \geq 2000$ *i.e.,* $5x_1 + 4x_2 \geq 25.$ ...(1)

The limitations on the available numbers of inspectors give the constraints

$x_1 \leq 10, 2 \leq 5$ ...(2)

Further the company is bearing two types of costs, the wages of inspectors and the costs of inspection errors.

The cost of each inspector per hour is as follows:

Grade I : Rs. $\left[4.50 + 1 \times \left(\frac{3}{100} \times 50\right)\right]$ = Rs. 6.00/hour

Grade II : Rs. $\left[2.50 + 1 \times \left(\frac{5}{100} \times 40\right)\right]$ = Rs. 4.50/hour.

Now the objective of the company is to minimize the total cost of inspection at the above rates for each day.

Thus the objective function is

$$\text{Minimize } Z = 8 \times 6.00 \times x_1 + 8 \times 4.50 \times x_2 = 48x_1 + 36x_2 \quad ...(3)$$

Hence the required L.P.P. is

$$\text{Minimize } Z = 48x_1 + 36x_2$$

subject to the constraints: $5x_1 + 4x_2 \geq 25$

$$x_1 \leq 10,\ x_2 \leq 5$$

and the non-negativity restrictions $x_1, x_2 \geq 0$.

Example 22:

Suresh has two factories of toys, one located in city X and the other in city Y. Both these factories manufacture the same type of toys. From these locations a certain number of toys are delivered to each of the three depots situated at places A, B and C. The weekly requirements of the depots are respectively 5, 5 and 4 units, while the production capacity of the factories at X and Y are respectively 8 and 6 units. The transportation cost in Rs. per unit from a factory to a depot is as given in the table.

	To Depot	*A*	*B*	*C*
From Factory				
X		*16*	*10*	*15*
Y		*10*	*12*	*10*

How many units should be transported from each factory to each depot in order that the transportation cost is minimum?

Solution:

Let x units and y units of toys be transported from the factory at X to the deputes at A and B respectively. Then 8 – x – y units will be transported from the factory at X to the depot at C, since the production capacity of the factory at X is 8 units.

Now the number of units supplied to the depots cannot be negative, therefore

$$x \geq 0,\ y \geq 0 \text{ and } 8 - x - y \geq 0 \Rightarrow x + y \leq 8.$$

The weekly requirement of the depot at A is 5 units. Since x units are supplied from the factory at X, the remaining 5 – x units are to be supplied from the factory at Y.

$\therefore \quad 5 - x \geq 0 \Rightarrow x \leq 5.$

Similarly, 5 – y units are to be supplied from the factory at Y to the depot at B.

Since the production capacity of the factory at Y is 6 units, therefore

$$6 - (5 - x + 5 - y),$$

i.e., $x + y - 4$

units of toys are to be supplied from this factory to the depot at C.

On account of the non-negative restrictions, we must have

$$x + y - 4 \geq 0$$

$$\Rightarrow \quad x + y \geq 4.$$

The total transportation cost Z in Rs. is given by

$$Z = 16x + 10y + 15(8-x-y) + 10(5-x) + 12(5 - y) + 10(x + y-4)$$

$$= x - 7y + 180.$$

Therefore, the LPP formulated for the given problem can be stated as:

Minimize $Z = x - 7y + 190$

subject to the constraints $x + y \leq 8$

$x \leq 5$

$y \leq 5$

$x + y \geq 4$

and the non-negative restrictions $x \geq 0$, $y \geq 0$.

Solving simultaneously the inequations of all the constraints and the non-negative restrictions by graphical method, the feasible region (the set of all points satisfying all the constraints and the non-negative restrictions) consists of the shaded region EFCGHD.

To find the minimum value of Z, we assign a particular value, say 190 to Z and draw the line Z = 190 (*i.e.,* x – 7y = 0), represented by OL, passing through the feasible region. It is an iso-cost line as the value of Z at each of its points is the same. At the corner point F(4, 0) of the feasible region, we have Z = 194 which is > 190. So we move the line OL parallel to itself away from the origin towards the positive direction of y-axis so that it passes through only one point [here the corner point D(0, 5)] of the feasible region.

This line is an iso-cost line having only one point viz. D in the feasible region which will give the minimum value of Z.

Thus, Z is minimum for x = 0 and y = 5 and the minimum value of Z in this case is $0 - 7 \times 5 + 190 = 155$.

Hencc, the optimal transportation strategy is to supply 0, 5 and 3 units from the factory at X and 5, 0 and 1 units from the factory at Y to the depots at A, B and C respectively. In this case the transportation cost is minimum and is Rs. 155.

Example 23:

Draw the seraph of the solution set of the inquisitions

$$x + y \leq 5,\ 4x + y \geq 4,\ x + 5y \geq 5,\ x \leq 4,\ y \geq 3.$$

Solution:

Consider the equations

$$x + y = 5,$$
$$4x + y = 4,$$
$$x + 5y = 5,$$
$$x = 4,$$
$$y = 3.$$

First we shall consider each inquisition separately.

Region represented by $x + y \leq 5$. The straight line $x + y = 5$ meets the x-axis at (5, 0) and y-axis at (0, 5). Since the given inequality is not strict, we join these points by a thick line. Clearly, the point (0, 0) not lying on the line $x + y = 5$ satisfies the inquisition $x + y \leq 5$. Therefore, out of the two portions of the xy-plane divided by the line $x + y = 5$, the one containing the origin (0, 0) along with the represents the solution set of the inquisition $x + y \leq 5$.

Region represented by $4x + y \geq 4$. The straight line $4x + y = 4$ meets x-axis at (1, 0) and y-axis at (0, 4). Since the given inequality is not strict, we join these points by a thick line. Clearly, the point (0, 0) not lying on the line $4x + y = 4$ does not satisfy the inquisition $4x + y \geq 4$. Therefore, out of the two portions of the xy-plane divided by the line $4x + y = 4$, the portion not containing the origin along with the line represents the solution set of the inquisition $4x + y \geq 4$.

Region represented by $x + 5y \geq 5$. The straight line $x + 5y = 5$ meets the x-axis at (5, 0) and the y-axis at (0, 1). Since the given inequality is not strict, we join these points by a thick line. Clearly, the point (0, 0) not lying on the line $x + 5y = 5$ does not satisfy the inquisition $x + 5y \geq 5$. Therefore, out of the two portions of the xy-plane divided by the line $x + 5y = 5$, the portion not containing the origin along with the line represents the solution set of the inquisition $x + 5y \geq 5$.

Region represented by $x \leq 4$. Clearly, the line $x = 4$ is parallel to y-axis at a distance of 4 units from the origin lying to the right hand side of the y-axis. Since the given inequality is not strict, we draw this line as a thick line. The point (0, 0) not lying on the line $x = 4$ satisfies the inquisition $x \leq 4$, therefore out of the two portions of the xy-plane divided by this line, the portion containing the origin along with the line represents the solution set of the inquisition $x \leq 4$.

Region represented by $y \leq 3$. Clearly, the line $y = 3$ is parallel to x-axis at a distance of 3 units from the origin lying above x-axis. Since the inequality is not strict, we draw this line as a thick line. The point (0, 0) not lying on the line $y = 3$ satisfies the inquisition $y \leq 3$, therefore out of the two portions of the xy-plane divided by this line, the portion containing the origin along with the line represents the solution set of the inquisition $y \leq 3$.

Hence, the shaded region *i.e.,* the region common to the given five inequations, represents the solution set of the given system of inequations.

EXERCISES

1. A company produces two types of leather belts, say type A and B. Belt A is of superior quality and belt B is of a lower quality. Profits on the two types of belts are 40 and 30 paise per belt, respectively. Each belt of type A requires twice as much time as required by a belt of type B. If all belts were of type B, the company would produce 1000 belts per day. But the supply of leather is sufficient only for 800 per day. Belt A requires a fancy buckle and 400 fancy buckles are available for this, per day. For belt of type B. only 700 buckles are available per day. How should the company manufacture the two types of belts in order to have maximum overall profit?

2. If $a_1 = \begin{bmatrix} 3 \\ 4 \end{bmatrix}$, $a_2 = \begin{bmatrix} -1 \\ 2 \end{bmatrix}$, $a_3 = \begin{bmatrix} 1 \\ 4 \end{bmatrix}$ and $b = \begin{bmatrix} 1 \\ 4 \end{bmatrix}$

   Then determine whether all possible basic solutions exist for the following set of equations $(a_1\ a_2\ a_3)\ x = b$.

3. A dietician decides a certain minimum intake of vitamins A, B and C for a family. The minimum daily needs of the vitamins A, B, C are 30, 20, 16 units respectively. For the supply of these, the dietician depends on two types of foods X and Y. The first one gives 7, 5, 2 units per gram

of vitamins A, B, C respectively. The second one gives 2, 4, 8 units per gram of these vitamins respectively. The first food costs Rs. 2 per gram and the second Re. 1 per gram.

How many grams of each food stuff should the family buy every day to keep the food expense at a minimum? Formulate a linear programming problem.

4. Find a B.F.S. of the system

$$x_1 + 2x_3 = 1,$$
$$x_2 + x_3 = 4, x_1,$$
$$x_2, x_3 \geq 0,$$

5. Do the system $x_1 + x_2 = 1$, $x_1 - x_3 = 2$, $x_1, x_2, x_3 \geq 0$ have a F.S.?

6. A person requires 10, 12 and 12 units of chemicals A, B and C respectively for his garden. A liquid product contains 5, 2 and 1 units of A, B and C respectively per jar. A dry product contains 1, 2 and 4 units of A, B and C per carton. If the liquid product sells for Rs 3 per jar and the dry product sells for Rs. 2 per carton. How many of each should be purchased to minimize the cost and meet the requirements?

7. Determine two different B.F.S. of the L.P.P.

$$\text{Max.} \quad Z = 2x_1 + 3x_2 + x_3 + 0.x_4 + 0.x_5 - M.x_6$$

$$\text{s.t.} \quad 2x_1 + 3x_2 + 4x_3 + x_4 = 6$$
$$x_1 + 2x_2 + 2x_3 - x_5 + x_6 = 3$$

and $x_1, x_2, x_3, x_4, x_5, x_6 \geq 0$.

8. Find all basic solutions for the system of simultaneous equations:

$$2x_1 + 3x_2 + 4x_3 = 5$$
$$3x_1 + 4x_2 + 5x_3 = 6.$$

9. Determine all basic feasible solutions of the system of equations:

$$2x_1 + x_2 + 4x_3 = 11$$
$$3x_1 + x_2 + 5x_3 = 14.$$

10. A furniture dealer in two items, viz. tables and chairs. He has Rs. 10000 to invest and a space to store at most 60 pieces (including both tables and chairs). A table costs him Rs. 500 and a chair Rs. 100. He can sell all the items that he buys, earning a profit of Rs. 50 for each table and Rs. 15 for each chair. Formulate this problem as a LPP so that he maximizes the profit.

11. Diet Problem. Consider two different types of foodstuffs, say F_1 and F_2. Assume that these foodstuffs contain vitamins V_1, V_2 and V_3 respectively. Minimum daily requirement of three vitamins are 1 kg. of V_1, 50 kg. of V_2 and 10 mg. of V_3. Suppose that the food stuff F_1 contains 1 mg. of V_1, 100 mg of V_2 and 10 mg. of V_3. Whereas the food stuff F_2 contains 1 mg. of V_1, 10 mg. of V_2 100 mg. of V_3. Cost of one unit of foodstuff F_1 is Rs. 1 and that of F_2 is Rs. 1.5.

    Find the minimum cost diet that would supply the body at least the minimum requirements of each vitamin by graphical method.

12. Find all the B.F.S. of the following system:

$$8x_1 + 6x_2 + 13x_3 + x_4 + x_5 = 6$$

$$9x_1 + x_2 + 2x_3 + 6x_4 + 10x_5 = 10.$$

13. A factory produces two products A and B. Each of the product A requires 2 hrs of moulding, 3 hrs of grinding and 4 hrs for polishing and each of the product B requires 4 hrs for moulding, 2 hrs for grinding and 2 hrs for polishing. The moulding machine can work for 20 hrs, grinding machine for 24 hrs and polishing machine available for 13 hrs. The profit is Rs. 5 per unit of A and Rs. 3 per unit of B. Assuming that the factory can sell all that it produces, formulate the problem as a LPP to maximize the profit.

14. Is $x_1 = 1, x_2 = 1/2, x_3 = x_4 = x_5 = 0$ a basic solution to the following equations:

$$x_1 + 2x_2 + x_3 + x_4 = 2,$$

$$x_1 + 2x_2 + \frac{1}{2}x_3 + x_5 = 2.$$

15. A toy company manufactures two types of dolls; an ordinary doll A and a deluxe doll B. Each type of doll B takes twice as long to produce as one of type A. It is given that the company would have time to make a maximum of 2000 dolls per day if it produces only the ordinary version.

    The supply of plastic is sufficient to produce 1500 dolls per day (both A and B combined). The deluxe version requires a fancy dress of which there are only 600 pieces per day available. If the company makes profit of Rs. 5 per doll respectively on doll A and doll B, formulate the problem as a linear programming problem to maximize the profit.

16. A factory produces two products A and B. To manufacture one unit of product A. A machine has to work 1½ hours and a craftsman has to work for 2 hours. To manufacture one unit of product B, the machine has to work 3 hours and the craftsman for one hour. In a week the factory can

avail of 80 hours of machine time and 70 hours of craftsman's time. The profit on the sale of each unit of A and B is of Rs. 10 and Rs. 8 respectively. If the manufacturer can sell all the items produced, how many of each should be produced to get the maximum profit per week? Formulate the problem as a LPP.

17. An automobile manufacturer makes automobiles and trucks in a factory that is divided into two shops. Shop A, witch performs the basic assembly operation, must work 5 man-days on each truck but only 2 man-days on each automobile.

    Shop B, which performs finishing operation. Must work 3 man-days for each automobile or truck that it produces. Because of men and machine limitations shop A has 180 man-days per week available while shop B has 135 man-days per week. If the manufacturer makes a profit of Rs. 300 on each truck and Rs. 200 on each automobile, how many of each should he produce to maximize his profit?

18. A company manufactures two kinds of leather purses, A and B. A is a high quality purse and B is lower quality. The sales of each of these purses A and B can profit of Rs. 4 and Rs. 3 respectively. Each purse of type A requires twice as much time a purse of type B, and if all purses are of type B, the company could make 1000 purses per day.

    The supply of leather is sufficient for only 800 purses per day (both A and B combined). Purse A requires a fancy buckle, and only 400 buckles per day are available. There are only 700 buckles available for purse B. What should be the daily production of each type of purse to get the maximum profit? Formulate the problem as a LPP.

Solve graphically the following linear programming problems:

19. Max. $Z = 3x_1 + 2x_2$

    s.t. $x_1 + x_2 \le 4,\ x_1 - x_2 \le 2,\ x_1, x_2 \ge 0.$

20. Max. $Z = 3x_1 + 4x_2$

    s.t. $x_1 - x_2 \le -1,\ -x_2 + x_2 \le 0,\ x_1, x_2 \ge 0.$

21. Min. $Z = x_1 + x_2,$

    s.t. $5x_1 + 10x_2 \le 5,$

    $x_1 + x_2 \ge 1,\ x_2 \le 4,$

    $x_1, x_2 \ge 0.$

22. Max. $Z = 0.75x_1 + x_2$

    s.t. $x_1 - x_2 \ge 0,\ -0.5x_1 + x_2 \le 1$

and $x_1, x_2 \geq 0.$

23. Max. $Z = 5x_1 + 7x_2$

s.t. $x_1 + x_2 \leq 4, 3x_1 + 8x_2 \leq 24,$

$10x_1 + 7x_2 \leq 35$

and $x_1, x_2 \geq 0.$

24. Min. $Z = 3x_1 + 5x_2$

s.t. $-3x_1 + x_2 \leq 12,$

$2x_1 - x_2 \geq -2,$

$2x_1 + 3x_2 \geq 12,$

$x_1 \leq 4, x_2 \geq 2$

and $x_1, x_2 \geq 0.$

25. Max. $Z = x_1 + x_2$

s.t. $x_1 - x_2 \geq 0, -3x_1 + x_2 \geq 3$

and $x_1, x_2 \geq 0.$

26. Max. $Z = 7x_1 + 3x_2$

s.t, $x_1 + 2x_2 \leq 3, x_1 + x_2 \leq 1,$

$0 \leq x_1 \leq \frac{5}{2}, \leq x_2 \leq \frac{3}{2}.$

27. Min. $Z = -x_1 + 2x_2$

s.t. $-x_1 + 3x_2 \leq 10, x_1 + x_2 \leq 6,$

$x_1 - x_2 \leq 2$

and $x_1, x_2 \leq 0.$

28. Min. $Z = 5x_1 - 2x_2$

s.t. $2x_1 + 3x_2 \geq 1, x_1, x_2 \geq 0.$

29. Max. $Z = 5x_1 + 3x_2$

s.t. $3x_1 + 5x_2 \leq 1, 3x_1 + x_2 \leq 4$

and $x_1, x_2 \geq 0.$

30. Max. $Z = x_1 + 2$

s.t. $x_1 + 2x_2 \leq 2000,$

$x_1 + x_2 \leq$

$x_2 \le 600$

and $x_1, x_2 \ge 0.$

31\. Max. $Z = 8x_1 + 7x_2$

s.t. $3x_1 + x_2 \le 66{,}000$

$x_1 + x_2 \le 45{,}000$

$x_1 \le 20{,}000$ $x_2 \le 40{,}000$

and $x_1, x_2 \ge 0.$

32\. Min. $Z = 1.5x_1 + 2.5x_2$

s.t. $x_1 + 3x_2 \ge 3,$

$x_1 + x_2 \ge 2$

and $x_1, x_2 \ge 0.$

33\. Max. $Z = 6x_1 - 2x_2$

s.t. $2x_1 - x_2 \le 2,\ x_1 \le 3$

and $x_1, x_2 \ge 0.$

34\. Max. $Z = 3x_1 + 4x_2$

s.t. $5x_1 + 4x_2 \le 200,\ 3x_1 + 5x_2 \le 150,$

$5x_1 + 4x_2 \ge 100,\ 8x_1 + 4x_2 \ge 80,\ x_1, x_2 \ge 0.$

35\. Max. $Z = x_1 + \frac{1}{2}x_2$

36\. Max. $Z = 2x_1 + 3x_2$

s.t. $x_1 + x_2 \le 1,\ 3x_1 + x_2 \le 4$

and $x_1, x_2 \ge 0.$

37\. Max. $Z = 2x_1 + x_2$

s.t. $x_1 + 2x_2 \le 10,\ x_1 + x_2 \le 6,$

$x_1 - x_2 \le 2,\ x_1 - 2x_2 \le 1$

and $x_1, x_2 \ge 0.$

38\. Obtain graphically the maximum value of

$Z = [\min (3x_1 - 10), \min (-5x_1 + 5)],\ 0 \le x_1 \le 5.$

s.t. $3x_1 + 2x_2 \le 12,\ 5x_1 \le 10,\ x_1 + x_2 \ge 8,$

$-x_1 + x_2 \ge 4,\ x_1, x_2 \ge 0.$

39. Min. $Z = 2x_1 - 10x_2$

s.t. $x_1 - x_2 \geq 0$, $x_1 - 5x_2 \geq -5$ and $x, x_2 \geq 0$.

40. Max. $Z = 3x_1 - 2x_2$

s.t. $x_1 + x_2 \leq 1$, $2x_1 + 2x_2 \geq 4$ and $x_1, x_2 \geq 0$.

41. Max. $Z = 6x_1 + 11x_2$

s.t. $2x_1 + x_2 \leq 104$,

$x_1 + 2x_2 \leq 76$

and $x_1, x_2 \geq 0$.

2

Replacement Problems

INTRODUCTION

A few replacement situations which are different from the situations discussed earlier in this chapter are as follows:

Staffing Problem

So far, we have discussed replacement problems which are not related with human beings working in an organization. The principles of replacement may be applied to formulate some useful recruitment and promotion policies for the stafff working in the organization. For this, we assume that life distribution for the service of staff in the organization is already known.

Equipment Renewal Problem

The term renewal here refers to either replacing old equipment by new or to repairing it so that the probability density function of its future life time is equivalent to that of a new piece of equipment. The future life time of the equipment is considered to be a random variable.

Definition : The probability that an equipment will need a renewal in the interval t to t + dt is called the *renewal rate* at time t, provided it is in running order at age f. It is given by r(f) dt (also called *renewal density function*).

REPLACEMENT OF ITEMS THAT FAIL COMPLETELY

Possibility of the failure of any item in a system always increases with passage of time. In some instances, the nature of the system may be such that if the item fails, may lead to complete breakdown of the system. If the replacement of the item is not available, the breakdown will result in loss of production, idle inventory, idle labour and many other losses causing heavy losses to the company. Obviously, in such a situation, a suitable replacement policy should be formulated. In many cases, the items may be replaced even while in working condition in order to reduce the probability of breakdown.

This category is concerned with items that work or fail completely, *i.e.,* work normal until a point of sudden failure is reached. There are two alternative approaches for the replacement, *i.e., individual replacement* and *group replacement*. In the former case, the items are replaced as and when they fail, while in the latter case, items are replaced at the end of a prefixed time (even without failure) and also as and when failure occurs. The approach to be adopted mainly depends on the number of identical parts and cost of each part.

For a given equipment, the period between installation and failure is not constant, but will follow some frequency of distribution. A conditional probability may be derived for the failure in some small interval of time ($t + \Delta t$). This conditional probability may increase with *t*, remain constant, or decrease with time.

Here, main consideration is to those items, which fail with increasing probability as they age.

The problem of replacing the failed items is insignificant in most situations. If an item is critical to the operation of a system, the productivity of the whole system will depend upon the replacement. For example, a pump in most chemical industries may force the entire plant to be closed. Therefore, the problem is to plan replacement of items, which have not failed. The replacement of a used item, but still functioning, is justified when

It is somehow difficult to predict that a particular equipment will fail at a particular time. This uncertainty can be avoided by deriving the probability distribution of failures. Here it is assumed that the failures occur only at the end of the period, say t. Thus, the objective becomes to find the value of t which minimizes the total cost involved for the replacement.

Mortality Tables

These tables are used to derive the probability distribution of life span of an equipment in question. Let,

$M(f)$ = number of survivors at any time t,

$M(t-1)$ = number of survivors at any time $t-1$,

N = initial number of equipments.

Then the probability of failure during time period t is given by

$$P(t) = \frac{M(t-1) - M(t)}{N}$$

The probability that an equipment has survived to an age (t – 1), and will fail during the interval (t – 1) to t can be defined as the conditional probability of failure. It is given by

$$P_s = \frac{M(t)}{N}$$

(i) The replacement cost after failure is significantly high, and

(ii) The new item reduces the probability of failure.

From the above, it may be concluded that the formulation of replacement policy in the situations of complete failure depends upon the probability of failure. Thus, a great importance is assigned to the computation of probability distribution of failures. The replacement of items, that fail completely, can be considered under the following two categories:

(i) Individual replacement policy

(ii) Group replacement.

INDIVIDUAL REPLACEMENT POLICY

Under this policy, an item (or equipment) is repalced just after its failure in the given system. This ensures smooth running of the system. This can be determined by Mortality Tables or life testing techniques as discussed below:

It is never possible to predict the time of failure of an item in the given system. However, theory of probability helps in solving such problems. The probability distribution of failures can be derived by number of methods. The basic assumption made is that failure happens only at the end of the period. Thus, the problem is to determine that value of *t* that minimizes total cost involved in the system.

In order to discuss such replacement policy, the problem of human population may be considered. In fact, no group of people ever existed under the following conditions:

(a) All deaths are replaced at once by births, and

(b) No other entries or exits take place.

In an industry, the death is equivalent to a failure of a part and birth is equivalent to a new replacement. Thus, the situation faced by the industries is also quite common as of population.

Theorem 1:

(Mortality Theorem). If all the deaths are immediately replaced by births and there are no other entries or exits, the age distribution ultimately becomes

stable and that the number of deaths per unit time becomes constant, i.e., equal to the size of population decided by the mean age death. This can be shown as following:

Proof :

For convenience, it may be assumed that individual can survive for more than $w+1$ units of time (year, month, etc.).

Suppose $f(t)$ = number of births at time t and

$p(x)$ = probability of dying just before the age $x + 1$, *i.e.,* at the age of x.

$f(t-x)$ = number of births at time $(t-x)$.

Obviously, the age of survivors at time t *of* the $f(t - x)$ births is equal to x, and their probability of dying at time t (just before time $t + 1$) will be equal to the probability $p(x)$ of those dying at age x (just before age $x + 1$).

Hence, the expected number of deaths out of the survivors aged x at time t (before reaching time $t + 1$) is $p(x)\,f(t - x)$.

Therefore, the total number of deaths expected before time $t + 1$ would be

$$\sum_{x=0}^{w} ft-x)p(x) \quad t = w, w + 1, w + 2. \ldots. \qquad \ldots (1)$$

Since all deaths are replaced by births, total number of births at time $(t + 1) = f(t + 1)$, then

$$f(t+1) = \sum_{x=0}^{w} f(t-x)p(x), \qquad \ldots (2)$$

The equation (2) is a difference equation in t and its solution can be given by

$f(t) = A\,\alpha^t$ where A is some constant.

Then the equation (2) can be written as

$$A\alpha^{t+1} = A \sum_{x=0}^{w} \alpha^{(t-x)}p(x)$$

Dividing both sides of above expression $A\alpha^{t/w}$

$$\alpha^{w+1} = A \sum_{x=0}^{w} \alpha^{(w-x)}p(x)$$

$$\alpha^{w+1} - A \sum_{x=0}^{w} \alpha^{(w-x)}p(x) = 0$$

$\alpha^{w+1} - [\alpha^w p(0) + \alpha^{w-1}p(1) + \alpha^{w-2}p(2) + ... + p(w) = 0$ . . . (3)

Since the sum of all the probabilities is 1,

or $\sum_{x=0}^{w} p(x) = 1$ or $1 - \sum_{x=0}^{w} p(x) = 0$

or $1 - [p(0) + p(1) + p(2) + ... + p(w) = 0$ . . . (4)

Now comparing equations (3) and (4), it is found that one solution of equation (3) is $\alpha_0 = 1$. But the equation (3), being an equation of degree $(w+1)$, must have $w+1$ roots. If the remaining roots are represented by α_1, α_2, α_3,.............. α_w, the solution of equation (2) will be of the form.

$$f(t) = A_0 + A_1\alpha_1^t + A_2\alpha_2^t + \text{.................} + A_w\alpha_w^t \quad ...(5)$$

Where, A_0, A_1, A_2,......................., A_w are arbitrary constants whose value can be found with the help of age distribution of some given point in time.

In equation (3), all the remaining roots (α_1, α_2, α_3, ... α_w) are less than unity, *i.e.*, $\alpha_i < 1$ for i = 1, 2, 3,.........w.

Therefore, $\alpha_1^t, \alpha_2^t, \alpha_3^t$,.................$\alpha_w^t$ tend to zero as t tends to infinite. As a result, $f(t) = A_0$, *i.e.*, number of deaths (as well as number of births) at any time becomes constant. The value of A_0 can be determined as described below:

Since births and deaths have settled down to a constant rate, A_0, the expected number of survivors ages x is also stable at $A_0\,p(x)$, where $p(x)$ = probability of members remaining alive longer than x.

Since the number of births are always equal the number of deaths, the size of total population, N is constant, *i.e.*,

$$\text{or} \quad N = A_0 \sum_{x=0}^{w} p(x) \quad ...(6)$$

$$\text{or} \quad A_0 = \frac{N}{\sum_{x-0}^{w} p(x)} \quad ...(7)$$

Now, the number of survivors aged 0, 1, 2, 3,..............can be determined from equation (6) as $A_0p(1)$, $A_0p(2)$,..........and so on.

The denominator in equation (7) is equivalent to mean age.

Theorem 2:

(*Group replacement policies*) (a) Group replacement should be made at the end of the period, t if the cost of individual replacements for the period t is greater than the average cost per period through the end of period t.

(b) Group replacement is not advisable at the end of period t if the cost of individual replacements at the end of period t – 1 is less than the average cost per period through the end of period t.

Proof :

Let us consider the following notations:

n = total number of items in the system

F(t) = number of items failing during time t

C(Q = total cost of group replacement until the end of period t

C_1 = unit cost of replacement in a group

C_2 = unit cost of individual replacement after time t, *i.e.,* failure

L = maximum life of any item

p(t) = probability of failure of any item at age t.

Rate of Replacement at Time t The number of failures at any time t is

$$F(t) = \begin{cases} np(t) + \sum_{x=1}^{t-1} P(x)\, F(t-x), & t \le L \\ \sum_{x=1}^{L} P(x)\, F(t-x), & t > L \end{cases} \qquad ...(1)$$

Cost of Replacement at Time t The cost of group replacement after time period t is given by

$$C(t) = nC_1 + C_2 \sum_{x=1}^{t} F(x) \qquad ...(2)$$

In Eqn. (3) nC_1 is the cost of replacing the items as a group, and C_2

$C_2 \sum_{x=1}^{t-1} F(x)$ is the cost of replacing the individual failures at the end of each of t – 1 periods before group is again replaced.

The average cost per unit period is then given by

$$\frac{C(t)}{t} = \frac{nC_1}{t} + \frac{C_2}{t} \sum_{x=1}^{t-1} F(x) \qquad ...(3)$$

For optimal replacement period t, the value of average cost per unit period given by Eqn. (3) should be minimum. The condition for minimum of C (t)/t is:

$$\Delta \left\{ \frac{C(t)}{t-1} \right\} < 0 < \Delta \left\{ \frac{C(t)}{t} \right\}$$

Now for $\Delta\left\{\frac{C(t)}{t}\right\} > 0$

we have $\Delta\left\{\frac{C(t)}{t}\right\} = \frac{C(t-1)}{t+1} - \frac{C(t)}{t} > 0$

From Eqn. (3), we get

$$\frac{C(t+1)}{t+1} - \frac{C(t)}{t} = nC_1\left(\frac{1}{t+1} - \frac{1}{t}\right) + C_2 \sum_{x=1}^{t-1} F(x)\left(\frac{1}{t+1} - \frac{1}{t}\right) + \frac{C_2 F(t)}{t+1}$$

$$= \left\{-nC_1 - C_2 \sum_{x=1}^{t-1} F(x) + tC_2 F(t)\right\} \Big/ t(t+1)$$

For $\frac{C(t+1)}{t+1} - \frac{C(t)}{t} > 0$, it is necessary that

$$t.C_2 F(t) > nC_1 + C_2 \sum_{x=1}^{t-1} F(x)$$

$$C_2 F(t) > \left\{nC_1 + C_2 \sum_{x=1}^{t-1} F(x)\right\} \Big/ t \qquad ...(4)$$

Similarly, for $\Delta\left\{\frac{C(t)}{t}\right\} = \frac{C(t-1)}{t} - \frac{C(t)}{t} > 0$, the following condition can be derived

$$C_2 F(t-1) < \left\{nC_1 + C_2 \sum_{x=1}^{t-2} F(x)\right\} \Big/ t-1 \qquad ...(5)$$

Inequalities (4) and (5) describe the necessary condition for optimal group replacement. In Eqn. (4), the expression

$$\left\{nC_1 + C_2 \sum_{x=1}^{t-1} F(x)\right\} \Big/ t$$

represents the average cost per period if all items are replaced at the end of period t. Whereas expressum $C_2 + F(t)$ represents the cost for the rth period if group replacement is not made at the end of period t.

GROUP REPLACEMENT

Sometimes, just after the complete breakdown of a system, the immediate replacement of the item(s) may not be available. This may result in heavy losses. In such circumstances a group replacement policy can be adopted.

Under this policy items are replaced: (i) individually as and when they fail during a specified time period, (ii) in groups at the end of some suitable time period without waiting for their failure, with the provision that if any item fails before the time specified, it may be replaced individually. Here, we have to see two things namely:

(i) rate of individual replacement during the specified time period,

(ii) total cost incurred for individual as well as group replacement during the specified time.

Obviously, the decision-maker will call a time period optimal for which total cost incurred is minimum. In order to calculate this optimal time period for replacement he has to keep the record of, (i) probability of failure, (ii) loss incurred due to these failures, (iii) cost of individual replacement, and (iv) cost of group replacement.

Remark : The group replacement policy is suitable for a large number of identical low cost items which are likely to fail with age and it is difficult as well as not justified to keep the record of their individual ages.

The rate of replacement and total cost involved in the group replacement and total cost involved in the group replacement is based on the following theorem.

A policy for group replacement consists of following two steps:

(a) Individual replacements at the time of failure of any unit in the system, which ensures running of the system, and

(b) Group replacement of existing live items at an appropriate time, which will reduce the probability of failure.

Thus, group replacement policy requires following two considerations:

(a) The rate of individual replacements during the period and

(b) The total cost incurred of individual and group replacement during the given period.

The period, corresponding to which the total cost incurred is minimum, would be the optimum period for replacement. Therefore, for the formulation of group replacement policy, following should be known:

(a) The probability of failure,

(b) Loss incurred due to these failures,

(c) Cost of individual replacements, and

(d) Cost of group replacements,

The procedure for computing the replacement rate and the total cost incurred in group replacement can be explained below:

In this system, it is proposed to replace all items at a definite interval "t" with the provision that the individual replacements can be made of failed items as and when they fail.

Let,

N_t = The number of items failing at time t,

N = Total number of items in the system,

$p(X)$ = Probability of failure of any item at age X,

$p(t–X)$ = Probability of failure of any item at age $(t–X)$,

$N_p(X)$ = Expected number of items to be replaced at time X.

$p(X).p(t–X)$= Probability of failure of any unit at age X and again it fails at age $(t–X)$

Similarly, p(X), p(b–X), p(t–b) = Probability of failure of any item at ages X, b–X, and t–b.

Therefore, the total number of replacements in time t can be given as

$$N_t = N\,[p(t) + \sum_{x=1}^{t-1} p(x),\, p(t–X) + \sum_{b=2}^{t-1}\sum_{x=1}^{t-1} p(X),\, p(b–X),\, p(t–b) + \dots\dots\dots \quad (1)$$

The equation (1) can be used to determine the number of items failing at the end of rth period in any system.

Now let

C_1 = Individual replacement cost on failure.

C_2 = Cost of replacement for item in a group.

$$\text{Then } C_t = C_1[N_1+N_2+\dots\dots\dots\dots\dots\dots + N_{t-1}] + C_2N$$

Average cost per unit period = C_t/t

$$= \frac{C_1(N_1 + N_2 + \dots\dots\dots\dots + N_{t-1}) + C_2N}{t} \quad \dots (2)$$

$N_1+N_2+\dots\dots\dots+ N_{t-1}$ can be calculated from equation . . . (3)

Now, in order to find the replacement age "t", the average cost per unit period $[C_t/t]$ should be minimum for which the condition would be

$$\frac{C_{t-1}}{t-1} > \frac{C_t}{t}$$

and $$\frac{C_{t-1}}{t-1} > \frac{C_t}{t} \qquad \ldots (4)$$

Now $$\frac{C_{t+1}}{t+1} - \frac{C_t}{t} = \frac{C_t + C_1 N_t}{t+1} - \frac{C_t}{t}$$

$$= \frac{tC_1N_t - Ct}{t(t+1)} = \frac{C_1N_t t - C_t/t}{t+1} \qquad \ldots (5)$$

Which must be greater than zero for minimum C_t/t *i.e.,*

$$C_1N_t > C_t/t \qquad \ldots (6)$$

Similarly, from $\frac{C_{t-1}}{t-1} > \frac{C_t}{t}$

following condition can be derived

$$C_1N_{t-1} > C_t/t \qquad (7)$$

Thus, from equations (6) and (7), the group replacement policy is completely established. This can be illustrated with the help of the following examples:

STAFFING (RECRUITMENT AND PROMOTION) PROBLEMS

The staff working in an organization can also be considered as a machine part. The problem of staff replacement may arise due to retirements or deaths, resignation, termination due to inefficiency of staff members from time to time. In order to maintain a required strength of staff members in a system, formulation of a useful recruitment and promotion policies would be required.

The problems can be solved through the analysis similar to that used in replacement of industrial items. For this, it is assumed that life distribution for the service of staff in a system is known.

REPLACEMENT THEORY

The problem of replacement is felt when the job performing units such as men, machines, equipments, parts, etc., become less effective or useless due to either sudden or gradual deterioration in their efficiency, failure or breakdown.

Any physical system (machine, trucks, etc.) is subjected to deterioration with time due to its use and many other reasons (temperature changes, vibrations, corrosion, wear, etc.). Sometimes, the item may even fail completely. The deterioration due to combined effect of all these factors on the system, is reflected as following:

(a) The system becomes incapable to take-up the specified load.

(b) Cost of production becomes higher due to rework and rejection.

(c) Operating cost rises sharply.

(d) The useful life of replacement spare and consumables becomes shorter.

By replacing them with new ones at frequent intervals, maintenance and other overhead costs can be reduced. However, such replacements would increase the need of capital cost for new ones. For example,

(i) A vehicle tends to wear out with time due to constant use. More money needs to be spent on it on account of increased repair and operating cost. A stage comes when it becomes uneconomical to maintain the vehicle and it is better to replace it with a new one. Here the replacement decision may be taken to balance the increasing maintenance cost with the decreasing money value of the vehicle as time passes.

(ii) In case of highway tubelights where time of failure is not predictable for individual tubes, replacement is done only after individual failure. However, it may be economical to replace such tubes on a schedule basis before their failure. Here the replacement decision may be taken to balance between the wasted life of a tube before failure and cost incurred when a tube fails completely during service.

Thus, the basic problem in such situations is to formulate a replacement policy to determine an age (or period) at which the replacement of the given machinery/equipment is most economical keeping in view all possible alternatives.

We shall discuss the replacement policies in the context of the following three types of replacement situations:

(i) Items such as machines, vehicles, tyres, etc., whose efficiency deteriorates with age due to constant use and which need increased operating and maintenance costs. In such cases deterioration level is predictable and is represented by

(a) increased maintenance/operational cost,

(b) its waste or scrap value and damage to item and safety risk.

(ii) Items such as light bulbs and tubes, radio and television parts, etc., which do not give any indication of deterioration with time but fail all of a sudden and become completely useless. Such cases require an anticipation of failures involving probabilities of failure. The optimum replacement policy is formulated to balance the wasted life of items replaced before failure against the costs incurred when items fail in service.

(iii) The existing working staff in an organization gradually reduces due to retirement, death, retrenchment and other reasons.

Although, systematic and regular maintenance can reduce the deterioration, but can not eliminate it completely. Thus, the operating inferiority goes on increasing with the age of the system reflected by increased maintenance costs, higher frequency of breakdowns, etc. The replacement is necessary because of the following reasons:

(a) *Obsolescence:* This is one of the major causes for developing operating inferiority. This happens due to availability of new, better or more efficient design of machine/equipment, improvements required in product design, changes in the specifications of materials used, etc.

(b) *Changes in Requirements:* Sharp rise in the demand of the product may lead to the major reorganization of the plant and machinery, *i.e.,* from batch to continuous production.

(c) *Expensive Maintenance/Work Badly:* When old item (machine/equipment) becomes in worse condition and does not yield the product of required quality/specification or the maintenance becomes expensive.

(d) *The Old Machine/Equipment Fails:* If the equipment has failed due to an accident or otherwise, and stops working or the old machine/equipment is expected to fail shortly.

TYPES OF FAILURE

The term 'failure' here will be discussed in the context of replacement decisions. There are two types of failures:

(i) Gradual failure, and

(ii) Sudden failure.

Gradual Failure

Gradual failure is progressive in nature. That is, as the life of an item increases, its operational efficiency also deteriorates resulting in

(i) increased running (maintenance and operating) costs.

(ii) decrease in its productivity.

(iii) decrease in the resale or salvage value.

Mechanical items like pistons, rings, bearings, etc., and automobile tyres fall under this category.

Sudden Failure

This type of failure occurs in items after some period of giving desired service rather than deterioration while in service. The period of giving desired service is not constant but follows some frequency distribution which may be progressive, 'retrogressive or random in nature.

In case of *progressive failure mechanism,* probability of failure increases with the increase in time of an item, *e.g.*, electric bulbs, automobile tyre tubes, etc.

In case of *retrogressive failure mechanism,* probability of failure is more in the early use of the items and then the chances of failure go down with the passage of time, *i.e.,* if an item survives in initial period, then its expected life increases. The examples are automobile and aircraft engines.

In case of *random failure mechanism,* the items fail due to some random causes (such as physical shock, accidents, etc.), but not related to age, *e.g.,* vacuum tubes.

(i) *Progressive Failure :* If the probability of failure of an item increases with the increase in its life, then such failure is called progressive failure. For example, light bulbs and tubes fail progressively.

(ii) *Retrogressive Failure :* If the probability of failure in the beginning of the life of an item is more but as time passes the chances of its failure become less, then such failure is said to be retrogressive.

(iii) *Random Failure :* In this type of failure, the constant probability of failure is associated with items mat fail from random causes such as physical shocks, not related to age. For example, vacuum tubes in air-born equipment have been found to fail at a rate independent of the age of the tube.

Thus, the problem of replacement is experienced in systems, where capital assets (machine, equipment, individuals, etc.) perform the main job. This calls for some suitable replacement policy regarding the items so that the system is maintained to give some required level of performance.

The replacement decisions can be placed into following four categories:

(a) Replacement of items, which fail gradually, *e.g.,* machines, tools, automobiles, planes, etc.

(b) Replacement of items, which fail completely, *e.g.,* light bulbs, light tubes and other consumable spares.

(c) Replacement of personnel in organization.

(d) Miscellaneous problems.

GENERAL APPROACH FOR REPLACEMENT DECISIONS

Although, the actual time of failure for any particular item cannot be predicted, the likely pattern can be established through observation. The optimum replacement policy can be obtained by generating the frequency distribution for a given system and then combining that with cost information. The analysis for replacement decisions requires the following informations:

(i) Probability estimation of the item failing at a given point of time,

(ii) Estimation of replacement cost in terms of:

- (a) Item's actual cost
- (b) Labour's direct cost involved in replacement, and
- (c) Disruption cost in terms of lost orders, lost production, etc.

There are four major approaches for replacement decisions, *i.e., average cost method, annual cost method, present value method, and MAPI method.*

Average Cost Method

In this method, the replacement decisions regarding, the systems failing gradually, consider the economic balance between the procurement cost and the operation cost. With increasing time of holding the system (machine/equipment), resale cost goes on decreasing while the maintenance cost increases and an economic balance between the two is determined. This method ignores the timings of the different costs which is not considered appropriate due to high interest rate or opportunity cost in the present time.

Present Value (PV) Method

The present value of numbers of expenditures, made over different periods of time, represents their value at the current time. Thus, in this method, all expenditures for each alternative are reduced (taking into account the interest factor) to their present value sum and the one with the least present value (PV) is selected. The present value of an alternative can be computed as following:

PV of the machine/equipment = Cost of acquisition of new equipment + sum of the PVs of the operating expenses for the holding period–PV of the salvage value of the new equipment.

PV of the old equipment = Net re-sale value of the old equipment + sum of PVs of the expenditures to the old one at the given rate and for given time + sum of PVs of the operating expenses at the given interest rate and specified additional life of the equipment – PV of the salvage value of the old equipment.

Annual Cost Method

If the interest factor (or opportunity cost) is considered in the average cost method, it may be called *annual uniform equivalent cost method.* This method employs time adjusted average of capital and running costs as a measure of replacement decision. In this method, the sums of uniform annual equivalent acquisition cost and annual equivalent operating cost of various alternatives known as annual uniform cost sums are compared and an alternative is selected which exhibits the lowest annual total cost sum. This can be computed as following:

$$\text{Annual uniform total cost} = \text{Annual uniform capital cost} + \text{Annual operating cost}$$

$$= \begin{bmatrix} \text{procurement cost} & \text{PV of the salvage} \\ \text{of the equipment} & \text{value} \end{bmatrix} \times \begin{bmatrix} \text{Capital} \\ \text{recovery} \\ \text{factor} \end{bmatrix}_i^k$$

$$+\left[\sum \text{PV of the running cost}\right] \times [\text{capital recovery factor}]_i^k$$

MAPI Method

The term MAPI refers to the name of the institute, which developed the method, *i.e., Machinery and Allied Products Institute of Washington.* The method was developed by the Institute's Director George Terborgh in 1950. The method is quite simple, and employs full provision of future depreciation and obsolescence on the new equipment. In this method, the lowest sum of the time adjusted average of capital cost and operating inferiority of the existing equipment is compared with that of the proposed equipment. If such a sum for the old equipment is higher than that of the proposed new equipment, the replacement is favoured.

REPLACEMENT OF ITEMS THAT DETERIORATE WITH TIME

In a machine, made system, the operation/maintenance cost always increases with time and a situation reaches when the maintenance cost becomes so high that it is preferable and economical to replace the equipment with a new one. Sometimes, a number of alternatives may be available and in such a situation, a comparison may be made between various alternatives by considering the costs involved in each alternative. The cost of each alternative will depend on a number of factors.

When operational efficiency of an item deteriorates with time (gradual failure), it is economical to replace the same with a new one. For example, the maintenance cost of a machine increases with time and a stage is reached when it may not be economical to allow machine to continue in the system. Besides, there could be a number of alternative choices and one may like to compare available alternatives on the basis of the running costs (average maintenance and operating costs) involved. In this section, we shall discuss various techniques for making such comparisons under different conditions. While making such comparisons it is assumed that suitable expressions for running costs are available.

Mode I : Replacement Policy for Items Whose Running Cost Increases with Time and Value of Money Remains Constant During a Period.

Model II : Replacement Policy for Items Whose Running Cost Increases with Time but Value of Money Changes with Constant Rate During the Period.

Value of Money Criterion

If the effect of the time value of money is to be considered, then replacement decision analysis must be based upon an equivalent annual cost. For example, if the interest rate on Rs. 100 is 10 per cent per year, then value of Rs. 100 to be spent after one year will be Rs. 110. This is also called value of money. Also, the value of money that decreases with constant rate is known as its depreciation ratio or discounted factor. The discounted value is the amount of money required at the time of the policy decision to build up funds at compound interest large enough to pay the required cost when due. For example, if the interest rate on Rs. 100 is r per cent per year, then present value (or worth) of Rs. 100 to be spent after n years will be

$$d = \frac{100}{(100 + r)^n}$$

where, d is the discount rate or depreciation value. After having the idea of discounted cost, the objective should be to determine the critical age at which an item should be replaced so that the sum of all discounted costs is minimum.

Present Worth Factor Criterion

In this case the optimal value of replacement age of an equipment can be determined under two different situations.

(i) The running cost of an equipment which deteriorates over a period of time increases monotonically and the value of the money decreases with a constant rate. If r is the interest rate, then

$$\text{Pwf} = (1 + r)^{-n}$$

is called the *Present Worth Factor* (Pwf) or present value of one rupee spent in n years from time now onwards. But if n = 1 the Pwf is given by

$$d = (1 + r)^{-1}$$

where, d is called the *discount rate or depreciation value.*

(ii) The money to be spent is taken on loan for a certain period at a given rate under the condition of repayment in instalments.

The replacement of items on the basis of Present Worth Factor (Pwf) includes the present worth of all future expenditure and revenues for each replacement alternatives. An item for which present worth factor is less is preferred. Let

C = purchase cost of an item,

R = annual running cost,

n = life of the item in years,

S = scrap (or salvage) value of the item at the end of its life,

r = annual interest rate.

Then the present worth of the total cost during n years is given by

Total cost = C + R (Pwf for r% interest rate for n years) – S (Pwf for r% interest rate for n years)

If the running cost of the item is different in its different operational life, then the present worth of the total cost during n years is given by

Total cost = C + R (Pwf for r% interest rate for i years) – S (Pwf for r% interest rate for i years) where i = 1, 2, . . ., n

Theorem 1:

The cost of maintenance of a machine is given as a function increasing with time and its scrap value is constant. If time is measured continuously, then the average annual cost will be minimized by replacing the machine when the average cost to date becomes equal to the current maintenance cost.

Proof :

The aim here is to determine the optimal replacement age of an equipment whose running cost increases with time and the value of money remains constant (*i.e.,* value is not counted) during that period.

Let,

C = capital or purchase cost of new equipment

S = scrap (or salvage) value of the equipment at the end of t/ years

R(t) = running cost of equipment for the year t

n = replacement age of the equipment.

When time 't' is a continuous variable : If the equipment is used for t years, then the total cost incurred over this period is given by

TC = Capital (or purchase) cost – Scrap value at the end of t years + Running cost for t years

$$= C - S + \int_0^n R(t)\, dt.$$

Therefore, the average cost per unit time incurred over the period of n years is:

$$ATC_n = \frac{1}{n}\left\{CS + \int_0^n R(t)\, dt\right\}. \qquad ...(i)$$

To obtain optimal value n for which ATC_n is minimum, differentiate ATC_n with respect to n, and set the first derivative equal to zero. That is, for minimum of ATC_n.

$$\frac{d}{dn}\{ATC_n\} = -\frac{1}{2}\{C-S\} + \frac{R(n)}{n} - \frac{1}{n^2}\int_0^n R(t)\, dt = 0$$

or

$$R(n) = \frac{1}{n}\left\{C - S + \int_0^n R(t)\, dt\right\},\ n \neq 0 \qquad ...(ii)$$

$$R(n) = ATC_n.$$

Hence, the following replacement policy can be derived with the help of eqn. (ii).

Policy Replace the equipment when the average annual cost for n years becomes equal to the current/annual running cost.

$$R(n) = \frac{1}{n}\left\{C - S + \int_0^n R(t)\, dt\right\}.$$

Theorem 2:

If time is measured in discrete units, then the average annual cost will be minimized by replacing s machine when the next period's maintenance cost becomes greater than the current average cost.

Proof :

When time 't' is a discrete variable The average cost incurred over the period n is given by

$$ATC_n \frac{1}{n}\left\{C - S + \sum_{t=0}^{n} R(t)\right\}. \qquad ...(iii)$$

If $C - S$ and $\sum_{t=0}^{n} R(t)$ are assumed to be monotonically decreasing and increasing, respectively, then there will exist a value ofn for which ATC_n is minimum. Thus, we shall have inequalities

$$ATC_n > ATC_n < ATC_{n+1}$$

or $\qquad ATC_{r-1} - ATC_n > 0$

and $\qquad ATC_{n+1} - ATC_n > 0.$

Rewriting eqn. (iii) for period n + 1, we get

$$ATC_{n+1} = \frac{1}{n+1}\left\{C - S + \sum_{t=1}^{n+1} R(t)\right\} = \frac{1}{n+1}\left\{C - S + \sum_{t=1}^{n} R(t) + R(n+1)\right\}$$

$$= \frac{n}{n+1}\,\frac{\left\{C - S + \sum_{t=1}^{n} R(t)\right\}}{n} = \frac{R(n+1)}{n+1}\;\frac{n}{n+1}.ATC_n + \frac{R(n+1)}{n+1}$$

Therefore,

$$ATC_{n+1} - ATC_n = \frac{n}{n+1} ATC_n + \frac{A(n+1)}{n+1} - ATC_n$$

$$= \frac{R(n+1)}{n+1} + ATC_n\left(\frac{n}{n+1} - 1\right) = \frac{R(n+1)}{n+1} - \frac{ATC_n}{n+1}$$

Since $ATC_{n+1} - ATC_n > 0$, we get

$$\frac{R(n+1)}{n+1} - \frac{ATC_n}{n+1} > 0$$

$$R(n + 1) - ATC_n > 0$$

$$R\,(n + 1) > ATC_n \qquad ...(iv)$$

Similarly, $ATCn_{n-1} - ATC_n > 0$, implies that $R(n + 1) < ATC_{n-1}$. This provides the following replacement policy.

Policy 1 : If the next year, running cost, R(n + 1) is more than average cost of nthyear, $ATC_{;r}$*, then it is economical to replace at the end of n years. That is*

$$R(n+1) > \frac{1}{n}\left\{C - S + \sum_{t=0}^{n} R(t)\right\}$$

Policy 2 : If the present year's running cost is less than the previous year's average cost, ATC_{n+1}, then do not replace. That is

$$R(n+1) < \frac{1}{n+1}\left\{C - S + \sum_{t=0}^{n-1} R(t)\right\}.$$

Theorem 3:

The maintenance cost increases with time and the money value decreases with constant rate, i.e., depreciation value is given. Then replacement policy will be:

(a) Replace if the running cost of next period is greater than the weighted average of previous cost.

(b) Do not replace if the running cost of the next period is less than the weighted average of the previous costs.

Proof :

Suppose that the item (machine or equipment) is available for use over a series of time periods of equal length, say one year. Let us use the following notations:

C = purchase price of a new item

R_n = running cost of the item at the beginning of nth year ($R_{n+1} > R_n$).

r = annual interest rate

d = depreciation value per unit of money during a year $\{1/(1 + r)\}$.

Let us assufne that the item is replaced after every n years of service and has no resale value (or price). The replacement policy can be formulated by calculating the total amount of money required for purchasing and running the item for n years. The period for which the total money is minimum will be considered best. The present worth (discounted value) of all future costs of purchasing and running the item with a policy of replacing it after every n years is given by

$$D_n = \{(C + R_1 + d\,R_2 + d^2 R_3 + \ldots + d^{n-1} R_n] \quad \text{(for 1 to n years)}$$

$$+ [d^n (C + R_1) + d^{n+1} R_2 + d^{n+2} R_3 + \ldots + d^{2n-1}R_n] \quad \text{(for n + 1 to 2n years)}$$

$$+ [d^{2n} (C + R_1) + d^{2n+1} R_2 + d^{2n+2} R_3 + \ldots + d^{3n-1}R_n] \quad \text{(for 2n + 1 to 3n years)}$$

$$+ \ldots$$

$$= [(C + R_1)(1 + d^n + d^{2n} + \ldots) + d\,R_2(1 + d^n + d^{2n} + \ldots) + \ldots + d^{n-1} R_n (1 + d^n + d^{2n} + \ldots)$$

$$= [(C + R_1) + d\,R_2 + \ldots + d^{n-1}]\,[1 + d^n + d^{2n} + \ldots]$$

$$= \left[C + \sum_{i=1}^{n} d^{i-1} R_i\right]\left[\frac{1}{1-d^n}\right] \quad \text{(sum of infinite G.P., } D < 1) \qquad \ldots(v)$$

The value of D_n in eqn. (v) is the money required to pay all future costs of purchasing and running the equipment with a replacement policy of every n years. Obviously, the minimum value of D_n will be preferred. In other words, if n is an optimal replacement interval, then D_n will be minimum because of the following inequality

$$D_{n+1} > D_n < D_{n-1}$$

From this, the two inequalities

$$D_{n+1} - D_n > 0 \text{ and } D_n - D_{n-1} < 0$$

can be established.

From eqn. (v), since

$$D_n = \frac{P(n)}{1-d^n},$$

$$\text{Therefore,} \quad D_{n+1} = \frac{P(n+1)}{1-d^{n+1}} = \frac{(1-d^n)\,D_n + d^n\,R_{n+1}}{1-d^{n+1}} = \frac{1-d^n}{1-d^{n+1}}.$$

$$D_n = \frac{d^n\,R_{n+1}}{1-d^{n+1}}$$

where $P(n) = C + R_1 + d\,R_2 + d^2\,R_3 + \ldots + d^{n+1}\,R_n$

Now, considering the inequality

$$D_{n+1} - D_n = \frac{P(n+1)}{1-d^{n+1}} - \frac{P(n)}{1-d^n}$$

$$= \frac{P(n+1)\,(1-d^n) - P(n)\,(1-d^{n+1})}{(1-d^n)\,(1-d^{n+1})}$$

$$= \frac{P\{P(n+1 - P(n)\} + d^{n+1}\,P(n) - d^n\,P(n+1)}{(1-d^n)\,(1-d^{n+1})}$$

$$= \frac{d^n R_{n+1} + d^{n+1}\,P(n) - d^n\,\{P(n) - d^n\,R_{n+1})}{(1-d^n)\,(1-d^{n+1})}$$

[Because $P(n+1) = P(n) + d^n\,R_{n+1}$]

$$= \frac{d^n\,(1-d^n)\,R_{n+1} - d^n\,(1-d)\,P(n)}{(1-d^n)\,(1-d^{n+1})}$$

$$= \frac{d^n (1-d)}{(1-d^n)(1-d^{n+1})}\left[\frac{1-d^n}{1-d} . R_{n+1} - P(n)\right] \quad ...(vi)$$

Since d < 1, and so $1 - d_n > 0$, therefore, $D_{n+1} + - D_{n+1}$ is always positive and has the same sign as the quantity in the bracket in eqn. (vi).

Similarly, putting n – 1 for n in eqn. (vi), we have

$$D_n - D_{n-1} = \frac{d^{n-1} (1-d)}{(1-d^{n-1})(1-d^n)}\left[\frac{1-d^{n-1}}{1-d} R_n - P(n-1)\right]$$

$$= \frac{d^{n-1} (1-d)}{(1-d^n)(1-d^{n-1})}\left[\frac{1-d^{n-1}}{1-d} R_n - \{P(n) - R_n \, d^{n-1}\}\right]$$

$$= \frac{d^{n-1} (1-d)}{(1-d^n)(1-d^{n-1})}\left[\frac{1-d^{n-1}}{1-d} .R_n - P(n)\right] \quad ...vii7)$$

Hence, the condition for minimum value of D_n from eqns. (vi) and (vii) can be expressed as:

$$(D_n - D_{n-1}) < 0 < (D_{n+1} - D_n)$$

$$R_n < \frac{C+(R_1 + d\, R_2 + d^2\, R_3 + ...+d^{n-1} R_n}{1 + d + d^2 + ...+ d^{n-1}} < R_{n+1}$$

The expression between R_n and R_{n+1} in eqn. (viii) represents the weighted average W(n) of all costs up to the period (n – 1) with weights 1, d, d^2, ... d^{n-1} respectively. The given weights are actually the discounted factors of the costs in the previous years. Hence, *the value of n satisfying the relationship (5) will be the best age for replacing the given item.*

However, the common costs in each choice at different stages need not be considered in the analysis. The various techniques for analyzing such alternative choices can be mainly divided into the following groups:

1. Unadjusted Average Cost Method, and
2. Adjusted Average Cost Method.

UNADJUSTED AVERAGE COST METHOD

In this technique, following assumptions are considered:

(a) The purchase cost of the equipment/machine does not change in future.

(b) The running cost (operating plus maintenance cost) per year of the equipment increases with the time of use of equipment.

(c) The running cost during a year is supposed to have been spent at the end of the year.

In the replacement decisions, the two costs involved are *acquisition cost* and *running cost.*

If C = Initial cost of the items

S_n = The salvage value of the item at the *n*th year

R_i = Running cost at time *i*

The acquisition cost uniform annual equivalent amount to be per year of the item recovered each year of the retentive period *n*

$$= \frac{C - S_n}{n}$$

Since the running cost incurred during "*n*" year becomes

$$= \int_0^n R_t dt \qquad \text{(when time is measured continuously)}$$

$$= \sum_{t=1}^{n} \frac{R_t}{n} \qquad \text{(when time } t \text{ is discrete variable)}$$

The total cost incurred on the item will be,

$$T_n = \int_0^n R_t dt + C - S_n$$

and the average total cost is given by

$$A_n = \frac{T_n}{n} = \frac{1}{n}\left[\int_0^n R_t dt + C - S_n\right] \qquad \ldots (1)$$

The acquisition cost and running cost are diametrically opposite to each other, and hence, to obtain retentive period, the sum of the two costs needs to be minimized. For this, the first derivative of equation (1) should be equal to zero, *i.e.*,

$$\frac{dA_n}{dn} = \frac{1}{n}R_n + \left\{-\frac{1}{n^2}\right\}\int_0^n R_t dt - \frac{C - S_n}{n^2}$$

$$= 0 \text{ for minimum of } A_n \qquad \ldots (2)$$

or

$$R_n = \frac{1}{n}\int_0^n R_t dt + \frac{C - S_n}{n}$$

$$= \frac{T_n}{n} \text{ (from equation 1)} \qquad \ldots (3)$$

Hence, running cost at time n = average capital cost in time n

When time "t" is a discrete variable

The cost equation (1) can be written as,

$$A_n = \frac{T_n}{n} = \sum_{t=1}^{n} \frac{R_t}{n} + \frac{C - S_n}{n} \quad \ldots (4)$$

While solving the problem, it is sufficient to compare the average cost only. In order to minimize the total cost, following relationship holds good,

i.e., $\frac{T_n}{n+1} > \frac{T_n}{n}$ and *vice-versa*

The two costs as well as total cost can be plotted against period of use (n). The total cost decreases in the first few years and then starts increasing. The point n_o represents the point of replacement.

Adjusted Average Cost Method

The simple average cost method (traditional concept), however, does not take into account the time of resale and/or expenses made. This leads to a considerable error in decision-making process. Adjusted average cost concept overcomes this deficiency by considering the time of payments received or given.

Acquisition cost per year is obtained by discounting the salvage value and multiplying the difference between the initial cost of the equipment and the present value of salvage price by the appropriate capital recovery factor. In this case, it is assumed that the items, which deteriorate over a period of time, operating costs increase monotonically.

If X = Initial cost of the equipment,

r = Interest rate per period which gives the depreciation ratio 1/(1 + r), say d,

1, 2, 3,......are the time periods of equal lengths,

C_1, C_2, C_3,.....are the respective operating costs incurred at the beginning of the periods.

Assuming that the equipment is desired to be replaced after every N years of service, the expenditure incurred in different years and their present values can be presented as shown in Table 1.

From Table 1, the present value of the total future expenditure incurred (F_n) N-yearly replacement decision policy, would be

Table 1

Year *i*	Capital cost	Operating cost	Total cost in *i*th year	Present Value of total expenditure
1	X	C_1	$X + C_1$	$X + C_1$
2	–	C_2	C_2	dC_2
3	–	C_3	C_3	d^2C_3
.	–	.	.	.
.	–	.	.	.
N	–	C_N	C_N	$d^{N-1}C_N$
N+1*	X*	C_1	$X^* + C^*_1$	$d^N(X + C_1)$
N+2	–	C^*_2	C_2	$d^{N+1}C_2$
2*N*	–	C^*_N	C_N	$d^{2N-1}C_N$
and so on				

* After *N* years, the equipment is to be replaced and the cycle of capital expenditure and annual operating expenditure will be repeated.

$$F_N = [\{X + C_1 + dC_2 + d^2C_3 + ...+ d^{N-1}C_N\} + \{(X+C_1)d^N + C_2d^{N+1} + ...+C_Nd\}^{2N-1} + ...\text{an infinite series}$$

$$= \left[X+\sum_{i=1}^{N} C_i d^{i-1}\right] + d^N\left[X+\sum_{i=1}^{N} C_i d^{i-1}\right] + d^{2N}\left[X+\sum_{i=1}^{N} C_i d^{i-1}\right] + ...$$

$$= \left[X+\sum_{i=1}^{N} C_i d^{i-1}\right][1+d^N+d^{2N}+....]$$

$$= \frac{X+\sum_{i=1}^{N} C_i d^{i-1}}{1-d^N} \qquad ...(5)$$

[The series $1 + d^N + d^{2N} + ...$ is an infinite G.P. series with common ratio of d^N, $d<1$ and thus it is equal to $1/(1-d^N)$.

In equation (5), F_N is the total amount of money required at present to pay all future costs of acquiring and operating the equipment with a replacement policy after every *N* years. It is obvious that the value of *N* has to be preferred for which F_N is minimum. For this situation, following two inequalities should be observed:

$$F_{N+1} > F_N$$
$$F_{N-1} > F_N$$

Now for $F_{N+1} > F_N$,

$$F_{N-1} - F_N > 0$$

From equation (4.5), we have

$$F_{N+1} - F_N = \frac{X + \sum_{i=1}^{N} C_i d^{i-1} + C_{N+1} D^N}{1 - d^{N+1}} - \frac{X + \sum_{i=1}^{N} C_i d^{i-1}}{1 - d^N} \quad \text{...(6)}$$

$$= \left[X + \sum_{i=1}^{N} C_i d^{i-1}\right]\left[\frac{1}{1-d^{N+1}} - \frac{1}{1-d^N}\right] + \frac{C_{N+1} d^N}{1-d^{N+1}}$$

$$= \frac{\left[X + \sum_{i=1}^{N} C_i d^{i-1}\right]\left[d^{N+1} - d^N\right]}{(1-d^{N+1})\, 1 - d^{N+1}} + \frac{C_{N+1} d^N}{1-d^{N+1}}$$

$$= \frac{F_N\left[d^{N+1} - d^N\right]}{(1-d^{N+1})} + \frac{C_{N+1} d^N}{1-d^{N+1}}$$

$$= \frac{\left[F_N(d-1) + C_{N+1}\right] d^N}{(1-d^{N+1})} = \frac{\left[C_{N+1} - F_N(1-d) d^N\right]}{(1-d^{N+1})} \quad \text{. . . (7)}$$

Since d is depreciation/interest rate, d will always be less than 1 and thus 1-d will always be positive and hence $d^N/(1-d^{N+1})$ will always be positive. Therefore, for

$$F_{N+1} - F_N > 0$$

we will have

$$C_{N+1} > F_N (1\text{-}d)$$

or $$F_N < \frac{C_{N+1}}{1-d}$$

or $$C_{N+1} > (1-d)\, F_N \quad \text{. . . (8)}$$

$$\text{Now } (1-d) F_N = (1-d)\, \frac{X + \sum_{i=1}^{N} C_i d^{i-1}}{1-d^N}$$

i.e., $$C_{N+1} > \frac{X + \sum_{i=1}^{N} C_i d^{i-1}}{(1-d^N)/(1-d)}$$

i.e.,
$$C_{N+1} > \frac{X + \sum_{i=1}^{N} C_i d^{i-1}}{1 + d + d^2 + ... + d^{N-1}}. \qquad ...(9)$$

The equation (8) gives the weighted average cost of all the previous N years with weight 1, d, d^2,................respectively.

Now, in equation (7) substituting N for by N–1, we get

$$\frac{\left[C_N - F_{N-1}(1-d)d^{N-1}\right]}{(1-d^N)}$$

Since $\quad F_N - F_{N-1} < 0$

$$C_N d^{N-1} - F_{N-1}(1 - d)d^{N-1} < 0$$

Since d < 1, dividing the above by d^{N-1},

$$C_N - F_{N-1}(1 - d) < 0$$

i.e.,
$$C_N(1 - d) < F_{N-1} \qquad ...(10)$$

Inequalities (8) and (10) should hold good for F_N to be minimum, *i.e.*, for replacement of the equipment after N periods for an optimal policy.

From expression (10), it follows that

$C_N < (1 - d)\, F_{N-1}$ and thus substituting the value of F_{N-1} (by substituting N – 1 for N in equation (9), we get the expression identical to expression (9).

i.e.,
$$C_N < \frac{X + \sum_{i=1}^{N-1} C_i d^{i-1}}{1 + d + d^2 + ... + d^{N-2}} \qquad ...(11)$$

The expression on the right hand side of the expression is the weighted average of all costs upto and including period (N–1).

As a result of these two inequalities, *i.e.,* expressions (9) and (11), minimizing rules can be given as

(i) If the next period's cost is less than the weighted average of previous costs, the equipment is not replaced.

(ii) If the next period's cost is greater than the weighted average of previous costs, the equipment is replaced.

Adjusted average cost method can be well understood with the help of the following example:

REPLACEMENT DECISION BASED ON MAPI CONCEPT

MAPI approach uses a set of terms, *i.e., defender, challenger, operating inferiority, capital cost, and adverse minimum.*

Defender is the term used for the equipment being considered for replacement. *Challenger* is the term used for the equipment being proposed as replacement for the defender.

Operating inferiority is the amount by which an equipment is operationally inferior to its best current alternative, *i.e.*, equals the amount by which a defender is inferior to challenger. Operating inferiority of defender develops over a period of time due to normal wear and tear as well as due to technological changes and other reasons.

Operating inferiority can be found by comparing the sum of income and operating expenses of the defender and the challenger, operating inferiority increases with the use of equipment and development of newer machines, which are capable of doing a job faster and better.

Capital cost means the annual cost of the capital recovery plus the interest. The capital cost decreases with passage of time.

Adverse minimum refers to the lowest sum of the two adverse costs, *i.e.*, sum of capital cost and operating cost (operating inferiority). In the beginning, the capital cost of an equipment is maximum, but its operating inferiority is minimum. As time passes, capital cost decreases and operating inferiority increases. Thus, the management has to make the choice between more capital cost and less imperfection, and less capital cost and more imperfection.

The optimum decision lies at the point where the sum of the two adverse costs is minimum The replacement is justified by comparing the sum of the two adverse costs of the challenger. Therefore, if the adverse minimum of the defender is observed to be lower than that of challenger, replacement is desirable.

The use of MAPI method involves the following steps:

(i) Next years's inferiority of the defender is computed which is equal to the differences of the sum of income and operating cost of the defender and challenger.

(ii) Next year's capital cost of the defender is calculated. This is equal to the reduction in resale price for retaining the equipment for one more year plus loss of interest for one year on the resale price today.

(iii) Defender's adverse minimum is calculated. This is obtained by adding its next year's operating inferiority to its next year's capital cost.

(iv) Inferiority gradient of the defender (G) is computed as following:

$$G = \frac{\text{Operating inf eriority of defender}}{\text{Service life of the defender}}$$

(v) Adverse minimum of the challenger is computed in the following manner:

Challenger will also acquire operating inferiority due to normal wear and tear and new technological developments. Since the data is not available for the challenger, following assumption is made.

Inferiority gradient of the challenger = Inferiority gradient of defender

$$= \frac{\text{Operating inferiority of defender}}{\text{Service life of the defender}}$$

Now, if A = Acquisition cost of the challenger

S = Salvage value

r = Interest rate

N = Period of service in years

G = Inferiority gradient of the defender

Since

Challenger's total adverse cost per year = Acquisition cost per year + Operating inferiority per year

= Straight line depreciation + average interest

$$\text{Average acquisition cost per year} = \frac{A-S}{N} + \frac{r(A+S)}{2}$$

Operating inferiority per year can be computed as follows:

In the first year, the challenger does not develop any operating inferiority and it is expected that inferiority is developed in future at the rate that of defender.

The challenger's operating inferiority at the time of its replacement say *N* years, would be

0 + G + 2G + 3G +..........+ NG (operating gradient of defender is G)

This is an arithmetic progression, hence this is equal to

$$0 + (0 + G) + (0 + 2G) + \ldots\ldots + (0 + NG)$$

$$= (N + 1)/2[2 \times 0 + (N)G].$$

Average operating inferiority of the challenger per year

$$= (N + 1)/2[2 \times 0 + (N)G)]1/N$$

$$= (N + 1)G/2$$

Therefore, total adverse

cost of the challenger (TAC)

$$= \frac{A-S}{N} + \frac{i(A+S)}{2} + \frac{G(N+1)}{2} \qquad \ldots (1)$$

For minimum value of TAC (Adverse minimum).

$$\frac{dTAC}{dN} = 0$$

$$\text{Thus} \quad \frac{dTAC}{dN} = -\frac{A-S}{N^2} + \frac{G}{2} = 0$$

$$\text{or} \quad N = [2(A - S)/G]^{1/2}$$

On substitution of the value of N in the equation (1), challenger's adverse minimum would be

$$= [2G(A-S)]^{\frac{1}{2}} + \frac{i(A+S)+G}{2} \qquad \ldots (2)$$

This method can be illustrated through the following example:

SOLVED EXAMPLES

Example 1:

A company, engaged in production of fasteners, is proposing to replace its 10 year old unit by a new unit costing Rs. 10 lakhs. The old unit is saleable for Rs. 1 lakh and its sale value a year later would be Rs. 50,000. The annual savings in labour cost and maintenance cost are estimated to be Rs. 15,000, and 20,000, respectively. Taxes and insurance for the new unit are expected to be Rs. 10,000 more. The new unit is expected to have a life of 12 years and its sale value at that time is expected to be at Rs. 1,50,000. If the interest rate is 10%, compute the economic feasibility of the proposal employing MAPI technique.

Solution

1. Calculation is made for the next year's operating inferiority of the old unit (defender), which is measured in terms of income and cost differences as below:

Expenditure details	Advantage of old unit (defender)	Advantage of new unit (challenger)
Labour	–	15,000
Maintenance and repair costs	–	20,000
Taxes and insurance	10,000	–
	10,000	35,000

Therefore, next year's operating inferiority of the defender (old unit) = Rs. 25,000.

2. Calculation is made for next year's capital cost of the old unit (defender)

   = Drop in resale price + Loss on interest for one year on resale price this year

   = 100,000 – 50,000 + 100,000 × 0.10 = Rs. 60,000.

3. Defender's adverse minimum is computed.

   Defender's adverse minimum = Capital cost + operating inferiority

   = 60,000 + 35,000 = 95,000

4. Challenger's adverse minimum is computed.

$$\text{Challenger's adverse minimum} = [2G(A-S)]^{\frac{1}{2}} + \frac{i(A+S)+G}{2}$$

$$= \left[2\frac{25000}{10}(10{,}00{,}000-150{,}000)\right]^{\frac{1}{2}} + \frac{0.1\left[(10{,}00{,}000+150{,}000)+\frac{25000}{10}\right]}{2}$$

$$= 1{,}29{,}030.$$

5. Adverse minimum of two units is compared.

Since adverse minimum of the new unit (challenger) is more than that of the adverse minimum of the old unit (defender), replacement is justified.

Example 2:

The data on the running costs per year and resale price of equipment A whose purchase price is Rs. 2,00,000 are as follows:

Year	*1*	*2*	*3*	*4*	*5*	*6*	*7*
Running cost (Rs.)	*30,000*	*38,000*	*46,000*	*58,000*	*72,000*	*90,000*	*1,10,000*
Resale value (Rs.)	*1,00,000*	*50,000*	*25,000*	*12,000*	*8,000*	*8,000*	*8,000*

(a) *What is the optimum period of replacement?*

(b) *When equipment A is two years old, equipment B which is a new model for the same usage is available. The optimum period for replacement is 4 years with an average cost of Rs. 72,000. Should equipment A be changed with equipment B? If so, when?*

Solution:

The calculations of average running cost per year during the life of the equipment A are shown in Table.

Table (a): Calculations of Average Running Cost.

Year of Service n	*Running Cost(Rs.) R(n)*	*Cumulative Running Cost(Rs.)ΣR(n)*	*Resale Price (Rs.) S*	*Depreciation Cost(Rs.) C–S*	*Total Cost (Rs.) TC*	*Average Cost(Rs.) ATC_n*
(1)	*(2)*	*(3)*	*(4)*	*(5)=20,000–S*	*(6)=(3)+(4)*	*(7)=(5)/(1)*
1.	30,000	30,000	1,00,000	1,00,000	1,30,000	1,30,000.00
2.	38,000	68,000	50,000	1,50,000	2,18,000	1,09.000.00
3.	46,000	1,14,000	25,000	1,75,000	2,89,000	96,333.33
4.	58,000	1,72,000	12,000	1,88,000	3,60,000	90,000.00
5.	72,000	2,44,000	8,000	1,92,000	4,36,000	87,200.00
6.	90,000	3,34,000	8,000	1,92,000	5,26,000	**87,666.66**
7.	1,10,000	4,44,000	8,000	1,92,000	6.36,000	90,857.14

From Table (a), it may be noted that the average cost per year is lowest in the fifth year, *i.e.,* Rs. 87,200. Hence, the equipment A should be replaced at the end of the fifth year.

Table (b): Average Running Cost When Equipment A is 2 Years Old

Year of Service	*Running Cost (Rs.)*	*Depreciation Cost (Rs.)*	*Total Cost (Rs.)*	*Cumulative Cost (Rs.)*	*Average Cost (Rs.)*
3.	46,000	50,000-25,000 = 25,000	71,000	71,000	71,000
		25,000-12,000 = 13,000			
4.	58,000	4,000	71,000	1,42,000	**71,000**
5.	72,000	–	76,000	2,18,000	72,666.66
6.	90,000	–	90,000	3,08,000	77,000
7.	1,10,000	–	1,10,000	4,18,000	83,600

Now to find the time of replacement of equipment A by equipment B, the average cost of equipment A in the successive years is computed as shown in Table (b).

Calculations in Table (b) indicate that the equipment A should be replaced with equipment B when it is four years old, otherwise the average cost per year would start increasing.

Example 3:

Truck tyres, which fail in service, can lead to expensive accidents. It is estimated that a failure in service results in an average cost of Rs. 5000 excluding the cost of replacing the burst tyre. Replacement of new tyres cost Rs. 2000 each and are subject to mortality as in table below (Table (a). If the tyres are to be replaced after a certain fixed kilometer running or on failure (whichever occurs first), find the replacement policy that minimizes the average cost per kilometer.

Table (a) : Truck Tyre Mortality

Age of tyre at failure (kilometers)	*Period after replacement*	*% of tyres that fail on that period*	*% of original tyres which have failed by the end of that period*
10,000	*0*	*0*	*0*
12,000	*1*	*10*	*10*
14,000	*2*	*15*	*25*
16,000	*3*	*25*	*50*
18,000	*4*	*30*	*80*
20,000	*5*	*20*	*100*

Initially, the system contains 1000 tyres. The cost records indicate that all the 1000 tyres can be replaced for Rs. 2000 each if done on group replacement basis. However, if a tyre fails, the cost will be Rs. 7000 (5000 + 2000). Hence, the cost of individual replacement is Rs. 7000 and the cost of group replacement is Rs. 2000 per tyre.

Solution

The average life of 1000 tyres is computed as following:

0.1×1 period $= 0.10$ period

0.15 × 2 period = 0.30 period

0.25 × 3 period = 0.75 period

0.30 × 4 period = 1.20 period

0.2 × 5 period = 1.00 period

Average life = 3.35 periods.

Therefore, the average number of failures per period, if replaced as and when they fail

= 1000/3.35 = 299 per period.

The replacement cost of each tyre under this situation would be Rs. 7000 and hence, total replacement cost per period will be

= 299 × 7000 = Rs. 20,93,000.

Perhaps, it would be possible to reduce the cost of this operation by replacing the tyres at a fixed interval (say 3 periods). However, even in this case, replacement has to be made of those tyres failing during this interval in order to maintain 1000 tyres.

If,

N_0 = original number (1000)

N_i = number replaced at the end of period *i* (*i* = 1, 2, 3, 4, 5)

P_i = probability of failing during period *i* (*i* = 1, 2, 3, 4, 5).

Now, replacement required each period can be computed as following:

$$N_1 = N_0 \times P_1$$

= The original ones are 1 period old = 100

$$N_2 = (N_0 \times P_2) + (N_1 \times P_1)$$

The original ones are 2 periods old, the tyres replaced at the end of period 2 are 1 period old.

Similarly,

$$N_3 = (N_0 \times P_3) + (N_1 \times P_2) + (N_2 \times P_1)$$

$$N_4 = (N_0 \times P_4) + (N_1 \times P_3) + (N_2 \times P_2) + (N_3 \times P_1)$$

$$N_5 = (N_0 \times P_5) + (N_1 \times P_4) + (N_2 \times P_3) + (N_3 \times P_2) + (N_4 \times P_1)$$

Thus, the number of tyres to be replaced in each period can be computed as following:

$N_1 = 1000 \times 0.1$ = 100

$$N_2 = 1000 \times 0.15 + 100 \times 0.1 = 160$$

$$N_3 = 1000 \times 0.25 + 100 \times 0.15 + 160 \times 0.1 = 281$$

$$N_4 = 1000 \times 0.30 + 100 \times 0.25 + 160 \times 0.15 + 281 \times 0.1 = 377$$

$$N_5 = 1000 \times 0.20 + 100 \times 0.30 + 160 \times 0.25 + 281 \times 0.15 + 377 \times 0.1 = 350$$

Now, the various alternatives available can be compared by the use of Table 4.11 as given below:

Table (b): The Replacement Costs

Replacement at the end of Period	Cost of Replacing 1000 Tyres at Rs. 2000 each	Cost of Replacing failed Tyres at Rs. 7000 each	Total Cost	Cost per Period
1	20,00,000	100 × 7000 = 700,000	27,00,000	27,00,000
2	20,00,000	260 × 7000 = 18,20,000	38,20,000	19,10,000
3	20,00,000	541 × 7000 = 37,87,000	57,87,000	19,29,000
4	20,00,000	918 × 7000 = 64,26,000	84,26,000	21,06,500
5	20,00,000	1268 × 7000 = 88,76,000	108,76,000	21,75,200

From Table (b), it can be observed that from the standpoint of total cost, the cost would be the least if all the tyres are replaced at the end of period-2. Those, failed during the period, would be replaced on individual basis. The total cost saved would be equal to 20,93,000 (the old method)–19,10,000 (new method) = 1,83,000 per period.

Example 4:

A company produces automobile batteries at a factory cost of Rs. 500 each. Battery life is subject to mortality as in the following table. (Table).

The company has a guarantee policy under which if a battery fails during the first month after purchase, the refund of the full price or a new battery is made, if it fails during the second month, a refund of 29/30 of the full price is given, during the third month 28/30, and so on until the 30th month after purchase, at which time the refund of 1/30 of full price is made.

At what unit price batteries should be sold so that on an average the company will have break-even? Assume that battery age is zero at the time of purchase.

Table : Mortality of Battery

Age in months	*Probability of failure in next month*	*Age in months*	*Probability of failure in next month*	*Age in months*	*Probability of failure in next month*
0	*0.050*	*11*	*0.000*	*21*	*0.010*
1	*0.010*	*12*	*0.000*	*22*	*0.010*
2	*0.000*	*13*	*0.000*	*23*	*0.015*
3	*0.000*	*14*	*0.000*	*24*	*0.015*
4	*0.000*	*15*	*0.000*	*25*	*0.020*
5	*0.000*	*16*	*0.000*	*26*	*0.025*
6	*0.000*	*17*	*0.010*	*27*	*0.030*
7	*0.000*	*18*	*0.010*	*28*	*0.035*
8	*0.000*	*19*	*0.010*	*29*	*0.040*
9	*0.000*	*20*	*0.010*	*30*	*0.710*
10	*0.000*				

Solution

If

K = Break even price.

p_i = probability that the new battery will fail during the $(i+1)$th month after purchase.

Then the average refund on failing batteries would be

$$= \sum_{i=0}^{29} \frac{30-i}{30} K_{pi}$$

Substituting the values of p_i from Table 4.8, this becomes

$$= [1 \times k \times 0.05 + \frac{29}{30} k \times 0 + \ldots\ldots\ldots\ldots + \frac{1}{30} k \times 0.040]$$

$$= 0.0908k.$$

Since the break-even price is the sum of a factory cost and the expected refund.

$$k = 500 + 0.0908k \qquad k = 550.$$

Thus, the break-even price of the battery is Rs. 550.

Example 5:

An airline, whose staff are subject to the same survival rates presently has a staff whose ages are distributed in the following table (Table). It is

estimated that for the next two years staff requirement will increase by 10% per year. If girls are to be recruited at the age of 21, how many should be recruited for next year and at what age will promotions take place? How many should be recruited for the following year and at what age will promotions take place?

Solution

If $p(x)$ = probability that a girl is in service at age x, will still be in service at age $x + 1$

$$= \frac{\lambda_{x+1}}{\lambda_x}.$$

Now, the values of $p(x)$ are calculated and the expected number of survivals from supervisors are computed for one year at each age as shown in Table.

Table : Number of Girls in Service at the Start of Each Year

Age (x)	Number of Supervisors	Probability of being in service for one year hence (p_x)	Expected number of supervisors next year	New Age
42	5	0.938	5.71	43
43	4	0.934	4.69	44
44	5	0.939	3.74	45
45	3	0.935	4.69	46
46	3	0.920	2.80	47
47	3	0.913	2.76	48
48	6	0.904	2.74	49
49	2	0.894	5.42	50
50	–	0.898	1.79	51
51	–	0.868	–	52
52	4	0.848	–	53
53	3	0.846	3.39	54
54	5	0.818	2.54	55
55	–	0.815	4.09	56
56	3	0.818	–	57
57	2	0.778	2.45	58
58	–	0.786	1.56	59
59	2	–	–	60
			≅ 43	

From the Table, it can be observed that only 43 supervisors will be in the service after one year. Further, total staff requirement will be 55 (10% increase). Thus, 12 hostesses will have to be promoted to supervisors on the basis of their age.

There are 6 hostesses of age 41 with 0.95 probability of survival for one year. Similarly, there are 8 hostesses of age 40 years with 0.954 probability of survival for one year. Hence, in a year's time, there will be

$$6 \times 0.95 = 5.7 \text{ hostesses aged } 42$$

and $8 \times 0.954 = 7.632$ hostesses aged 41.

Thus, after one year from present age, 13.3 (5.7 + 7.63) seniormost hostesses will be of age 42 and 41 years, 12 out of them have to be promoted as supervisors after one year. In the following year, supervisors required would be 61. But in between the ages of 41 and 59, there are only 57.86 ($\cong$ 58) girls as supervisors and thus 3 will be promoted at the age of 39 from hostesses to supervisors, since no hostess will be available at the age of 40.

Now, since assistant hostesses required in the next year = 220 (10% increase), and upto the age of 23, there would be 237 girls and thus 237 – 220 = 17 girls have to be promoted to hostesses. Further, in the following year, number of assistant hostesses required would be 242 and upto the age of 22, there would be 254 girls, and hence, 12 (254 – 242) assistant hostesses will be promoted to hostesses at the age of 22.

Therefore, with the help of the Table, the solution may be summarized as following:

1. 21 year old recruits should be 143 next year and 168 in the following year.
2. Next year all the girls aged 24 will be promoted to hostesses and also 17 girls aged 23 will be promoted.
3. 3 girls aged 39 will be promoted to supervisors, and 6 girls aged 41 will be promoted to supervisors.

Example 6:

Machine A costs Rs. 45,000 and the operating costs are estimated at Rs. 1,000 for the first year increasing by Rs. 10,000 per year in the second and subsequent years. Machine B costs Rs. 50,000 and operating costs are Rs. 2,000 for the first year, increasing by Rs. 4,000 in the second and subsequent years. If we now have a machine of type A, should we replace it with B? If so when? Assume that both machines have no resale value and future costs are not discounted.

Solution:

The calculations of average running cost per year during the life of machines A and B are shown in Tables (a) and (b), respectively,.

Table (a): Calculations of Average Running Cost for Machine A

Year of Service n	*Running Cost (Rs.)* $R(n)$	*Cumulative Running Cost (Rs.)* $\Sigma R(n)$	*Depreciation Cost(Rs.)* $C–S$	*Total Cost (Rs.)* TC	*Average Cost (Rs.)* ATC_n
(1)	*(2)*	*(3)*	*(4)*	*(5)=(3)+(4)*	*(6)=(5)/(1)*
1.	1,000	1,000	45,000	46,000	46,000
2.	11,000	12,000	45,000	57,000	28,500
3.	21,000	33,000	45,000	78,000	**26,000**
4.	31,000	64,000	45,000	1,09,000	27,250
5.	41,000	1,05,000	45,000	1,50,000	30,000
6.	51,000	1,56,000	45,000	2,01,000	33,500

From Table 4.13, it may be noted that the average running cost per year is lowest in the third year, *i.e.,* Rs. 26,000. Hence, machine A should be replaced after every three years of service..

Table (b): Calculations of Average Running Cost for Machine B.

Year of Service n	*Running Cost (Rs.)* $R(n)$	*Cumulative Running Cost(Rs.)* $\Sigma R(n)$	*Depreciation Cost(Rs.)* $C–S$	*Total Cost (Rs.)* TC	*Average Cost (Rs.)* ATC_n
(1)	*(2)*	*(3)*	*(4)*	*(5)=(3)+(4)*	*(6)=(5)/(1)*
1.	2,000	2,000	50,000	52,000	52,000
2.	6,000	8,000	50,000	58,000	29,000
3.	10,000	18,000	50,000	68,000	22,667
4.	14,000	32,000	50,000	82,000	20,500
5.	18,000	50,000	50,000	1,00,000	**20,000**
6.	22,000	72,000	50,000	1,22,000	20,333

The average running cost per year is lowest in the fifth year, *i.e.,* Rs. 20,000. This cost is less than the lowest average running cost (Rs. 26,000) per year for machine A. Hence, machine A should be replaced by machine B.

Now, to find the time of replacement of machine A by machine B, the total cost of machine A in the successive years is computed as follows:

Year	:	1	2	3	4
Total cost incurred (Rs.)	:	46,000 –	57,000–46,000 = 11,000	78,000–57,000 = 21,000	1,90,000–78,000 = 31,000

Machine A should be replaced by machine B at the time (age) when its running cost for the next year exceeds the lowest average running cost (Rs. 20,000) per year of machine B.

Calculations show that the running cost (Rs. 21,000) of machine A in the third year is more than lowest average cost (Rs. .20,000) of machine B. Hence, machine A should be replaced by machine B after two years.

Example 7:

A computer contains 10,000 resistors. When any one of the resistors fails, it is replaced. The cost of replacing a single resistor is Re. 1 only. If all the resistors are replaced at the same time, the cost per resistor would be reduced to 35 paise. The percent surviving by the end of the month i is as follows:

Month (t):	*0*	*1*	*2*	*3*	*4*	*5*	*6*
%Surviving by the end of month:	*100*	*97*	*90*	*70*	*30*	*15*	*0*

What is the optimum plan?

Solution

The problem can be considered in two parts, *i.e.*,

1. Policy for individual replacement,
2. Policy for group replacement.

The probabilities $p(t)$ of failure during the month t can be given as

$p(1)$	$p(2)$	$p(3)$	$p(4)$	$p(5)$	$p(6)$	Total
0.03	0.07	0.20	0.40	0.15	0.15	1.00

It may be observed that no resistor survives for more than 6 months and hence, a resistor surviving for 5 months, will definitely fail during 6th month. It is assumed that the resistors, which fail during a month, are replaced just at the end of the month.

If N_i denotes the number of resistors replaced at the end of ith month, the different values of N_i can be computed as following:

$N_0 = 10{,}000$

$N_1 = N_0 \times p(1) = 10{,}000 \times 0.03 = 300$

$N_2 = N_0 p(2) + N_1 p(1) = 10{,}000 \times 0.07 + 300 \times 0.03 = 709$

$N_3 = N_0p(3) + N_1p(2) + N_2p(1) = 10{,}000 \times 0.20 + 300 \times 0.07 + 709 \times 0.03 = 2042$

$N_4 = N_0p(4) + N_1p(3) + N_2p(2) + N_3p(1) = 10{,}000 \times 0.40 + 300 \times 0.20 + 709 \times 0.07 + 2042 \times 0.03 = 4171$

$N_5 = N_0p(5) + N_1p(4) + N_2p(3) + N_3p(2) + N_4p(1) = 10{,}000 \times 0.15 + 300 \times 0.40 + 709 \times 0.02 + 2042 \times 0.07 + 4171 \times 0.03 = 2030$

$N_6 = N_0p(6) + N_1p(5) + N_2p(4) + N_3p(3) + N_4p(2) + N_5p(1) = 10{,}000 \times 0.15 + 300 \times 0.15 + 709 \times 0.40 + 2042 \times 0.20 + 4171 \times 0.07 + 2030 \times 0.03 = 2590$

The average (expected) life of each resistor

$= \sum_{i=1}^{6} x_i p(i)$ (x_i is the month and p_i is the corresponding probability of failure)

$= 1 \times 0.03 + 2 \times 0.07 + 3 \times 0.20 + 4 \times 0.40 + 5 \times 0.15 + 6 \times 0.15$

$= 4.02$ months.

Average number of replacements each month

$= N_0/\text{mean age} = 10{,}000/4.02$

$\cong 2488.$

Hence, average cost of monthly individual replacement

$=$ Rs. $2488 \times 1 = 2488.$

Under group replacement, the computation results are obtained as in Table.

Table : Group Replacement Computation

End of month replacement (Rs.)	Cost of individual (Rs.)	Total cost of group replacement	Average cost per month (Rs.)
1	300	10,000 × 0.35 + 300 × 1 = 3800	3800.00
2	709	3800 + 709 × 1 = 4509	2254.50
3	2042	4509 + 2042 × 1 = 6551	2183.66
4	4171*	6551 + 4171 × 1 = 10722	2680.50
5	2030	10722 + 2030 × 1 =12752	2550.40
6	2590	12752 + 2590 × 1 = 15342	2557.00

The cost of individual replacement in the 4th month exceeds the average cost for 3 months (Rs. 2183.66). Thus, optimal policy for replacement is group replacement of all resistors after every 3 months.

Example 8:

A company has the option to buy one of the mini computers: MINICOMP and CHIPCOMP. MINICOMP costs Rs. 5 lakh, and running and maintenance costs are Rs. 60,000 for each of the first five years, increasing by Rs. 20,000 per year in the sixth and subsequent years. CHIPCOMP has the same capacity as MINICOMP, but costs only Rs. 2,50,000. However, its running and maintenance costs are Rs. 1,20,000 per year in the first five years, and increase by Rs. 20,000 per year thereafter. If the money is worth 10 per cent per year, which computer should be purchased? What are the optimal replacement periods for each of the computers? Assume that there is no salvage value for either computer. Explain your analysis.

Solution:

Since money is worth 10 per cent per year, the discounted factor (or rate) over a period of one year is given by

$$d = 1/(1 + 0.10) = 0.9091$$

It is also given that C = Rs. 5 lakh.

The optimum replacement age n must satisfy the condition $R_n < W(8) < R_{n+1}$.

The calculations for best replacement age (period), n for both computers.

Table shows that the running cost, R_{10} is more than the weighted average cost, W(9) for 9th year. Aiso the inequality

Table (a) : Weighted Average Cost for MINICOMP Computer

Year of Service n	*Running Cost(Rs.)* R_n	*Discounted Factor* d^{n-1}	$R_n d^{n-1}$	*Cumulative* $\Sigma R_i d^{i-1}$	$C + SR_i d^{i-1}$	*Cumulative* Σd^{i-1}	$W(n)$
(1)	(2)	(3)	(4)	(5)	(6)=5,00.000+(5)	(7)	(8)=(6)/(7)
1.	60,000	1.0000	60,000	60,000	5,60,000	1.0000	5,60,000
2.	60,000	0.9091	54,546	1,14,546	6,14,546	1.9091	3,21,904
3.	60,000	0.8264	49,584	1,64,130	6,64,130	2.7355	2,42,782
4.	60,000	0.7513	45,078	2,09,208	7,09,208	3.4868	2,03,398
5.	60,000	0.6830	40,980	2,50,188	7,50,188	4.1698	1,79,910
6.	80,000	0.6209	49,672	2,99,860	7,99,860	4.7907	1,66,961
7.	1,00,000	0.5645	56,450	3,56,310	8,56,310	5.3552	1,59,903
8.	1,20,000	0.5132	61,584	4,17,894	9,17,894	5.8684	1,56,413
9.	1,40,000	0.4665	65,310	4,83,204	9,83,204	6.3349	**1,55,204**
10.	1,60,000	0.4241	67,586	5,51,060	10,51,060	6.7590	1,55,505

$R_9 < W(9) < R_{10}$,

i.e., 1,40,000 < 1,55,204 < 1,60,000

is satisfied, therefore MINICOMP computer should be replaced after nine years.

Table (b) : Weighted Average Cost for CHIPCOMP Computer

Year of Service n	*Running Cost(Rs.)* R_n	*Discounted Factor* d^{n-1}	$R_n d^{n-1}$	*Cumulative* $\Sigma R_i d^{i-1}$	$C + SR_i\, d^{i-1}$	*Cumulative* Σd^{i-1}	$W(n)$
(1)	(2)	(3)	(4)	(5)	(6)=2,500,000+(5)	(7)	(8)=(6)/(7)
1.	1,20,000	1,0000	1,20,000	1,20,000	3,70,000	1.0000	3,70,000.00
2.	1,20,000	0.9091	1,09,092	2,29,092	4,79,092	1.9091	2,50,951.76
3.	1,20,000	0.8264	99,168	3,28,260	5,78,260	2.7355	2,11,390.97
4.	1,20,000	0.7513	90,156	4,18,416	6,68,416	3.4868	1,91,698.97
5.	1,20,000	0.6830	81,960	5,00,376	7,50,376	4.1698	1,79,954.91
6.	1,40,000	0.6209	86,926	5,87,302	8,37,302	4.7907	1,74,776.54
7.	1,60,000	0.5645	90,320	6,77,622	9,27,622	5.3552	**1,73,218.92**
8.	1,80,000	0.5132	92,376	6,69,998	10,19,998	5.8684	1,73,811.94
9.	2,00,000	0.4665	93,300	8,63,298	11,13,298	6.3349	1,75,740.42
10.	2,20,000	0.4241	93,302	9,56,600	12,06,600	6.7590	1,78,517.53

From Table 4.36, since the condition $R_6 < W(7) < R_8$ is satisfied, the replacement period for CHIPCOMP computer is after six years.

Example 9(a):

A piece of equipment either can fail completely, so that it has to be scrapped (no salvage value), or may suffer a minor defect, which can be repaired. The probability that it will not have to be scrapped before age t is f(t). The conditional probability that it will need a repair in the instant t + dt, knowing that it was in running order at t, is r(t)dt. The probability of a repair or complete failure is dependent only on the age of the equipment, and not on the previous repair history.

Each repair costs Rs. C, and complete replacement costs Rs. K. For some considerable time, the policy has been to replace only on failure.

(a) *Derive a formula for the expected cost per unit time of the present policy of replacing only on failure.*

(b) *It has been suggested that it might be cheaper to scrap equipment at some fixed age T, thus avoiding the higher risk of repairs with advancing age. Show that the expected cost per unit time of such policy is*

$$\frac{\left[C\int_0^T f(u)\, r du + K\right]}{\int_0^T f(u)\, du}$$

Solution:

The probability that the equipment will have to be scrapped before age t is f(t). Therefore, the equipment will fail at some time and is given by

$$\int_0^\infty f(t)\, dt = 1$$

Further, the probability that the equipment will need renewal in the interval t and t + dt, knowing that it was in running order at time t is given by r(t) dt.

(a) Probability that equipment needs repair between age u and u + du is f(u) du. Thus expected cost and total expected cost of repair will be

$$\text{Expected cost} = C\int_0^\infty f(u)\, r(u)\, du$$

$$\text{Total expected cost} = \frac{\left[K + C\int_0^\infty f(u)\, r(u)\right]}{\int_0^T f(u) du}$$

$$= K + C\int_0^\infty f(u)\, r(u)\, du; \quad \int_0^\infty f(u) d = 1$$

(b) Under the policy of scrapping at the age T, the total expected cost of repair will be

$$K + C\int_0^T f(u)\, r(u)\, du$$

Hence, the expected cost per unit of time will be

$$E(T) = \frac{\left[K + C\int_0^T f(u) r(u) du\right]}{\int_0^T f(u) du}$$

Example 9(b):

An airline requires 200 assistant hostesses, 300 hostesses and 50 supervisors. Girls are recruited at the age of 21, if still in service, retire at the age of 60 years. Given the following life table.

Compute:

(i) How many girls should be recruited in each year?

(ii) At what age promotion should take place.

Table : Airline Hostesses Life Record

Age	*Number in service*	*Age*	*Number in service*	*Age*	*Number in service*	*Age*	*Number in service*
21	1000	31	173	41	119	51	53
22	600	32	167	42	113	52	46
23	480	33	161	43	106	53	39
24	384	34	155	44	99	54	33
25	307	35	150	45	93	55	27
26	261	36	146	46	87	56	22
27	228	37	141	47	80	57	18
28	206	38	136	48	73	58	14
29	190	39	131	49	66	59	11
30	181	40	125	50	59	–	–

Solution:

If x = age

λ_x = number of girls in service at age x

The total number of girls recruited at the age of 21 and those serving upto the age of 59 is

$$\sum_{x=21}^{59} \lambda_x = 6480$$

In all, 200 + 300 + 50 = 550 girls are required in the system:

Each year, the recruitment is 1000, when total number of girls are 6480 after 59 years. Hence, to maintain a strength of 550 girls, recruitment should be of

$$\frac{1000 \times 550}{6480} \sim 85 \text{ girls each year}$$

If promotion from assistant hostess to hostess is given at the age Y, then 200 assistant hostesses will be required upto the age of $Y - 1$. Among 550, there are 200 assistant hostesses. Hence, out of a strength of 1000, there will be

$$\frac{200 \times 1000}{550} = 364 \text{ assistant hostesses,}$$

and from the given life table in the problem, this number is available upto the age of 24 years. Therefore, the promotion of assistant hostesses will be due in 25th year.

Further, out of 550 recruitments, only 300 hostesses would be required. Therefore, if 1000 girls are recruited, then only hostesses required would be

$$\frac{1000 \times 300}{550} = 545.$$

Therefore, the number of hostesses and assistant hostesses in a recruitment of 1000 would be

$$545 + 364 = 909.$$

This gives that number of supervisors needed would be

$$1000 - 909 = 91$$

Whereas at the age of 46, only 87 will survive, and thus promotion of hostesses to supervisors will be due in 46*th* year.

The solution can thus be summarized as

1. 85 assistant hostesses of age 21 will be recruited every year.
2. Promotion of assistant hostesses to hostesses will be due in 25th year.
3. Promotion of hostesses to supervisors will be due in 46th year.

Example 9(c):

A firm has a machine whose purchase price is Rs. 1,00,000. Its running cost and resale price at the end of different years are as follows:

Year	:	*1*	*2*	*3*	*4*	*5*	*6*
Running cost (Rs.)	:	*7,500*	*8,500*	*10,000*	*12,500*	*17,500*	*27,500*
Resale price (Rs.)	:	*85,000*	*76,500*	*70,000*	*60,000*	*40,000*	*15,000*

(a) *Obtain the economic life of the machine and the minimum average cost.*

(b) *The firm has obtained a contract to supply the goods produced by the machine, for a period of five years from now. After this time period, the firm does not intend to use the machine. If the firm has a machine of this type which is one year old, what replacement policy should it adopt if it intends to replace the machine not more than once?*

Solution:

(i) The calculations of average running cost per year during the life of the machine are shown in Table.

From Table , it may be noted that the economic life of the machine is three years with corresponding minimum average cost of Rs. 18,667.

Table (a): Calculations of Average Running Cost

Year of Service *n*	*Running Cost (Rs.)* *R(n)*	*Cumulative Running Cost (Rs.)* *Σ R(n)*	*Resale Price(Rs.)* *S*	*Depreciation Cost (Rs.)* *C–S*	*Total Cost (Rs.)* *TC*	*Average Cost (Rs.)* *ATC,*
(1)	(2)	(3)	(4)	(5)=C–(4)	(6)= (3)+(5)	(7)=(6)/(1)
1.	7,500	7,500	85,000	15,000	22,500	27,500
2.	8,500	16,000	76,500	23,500	39,500	19,750
3.	10,000	26,000	70,000	30,000	56,000	**18,667**
4.	12,500	38,500	60,000	40,000	78,500	19,625
5.	17,500	56,000	40,000	60,000	1,16,000	23,200
6.	27,500	83,500	15,000	85,000	1,68.500	28,083

(ii) The yearly cost of maintaining one year old machine in subsequent years of its life is shown in Table (b).

Table (b) : Yearly Cost of Existing Machine

Year of Service	*Running Cost (Rs.)*	*Depreciation Cost (Rs.)*	*Total Cost (Rs.)*	*Cumulative Cost (Rs.)*	*Average Cost (Rs.)* ATC_n
(1)	(2)	(3)	(4)=(2)+(3)	(5)	(6)=(5)/(1)
2.	8,500	23,500-15,000=8,500	17,000	17,000	8,500
3.	10,000	30,000-23,500=6,500	16,500	33,500	11,166.66
4.	12,500	10,000	22,500	56,000	14,000
5.	17,500	20,000	37,500	93,500	18,700
6.	27,500	25,000	52,500	1,46,000	24,333.33

The alternative policies of retaining the old machine and buying the new machine are enumerated as shown in Table (c).

Table (c) : Alternative Policies and Associated Costs.

Policy	*Total associated cost (Rs.)*
(i) Do not retain old machine and buy new one for five years	0 + 1,16,000 = 1,16,000
(ii) Retaining old machine for one year and buying new one for four years	17,000 + 78,500 = 95,500

(iii) Retaining old machine for two years and buying new one for three years	33,500 + 56,000 = 89,500
(iv) Retaining old machine for three years and buying new one for two years	56,000 + 39,500 = 95,500
(v) Retaining old machine for four years and buying new one for one year	93,500 + 22,500 = 1,16,000
(vi) Keep old machine for five years and do not buy new one	1,46,000 + 0 = 1,46,000

Since total cost associated with policy (iii) is lowest among all alternative policies, this policy is the optimal policy.

Example 10:

(a) A fleet owner finds from his past records that the cost per year of an auto whose purchase price is Rs. 60,000 is as given below:

Year	:	*1*	*2*	*3*	*4*	*5*	*6*	*7*	*8*
Running cost (Rs.)	:	*10,000*	*12,000*	*14,000*	*18,000*	*23,000*	*28,000*	*34,000*	*40,000*
Resale value (Rs.)	:	*30,000*	*15,000*	*7,500*	*3,750*	*2,000*	*2,000*	*2,000*	*2,000*

Determine at what age is its replacement due?

(b) Let the owner have three autos, two of which are two years old and the third, one year old. The cost price, running costs and resale value of these autos is same as given in part (a). Now he is considering a new type of auto with 50 per cent more capacity than one of the old ones at a unit price of Rs. 80,000. He estimates that the running costs and resale price for the new auto will be as follows:

Year	:	*1*	*2*	*3*	*4*	*5*	*6*	*7*
Running cost (Rs.)	:	*12,000*	*15,000*	*18,000*	*24,000*	*31,000*	*40,000*	*50,000*
Resale value (Rs.)	:	*40,000*	*20,000*	*20,000*	*5,000*	*3,000*	*3,000*	*3,000*

Assuming that the loss of flexibility due to fewer autos is of no importance, and that he will continue to have sufficient work for three of the old autos, what should his policy be?

Solution:

(a) The calculations of average cost per year during the life of the auto are shown in Table (a).

From Table (a), it may be noted that the average cost per year ATC_n is minimum in the 5th year. Hence, the autos should be replaced after every 5th year, otherwise the average cost per year would start increasing.

Table (a) : Average Cost of Old Auto

Year of Service *n*	*Running Cost (Rs.)* *R(n)*	*Cumulative Running Cost (Rs.)* $\Sigma R(n)$	*Depreciation Cost (Rs.)* *C–S*	*Total Cost (Rs.)* *TC*	*Average Cost (Rs.)* ATC_n
(1)	(2)	(3)	(4)	(5)=(3)+(4)	(6)–(5)/(1)
1.	10,000	10,000	30,000	40,000	40,000.00
2.	12,000	22,000	45,000	67,000	33,500.00
3.	14,000	36,000	52,500	88,500	29,500.00
4.	18,000	54,000	56,250	1,10,250	27,562.50
5.	23,000	77,000	58,000	1,35,000	**27,000.00**
6.	28,000	1,05,000	58,000	1,63,000	27,166.66
7.	34,000	1,39,000	58,000	1,97,000	28,142.85
8.	40,000	1,79,000	58,000	2,37,000	29,625.00

As in part (a), first calculate average cost per year for the new auto as shown in Table (b).

Table (b) : Average Cost of New Auto.

Year of Service *n*	*Running Cost (Rs.)* *R(n)*	*Cumulative Running Cost (Rs.)* $\Sigma R(n)$	*Depreciation Cost (Rs.)* *C–S*	*Total Cost (Rs.)* *TC*	*Average Cost (Rs.)* ATC_n
(1)	(2)	(3)	(4)	(5)=(3)+(4)	(6)=(5)/(1)
1	12,000	12,000	40,000	52,000	52,000.00
2	15,000	27,000	60,000	87,000	43,500.00
3	18,000	45,000	70,000	1,15,000	38,333.33
4	24,000	69,000	75,000	1,44,000	36,000.00
5	31,000	1,00,000	77,000	1,77,000	**35,400.00**
6	40,000	1,40,000	77,000	2,17,000	36,166.66
7	50,000	1,90,000	77,000	2,67,000	38,142.85
8	61,000	2,51,000	77,000	3,28,000	41,000.00

In Table (b), since $ATC_n < ATC_n$, therefore, new auto should be replaced after every 5th year. The average yearly cost would be Rs. 35,400.

Since the capacity of the new auto is 50 per cent more than that of the old auto, therefore, capacity of two new autos is equivalent to three smaller auto. Thus, the minimum average yearly cost for the new Replacement and

Maintenance Models 745 auto will be equal to Rs. 23,600 {= 35,400 × (2/3)}. But this is less than the minimum average yearly cost (Rs. 27,000) for one of the old autos (see Table a). Hence the old, smaller auto should be replaced by a new auto.

After deciding that the old type of autos should be replaced with the new autos, we must decide as to when the new autos should be purchased. For uniformity, let us assume that the replacement will involve two new autos and all three old autos. The new autos should be purchased to replace three old autos when the running cost for the next year of the three old autos exceeds the average yearly cost for two new autos. The total cost of old autos in the subsequent years is computed as shown in Table (c).

Table (c) : Yearly Cost of Old Auto

Year of Service →	*1*	*2*	*3*	*4*	*5*	*6*
Yearly total cost of old autos (Rs.):	67,000– 40,000 4,000	88,500– 67,000 = 27,000	1,10,250– 88,500 = 21,500	1,35,500– 1,10,250 = 21,750	1,35,500 = 25,250	1,63,000– = 27,500

The average cost for two new autos will be Rs. 70,800 (= 2 × 35,400) and for three old autos will be Rs. 81,000 (= 3 × 27,000). Further, it is given that two autos are two years old and one is one year old; therefore, total average cost during first year will be Rs. 70,000 (= 2 × 21,500 + 27,000) because two of the autos would be running in the third year and the third one in the second year. Similarly, the average cost in the subsequent years will be

2 × 21,750 + 21,500 = Rs. 65,000 (2nd year)

2 × 25,250 + 21,750 = Rs. 72,250 (3rd year)

2 × 27,500 + 25,250 = Rs. 80,250 (4th year)

From these calculations, we conclude that the total cost of three old autos up to the third year, *i.e.*, Rs. 65,000 is less than total average cost for new autos. But the total cost of three old autos during fourth year, *i.e.*, Rs. 72,250 is more than the total average cost for new autos, *i.e.*, Rs. 70,800. Hence, all the three old autos should be replaced after two years of service without waiting for their normal replacement age of five years.

Example 11:

Let the value of the money be assumed to be 10 per cent per year and suppose that machine A is replaced after every three years whereas machine

B is replaced every six years. The yearly costs (in Rs.) of both the machines are given as under:

Year	:	*1*	*2*	*3*	*4*	*5*	*6*
Machine A	:	*1,000*	*200*	*400*	*1000*	*200*	*400*
Machine B	.	*1,700*	*100*	*200*	*300*	*400*	*500*

Determine which machine should be purchased.

Solution:

The discounted cost (present worth) at 10 per cent rate per year for machine A for three years and B for six years is given in Tables (a) and (b), respectively.

Table (a) : Discounted Cost of Machine A

Year	*Discounted Cost at 10% Rate (Rs.)*		
	Cost	*Present Worth*	
1	1,000	$100 \times 1{,}000$	= 1,000
2	200	$20\left(\frac{100}{100+10}\right) = 200 \times 0.9091$	= 181.82
3	400	$400\left(\frac{100}{100+10}\right)^2 = 400 \times 0.8264$	= 330.56
Total			Rs. 1,512.38

Thus average yearly cost of machine A is 1512.38/3 = Rs. 504.13.

Table (b) : Discounted Cost of Machine B

Year	*Discounted Cost at 10% Rate (Rs.)*		
	Cost	*Present Worth*	
1.	1,700	1,700 × 1,000	= 1,700.00
2.	100	100 × (10/11) = 100 × 0.9091	= 90.91
3.	200	200 × (10/11)2 = 200 × 0.8264	= 165.28
4.	300	300 × (10/11)3 = 200 × 0.7513	= 225.39
5.	400	400 × (10/11)4 = 400 × 0.6830	= 273.20
6.	500	500 × (10/11)5 = 500 × 0.6209	= 310.45
			Total Rs. 2,765.23

Thus, average yearly cost of machine B is 2,765.23/6 = Rs. 460.87.

With the data on average yearly cost of both the machines, the apparent advantage is in purchasing machine B. But, the periods for which the costs are considered are different. Therefore, let us first calculate total present worth of machine A for six years.

Total present worth = $1{,}000 + 200 \times 0.9091 + 400 \times 0.8264 + 1{,}000 \times 0.7513 + 200 \times 0.6830 + 400 \times 0.6209$

= Rs. 2,648.64

This is less than the total present worth of machine B. Thus machine A should be purchased.

Example 12(a):

A pipeline is due for repairs. It will cost Rs. 10,000 and lasts for three years. Alternately, new pipeline can be laid at a cost of Rs. 30,000 and lasts for 10 years. Assuming cost of capital to be 10 per cent and ignoring salvage value, which alternative should be chosen?

Solution:

Consider the two types of pipelines for infinite replacement cycles of ten years for the new pipeline and three years for the existing pipeline. Since the discount rate of money per year is 10 per cent, then the present worth of the money to be spent over a period of one year is

$$d = 10/000 + 10) = 0.901.$$

Let D_n denote the discounted value of all future costs associated with a policy of replacing the equipment after n years. Then we shall have,

$$D_n = c + c \times d^n = c \times d^{2n} + \ldots$$

$$= c(1 + d^n + d^{2n} + \ldots)$$

$$= \frac{c}{1-d^n} \text{ (sum of infinite GP).}$$

where c is the initial cost.

Now, substituting the values of c, d's and n for two types of pipelines, we get

$$D_3 = \frac{10{,}000}{1-(0.9091)^3} = \text{Rs. } 4{,}021, \text{ for existing pipeline}$$

and $$D_{10} = \frac{30{,}000}{1-(0.9091)^{10}} = \text{Rs. } 48{,}820, \text{ for new pipeline}$$

Since the value of $D_3 < D_{10}$ the existing pipeline should be continued. Alternatively, the comparison may be made over 3 × 10 = 30 years.

Example 12(b):

A company is considering the purchase of a new machine at Rs. 15,0C0. The economic life of the machine is expected to be 8 years. The salvage value of the machine at the end of the life will be Rs. 3,000. The annual running costs are estimated to be Rs. 7,000.

(a) Assuming an interest rate of 5 per cent, determine the present worth of future costs of the proposed machine.

(b) Compare the new machine with the presently owned machine that has an annual operating cost of Rs. 5,000 and cost of repair Rs. 1,500 in the second year with an annual increase of Rs. 500 in the subsequent years of life.

Solution :

(a) New Machine

(i) Purchase cost C = Rs. 15,000

(ii) Present worth of annual operating cost

= 7,000 x Pwf at 5% interest for 8 years

= 7,000 × 6.4632

= Rs. 45,242.40

(iii) Present worth of the salvage value

= 3,000 × Pwf at 5% interest for 8 years

= 3,000 × 0.6768

= Rs. 2,030.40.

Thus, present worth of total future costs for new machine for eight years will be

15,000 + 45,242.4 + 2,030

= Rs. 58,212.

(b) Old Machine : The calculations of the present worth of the old machine are shown in Table.

Since the present worth of old machine as shown in Table 4.25 is less than that of the new machine, new machine should not be purchased.

Table : Present Worth of Old Machine

Year of Service	*Operating Cost (Rs.)*	*Repair Cost (Rs.)*	*Total Operating and Repair Cost (Rs.)*	*Pwf for Single Payment*	*Present Worth (Rs.)*
1.	5,000	–	5,000	0.9524	5,000 × 0.9524 = 4762.00
2.	5,000	1,500	6,500	0.9072	5,895.50
3.	5,000	2,000	7,000	0.8638	6,046.60
4.	5,000	2,500	7,500	0.8227	6,252.52
5.	5,000	3,000	8,000	0.7835	6,268.00
6.	5,000	3,500	8,500	0,7462	6,342.70
7.	5,000	4,000	9,000	0.7107	6,396.30
8.	5,000	4,500	9,500	0.6778	6,429.60
				Total	44,103.20

Example 12(c):

A person is considering to purchase a machine for his own factory. Relevant data about alternative machines are as follows:

	Machine A	*Machine B*	*Machine C*
Present investment (Rs.)	*10,000*	*12,000*	*15,000*
Total annual cost (Rs.)	*2,000*	*1,500*	*1,200*
Life (years)	*10*	*10*	*10*
Salvage value (Rs.)	*500*	*1,000*	*1,200*

As an adviser to the buyer, you have been asked to select the best machine, considering 12 per cent normal rate of return.

You are given that:

(a) Single payment present worth factor (Pwf) at 12 per cent interest for 10 years (= 0.322).

(b) Annual series present worth factor (Pwf) at 12 per cent interest for 10 years (= 5.650).

Solution:

The present value of total cost of each of the three machines for a period of ten years is given in Table.

Table : Present Value of Total Cost for Three Machines.

Machine	*Present Investment*	*Preset Value of Total Annual Cost*	*Present Value of Salvage Value*	*Net Cost (Rs.)*
(1)	*(2)*	*(3)*	*(4)*	*(5) =(2) +(3)–(4)*
A	10,000	2,000×5.65=11,300	500×0.322=161.00	21,139.00
B	12,000	1,500×5.65=8,475	1,000×0.322=322.00	20,153.00
C	15,000	1,200×5.65=6,780	1,200×0.322=386.40	21,393.60

Table 4.26 shows that the present value of total cost for machine B is the least and hence, machine B should be purchased.

Example 13:

An engineering company is offered a material handling equipment A. It is priced at Rs. 60,000 including cost of installation, and the costs for operation and maintenance are estimated to be Rs. 10,000 for each of the first five years, increasing every year by Rs. 3,000 in the sixth and subsequent years. The company expects a return of 10 per cent on all its investment. What is the optimal replacement period?

Solution:

Since money is worth 10 per cent per year, the discounted factor over a period of one year is given by

Table : Calculations of Replacement Period.

Year of Service n	*Running Cost (Rs.) Rn*	*Discounted Factor d^{n-1}*	*Rn d^{n-1}*	*Cumulative* $\sum_{i=1}^{10} R_i d^{i-1}$	$C+\sum_{i=1}^{10} R_i d^{i-1}$	*Cumulative* $\sum_{i=1}^{10} R_i d^{i-1}$	*W(n)*
(1)	(2)	(3)	(4) = (2) × (3)	(5)	(6)=60,000+(5)	(7)	(8)=(6)/(7)
1.	10,000	0.909	9,090	9,090	69,090	1.909	36,192
2.	10,000	0.826	8,260	17,350	77,350	2.735	28,282
3.	10,000	0.751	7,510	24,860	84,860	3.486	24,343
4.	10,000	0.683	6,830	31,690	91,690	4.169	'21,993
5.	10,000	0.621	6,210	37,900	97,900	4.790	20,438
6.	13,000	0.564	7,332	45,232	1,05,232	5.354	19,655
7.	16,000	0.513	8,208	53,440	1,13,440	5.867	19,335
8.	19,000	0.466	8,854	62,294	1,22,294	6.333	19,311
9.	22,000	0.424	9,328	71,622	1,31,622	6.757	19,479
10.	25,000	0.385	9,650	81,247	1,41,247	7.142	19,777

$$d = 1/(1 + 0.10) = 0.9091$$

It is also given that C = Rs. 60,000.

The optimum replacement age must satisfy the condition $R_n < W(n) < R_{n+1}$.

The calculations for best replacement period are shown in Table 4.27. From this table, we find that the running cost R_q Rs. 22,000 is more than the weighted average cost Rs. 19,311 for eight years. Hence, the equipment needs to be replaced after every 8 years at an average cost of Rs. 19,311.

Example 14(a):

A company has the option to buy one of the mini computers: MINICOMP and CHIPCOMP. MINICOMP costs Rs. 5 lakh, and running and maintenance costs are Rs. 60,000 for each of the first five years, increasing by Rs. 20,000 per year in the sixth and subsequent years. CHIPCOMP has the same capacity as MINICOMP, but costs only Rs. 2,50,000.

However, its running and maintenance costs are Rs. 1,20,000 per year in the first five years, and increase by Rs. 20,000 per year thereafter. If the money is worth 10 per cent per year, which computer should be purchased? What are the optimal replacement periods for each of the computers? Assume that there is no salvage value for either computer. Explain your analysis.

Solution:

Since money is worth 10 per cent per year, the discounted factor (or rate) over a period of one year is given by

$$d = 1/(1 + 0.10) = 0.9091$$

It is also given that C = Rs. 5 lakh.

The optimum replacement age n must satisfy the condition $R_n < W(8) < R_{n+1}$.

The calculations for best replacement age (period), n for both computers are shown in Tables (a) and (b).

Table (a) shows that the running cost, R_{10} is more than the weighted average cost, W(9) for 9th year. Also the inequality

$$R_9 < W(9) < R_{10},$$

i.e., 1,40,000 < 1,55,204 < 1,60,000

is satisfied, therefore MINICOMP computer should be replaced after nine years.

Table (a): Weighted Average Cost for MINICOMP Computer

Year of Service n	*Running Cost(Rs.)* R_n	*Discounted Factor* d^{n-1}	$R_n d^{n-1}$	*Cumulative* $\Sigma R_i d^{i-1}$	$C + SR_i d^{i-1}$	*Cumulative* Σd^{i-1}	$W(n)$
(1)	(2)	(3)	(4)	(5)	(6)=5,00.000+(5)	(7)	(8)=(6)/(7)
1.	60,000	1.0000	60,000	60,000	5,60,000	1.0000	5,60,000
2.	60,000	0.9091	54,546	1,14,546	6,14,546	1.9091	3,21,904
3.	60,000	0.8264	49,584	1,64,130	6,64,130	2.7355	2,42,782
4.	60,000	0.7513	45,078	2,09,208	7,09,208	3.4868	2,03,398
5.	60,000	0.6830	40,980	2,50,188	7,50,188	4.1698	1,79,910
6.	80,000	0.6209	49,672	2,99,860	7,99,860	4.7907	1,66,961
7.	1,00,000	0.5645	56,450	3,56,310	8,56,310	5.3552	1,59,903
8.	1,20,000	0.5132	61,584	4,17,894	9,17,894	5.8684	1,56,413
9.	1,40,000	0.4665	65,310	4,83,204	9,83,204	6.3349	**1,55,204**
10.	1,60,000	0.4241	67,586	5,51,060	10,51,060	6.7590	1,55,505

Table (b): Weighted Average Cost for CHIPCOMP Computer

Year of Service n	*Running Cost(Rs.)* R_n	*Discounted Factor* d^{n-1}	$R_n d^{n-1}$	*Cumulative* $\Sigma R_i d^{i-1}$	$C + SR_i d^{i-1}$	*Cumulative* Σd^{i-1}	$W(n)$
(1)	(2)	(3)	(4)	(5)	(6)=2,500,000+(5)	(7)	(8)=(6)/(7)
1.	1,20,000	1,0000	1,20,000	1,20,000	3,70,000	1.0000	3,70,000.00
2.	1,20,000	0.9091	1,09,092	2,29,092	4,79,092	1.9091	2,50,951.76
3.	1,20,000	0.8264	99,168	3,28,260	5,78,260	2.7355	2,11,390.97
4.	1,20,000	0.7513	90,156	4,18,416	6,68,416	3.4868	1,91,698.97
5.	1,20,000	0.6830	81,960	5,00,376	7,50,376	4.1698	1,79,954.91
6.	1,40,000	0.6209	86,926	5,87,302	8,37,302	4.7907	1,74,776.54
7.	1,60,000	0.5645	90,320	6,77,622	9,27,622	5.3552	**1,73,218.92**
8.	1,80,000	0.5132	92,376	6,69,998	10,19,998	5.8684	1,73,811.94
9.	2,00,000	0.4665	93,300	8,63,298	11,13,298	6.3349	1,75,740.42
10.	2,20,000	0.4241	93,302	9,56,600	12,06,600	6.7590	1,78,517.53

From Table (b), since the condition $R_6 < W(7) < R_8$ is satisfied, the replacement period for CHIPCOMP computer is after six years.

Example 14(b):

At time zero, all items in a system are new. Each item has a probability p of failing immediately before the end of the first month of life, and a probability q = 1 – p of failing immediately before the end of the second month (i.e., all items fail by the end of the second month). If all items are replaced as they fail then show that the expected number of failures f(x) at the end of month x is given by

$$f(x) = \frac{N}{1+q}\left\{-(-q)^{x+1}\right\},$$

where, N is the number of items in the system.

(b) If the cost per item of individual replacement is C_1 and the cost per item of group replacement is C_2 find the conditions under which (i) a group replacement policy at the end of each month is the most profitable; (ii) no group replacement policy is better than that of pure individual replacement.

Solution:

(a) Let N_1 be the expected number of items to fail at the end of the fth month. Then,

N_0 = number of items in the system in the beginning (= N)

N_1 = expected number of failures at the end of the first month

$= N_0 p$

$= N(1 - q)$, since $p = 1 - q$

N = expected number of failures at the end of the second month

$= N_0 q + N_1 p = Nq + N_1(1 - q)$

$= Nq + N(1 - q)^2 = N(1 - q + q^2)$.

N = expected number of failures at the end of the third month

$= N_0\, q + N_1\, q + N_2 p = N\,(1 - q)\, q + N\,(1 - q + q^2)\,(1 - q)$

$= N(1 - q + q^2 - q^3)$

and so on. In general

$N_k = N\{1 - q + q^2 - q^3 + \ldots + (-q^k\}$, therefore

$N_{k+1} = N_{k-1} + N_k P$

$= N\{1 - q + q^2 + \ldots + (-9)^{k-1}\}q + N\{1 - q + q^2 + \ldots + (-q)^k\}(1 - q)$

$= N\{1 - q + q^2 + \ldots + (-q)^{k+1}\}$

By mathematical induction, the expected number of items to fail, f(x), at the end of month x is then given by

$$f(x) = N\{1 - q + q^2 + \ldots + (-q)^x\}$$

$$= \frac{N\{1-(-q)^{x+1}\}}{1+q}$$

sum of G.P. of x + 1 terms with common ratio – q.

(b) The value of f(x) at the end of month x will vary for different values of $(-q)^{x+1}$ and it will reach in steady state as $x \to \infty$. Hence in the steady state the expected number of failures becomes

$$\lim_{x\to\infty} f(x) = \lim_{x\to\infty} \frac{N}{1+q} \{1-(-q)^{x+1}\}$$

$$= \frac{N}{1+q},\ q < 1 \text{ and } (-q)^{x+1} + 0 \text{ as } x \to \infty,$$

where (1 + q) represents the mean age at failure and is given by p + 2q = (1 – q) + 2q = 1 + q. Since C_2 is the cost of replacement per item individually, the average cost per month for an individual replacement policy will be $NC_2/(1 + q)$

(i) The average cost for group replacement policy at the end of every month is given by

$$NC_1 + Np\,C_2 = NC_1 + N(1-q)C_2$$

(ii) A group replacement policy at the end of each month is the most profitable, when

$$NC_1 + NpC_2 < \frac{NC_2}{1+q}$$

or $$C_1 < \frac{q^2}{1+q} C_2 \text{ or } C_2 > \frac{1+q}{q^2} C_1$$

Then individual replacement policy is always better than any group replacement policy.

Example 14(c):

A computer contains 10,000 resistors. When any resistor fails, it is replaced. The cost of replacing a resistor individually is Re 1 only. If all the resistors are replaced at the same time, the cost per resistor would be reduced to 35 paise. The percentage of surviving resistors say S(t) at the end of month t and the probability of failure P(t) during the month t are:

t	:	*0*	*1*	*2*	*3*	*4*	*5*	*6*
s(t)	:	*100*	*97*	*90*	*70*	*30*	*15*	*0*
P(i)	:	–	*0.03*	*0.07*	*020*	*0.40*	*0.15*	*0.15*

What is the optimal replacement plan?

Solution:

Let N_i be that number, of resistors replaced at the end of the ith month. Then different values of N_i can be calculated as follows:

N_0 = number of resistors in the beginning = 10,000

N_1 = number of resistors being replaced by the end of first month

$= N_0p_1 = 10{,}000 \times 0.03 = 300$

N_2 = number of resistors being replaced by the end of second month.

$= N_0p_2 = N_1p_1 = 10{,}000 \times 0.07 + 300 \times 0.30 = 709$

$N_3 = N_0p_3 = N_1p_2 + N_2p_1$

$= 10{,}000 \times 0.20 + 300 \times 0.07 + 709 \times 0.03 = 2{,}042$

$N_4 = N_0p_4 + N_1p_3 + N_2p_2 + N_3p_1$

$= 10{,}000 \times 0.40 + 300 \times 0.20 + 709 \times 0.07 + 2{,}042 \times 0.03 = 4{,}171$

$N_5 = N_0p_5 + N_1p_4 + N_2p_3 + N_3p_2 + N_4p_1$

$= 10{,}000 \times 0.15 + 300 \times 0.40 + 709 \times 0.20 + 2{,}042 \times 0.07 + 4{,}171 \times 0.03 = 2{,}030$

$N_6 = N_0p_6 + N_1p_5 + N_2p_4 + N_3p_3 + N_4p_2 + N_5p_1$

$= 10{,}000 \times 0.15 + 300 \times 0.15 + 709 \times 0.40 + 2{,}042 \times 0.20 + 4{,}171 \times 0.07 + 2{,}030 \times 0.03 = 2{,}590$

From the values of N_i ($i = 0, 1, 2, ..., 6$) so calculated, it can be seen that the expected number of resistors failing each month increases up to fourth month and then starts decreasing and later increases in the sixth month. Thus, N_i will oscillate till the system acquires a steady state. The expected life of each resistor is given by

$$\text{Expected life} = \sum_{i=1}^{6} x_i p(x)$$

$= 1 \times 0.03 + 2 \times 0.07 + 3 \times 0.20 + 4 \times 0.40 + 5 \times 0.15 + 6 \times 0.15$

$= 4.02$ months.

Average number of failures per month is

$$\frac{N}{\text{Mean age}} = \frac{10{,}000}{4.02} = 2{,}488 \text{ resistors (approx.)}$$

Hence, the total cost of individual replacement at the cost of Re 1 per resistor will be Rs. (2,488 × l) = Rs. 2,488. The cost of replacement of all the resistors at the same time can be calculated as follows:

End of Month	*Total Cost of Group Replacement (Rs.)*	*Average Cost per Month (Rs.)*
1.	300 × 1 + 10,000 × 0.35 = 3,800	3,800.00
2.	(300 + 709) × 1 + 10,000 × 0.35 = 4,509	2,254.50
3.	(300 + 709 + 2,042) × 1 + 10,000 × 0.35 = 6,551	**2,183.66**
4.	(300 + 709 + 2,042 + 4,171) × 1 + 10,000 × 0.35 = 10,722	2,680.50
5.	(300 + 709 + 2,042 + 4,171 + 2,030) × 1 + 10,000 × 0.35 = 12,752	2,550.40
6.	(300+709+2,042+4,171+2,030+2590)×1+10,000×0.35 = 15,442	2,557.00

Since the average cost per month of Rs. 2,183.66 is obtained in the third month, it is optimal to have a group replacement after every third month.

Example 15:

The following mortality rates have been observed for a certain type of fuse:

Week	:	*1*	*2*	*3*	*4*	*5*
Per cent failing by the end of week	:	*5*	*15*	*35*	*57*	*100*

There are 1,000 fuses in use and it costs Rs. 5 to. replace an individual fuse. If all fuses were replaced simultaneously it would cost Rs. 1.25 per fuse. It is proposed to replace all fuses at fixed intervals of time, whether or not they have burnt out, and to continue replacing burnt out fuses as they fail.

At what intervals the group replacement should be made? Also prove that this optimal policy is superior to the straight forward policy of replacing each fuse only when it fails.

Solution:

Let p_i be the probability that a fuse which was new when placed in position for use, fails during the ith week of its life. Then the following probability distribution is obtained assuming to replace burnt out fuses as and when they fail.

Week	:	1	2	3	4	5
Probability of failure	:	5/100 = 0.05	(15-5)/100 = 0.10	(35-15)/100 = 0.20	(75-35)/100 = 0.40	(100-75)/100 = 0.25

Furthermore, assume that

(i) fuses that fail during a week are replaced just before the end of that week, and

(ii) the actual percentage of failures during a week for a sub-population of fuses with the same age is the same as the expected percentage of failures during the week for that sub-population.

Let N_i be the number of replacements made at the end of the ith week, when all $N_0 = 1{,}000$ fuses are new initially. Thus expected number of failures at different weeks can be calculated as shown in Table (a).

Table (a): Number of Failures at Different Weeks

End of Week	*Expected Number of Failures {Replacements)*
1.	$N_1 = N_0p_1 = 1{,}000 \times 0.05 = 500$
2.	$N_2 = N_0P_2 + N_1p_1 = 1{,}000 \times 0.10 + 50 \times 0.05 = 102$
3.	$N_3 = N_0\ p_3 + N_1p_2 + N_2p_1 = 1{,}000 \times 0.20 + 50 \times 0.10$ $+ 102 \times 0.05 = 210$
4.	$N_4 = N_0p_4 + N_1p_3 + N_2p_2 + N_3\ p_1$ $= 1{,}000 \times 0.4 + 50 \times 0.2 + 102 \times 0.10 + 210 \times 0.05 = 430$
5.	$N_0 = N_0p_4 + N_2p_3 + N_3p_3 + N_4p_1 + N_4p_1$ $= 1{,}000 \times 0.25 + 50 \times 0.40 + 120 \times 0.20 + 210 \times 0.10 + 430$ $\times 0.05 = 333$

From Table (a), it is observed that the expected number of fuses failing each week increases till the fourth week and then start decreasing.

Thus the value of N_i will oscillate till the system acquires a steady state in which the proportion of bulbs failing each month is reciprocal of their average life. The expected life of fuse can be calculated as follows:

$$\text{Expected life} = 1 \times p_1 + 2 \times p_2 + 3 \times p_3 + 4 \times p_4 + 5 \times p_5$$
$$= 1 \times 0.05 + 2 \times 0.10 + 3 \times 0.20 + 4 \times 0.40$$
$$+ 5 \times\times 0.25$$
$$= 3.70 \text{ weeks.}$$

Expected number of failures during a week in steady-state condition becomes 1,000/3.70 = 270 fuses. Under individual replacement policy the cost of replacement only on failure is

Expected number of failures × Cost per fuse = 270 × 5 = Rs. 1,350.

Under the group replacement policy along with individual replacement, the cost of replacement is shown in Table (b).

Table (b)

End of Week	Cost of Individual Replacement	Total Cost of Replacement Individual + Group	Average Cost per Week
1	50 × 5 = 250	50 × 5 + 1,000 × 1.25 = 1,500	1,500
2	102 × 5 = 510	102 × 5 + 1,250 = 1,760	880
3	210 × 5 = 1,050	210 × 5 + 1,250 = 2,300	766.66

Table (b) shows that the cost of individual replacement in the third week (Rs. 1,050) is more than the average cost for two weeks. Hence, it is economical to replace all the fuses after every two weeks, otherwise the average cost will start increasing.

Example 16:

A computer has a large number of electronic tubes. They are subject to mortality as given below:

Period	Age of Failure (hrs.)	Probability of Failure
1	*0-200*	*0.10*
2	*201-400*	*0.26*
3	*401-600*	*0.35*
4	*601-800*	*0.22*
5	*801-1000*	*0.07*

If the tubes are group replaced, the cost of replacement is Rs. 15 per tube. Group replacement can be done at fixed intervals in the night shift when the computer is not normally used. Replacement of individual tubes which fail in service costs Rs. 60 per tube. How frequently should the tubes be replaced?

Solution:

Consider each block of 200 hours as one period and assume that there are 1,000 tubes initially. Let N, be the number of replacements made at the end of the rth period, if all the 1,000 tubes are new initially. Thus, the expected number of failures at different weeks can be calculated as shown in Table(a).

From Table (b), it may be observed that the number of tubes failing in each period increases till the third period, and then starts decreasing. Thus, the value of N_1 will oscillate till the system settles down to a steady state. In the steady state, the proportion of tubes failing during each period is the reciprocal of their average life

Table (a) : Expected Number of Failures (Replacements)

End of Period (hrs.)	*Expected Number of Replacements*
1.	$N_1 = N_0p_1 = 1{,}000 \times 0.10 = 100$
2.	$N_2 = N_0p_2 + N_1p_2 = 1{,}000 \times 0.26 + 100 \times 0.15 = 270$
3.	$N_3 = N_0p_3 + N_1p_2 + N_2p_1$ $= 1{,}000 \times 0.35 + 100 \times 0.26 + 270 \times 0.10 = 403$
4.	$N_4 = N_0p_4 + N_1p_3 + N_2p_2 + N_4p_1$ $= 1{,}000 \times 0.22 + 100 \times 0.35 + 270 \times 0.26 + 403 \times 0.1.0 = 365$
5.	$N_5 = N_0p_5 + N_1p_4 + N_2p_3 + N_3p_2 + N_4p_1$ $= 1{,}000 \times 0.07 + 100 \times 0.22 + 270 \times 0.35 + 403 \times 0.26 +$ $365 \times 0{,}10 = 328$

Expected life of a tube = $1 \times 0.10 + 2 \times 0.26 + 3 \times 0.35 + 4 \times 0.22 + 5 \times 0.07 = 2.90$ periods.

Expected number of failures per period = 1,000/2.90 = 345

Cost of individual replacements per period = 345×60 = Rs. 20,700

The average cost per period due to group replacement at fixed intervals is shown in Table (a).

Table (b) : Group Replacement Calculations.

End of Period (hrs)	*Total Cost of Replacement Individual + Group*	*Average Cost per Period (hrs)*
1. (1-200)	$100 \times 60 + 1{,}000 \times 15 = 21{,}000$	21,000
2. (201-400)	$270 \times 60 + 1{,}000 \times 15 = 37{,}200$	**18,600**
3. (401-600)	$403 \times 60 + 1{,}000 \times 15 = 61{,}380$	20,460
4. (601-800)	$365 \times 60 + 1{,}000 \times 15 = 83{,}280$	20,820
5. (801-1,000)	$328 \times 60 + 1{,}000 \times 15 = 1{,}02{,}960$	20,592

Table (b) shows that the group replacement is optimal after every second period, *i.e.,* after every 400 hour. This will cost Rs. 18,600 which is less than the cost associated with individual replacement of tubes.

Example 17(a):

An airline requires 200 assistant hostesses, 300 hostesses, and 50 supervisors. Women are recruited at the age of 21, and if still in service retire at 60. Given the following life table, determine

(i) How many women should be recruited in each year?

(ii) At what age should promotion take place?

Airline Hostesses' Life Record

Age	*21*	*22*	*23*	*24*	*25*	*26*	*27*	*28*
No. in Service	*1,000*	*600*	*480*	*384*	*307*	*261*	*228*	*206*
Age	*29*	*30*	*31*	*32*	*33*	*34*	*35*	*36*
No. in Service	*190*	*181*	*173*	*167*	*161*	*155*	*150*	*146*
Age	*37*	*38*	*39*	*40*	*41*	*42*	*43*	*44*
No. in Service	*141*	*136*	*131*	*125*	*119*	*113*	*106*	*99*
Age	*45*	*46*	*47*	*48*	*49*	*50*	*51*	*52*
No. in Service	*93*	*87*	*80*	*73*	*66*	*59*	*53*	*46*
Age	*53*	*54*	*55*	*56*	*57*	*58*	*59*	–
No. in Service	*39*	*33*	*27*	*22*	*18*	*14*	*11*	–

Solution:

If 1,000 women had been recruited each year for the past 39 years, then the total number of them recruited at the age of 21 and those serving up to the age of 59 is 6,480. Total number of women recruited in the airline are: 200 + 300 + 50 = 550.

(a) Number of women to be recruited every year in order to maintain a strength of 550 hostesses 550 × (1,000/6,480) = 85 approx.

(b) If the assistant hostesses are promoted at the age of x, then up to age (x – 1), 200 assistant hostesses will be required. Among 550 women, 200 are assistant hostesses. Therefore, out of a strength of 1,000 there will be: 200 × (1,000/550) = 364 assistant hostesses. But from the life table given in the question, this number is available up to the age of 24 years. Thus, the promotion of assistant hostesses is due in the 25th year.

Since out of 550 recruitments only 300 hostesses are needed, if 1,000 girls are recruited, then only 1000 × (300/550) = 545 (approx.) will be hostesses.

Hence, total number of hostesses and assistant hostesses in a recruitment of 100 will be: 545 + 364 = 909. This means, only 1,000-909 = 91 supervisors are required. But from life table this number is available up to the age of 46 years. Thus promotion of hostesses to supervisors will be due in 47th year.

Example 17(b):

It is planned to raise a research team to a strength of 50 chemists, which is to be maintained. The wastage of recruits depends on their length of service which is as follows:

Year	:	*1*	*2*	*34*	*5*	*6*	*7*	*8*	*9*	*10*
Total percentage who have left by end of year	:	*5*	*36*	*55*	*63*	*68*	*73*	*79*	*87*	*97*	*100*

What is the recruitment per year necessary to maintain the required strength? There are 8 senior posts for which the length of service is the main criterion. What is the average length of service after which the new entrant expects promotion to one of the posts?

Solution:

The probability of a chemist being in service at the end of the year can be calculated with help of the given data as shown in Table.

Table : Probability of Chemists in Service

Year	*Number of Chemists Who Left at the End of the Year*	*Number of Chemists in Service at the End of the Year*	*Probability of Leaving at the End of Year*	*Probability of in Service at the End of the Year*
1.	0	100	0	1.00
2.	5	95	0.05	0.95
3.	36	64	0.36	0.64
4.	56	44	0.56	0.44
5.	63	37	0.63	0.37
6.	68	32	0.68	0.32
7.	73	27	0.73	0.27
8.	79	21	0.79	0.21
9.	87	13	0.87	0.13
10.	97	3	0.97	0.03
10.	100	1.00	0	
		436		

Table shows that if 100 chemists are recruited each year, then total number of chemists present at the end of the year will be 436. Thus to maintain a strength of 50 chemists in the organization, a recruitment of [(100/436) × 50 = 12] chemists has to be done each year.

If P_n is the probability of a person to be in service at the end of the year, then out of 12 new recruits as calculated above, the number of survivals (chemists who will remain in service) at the end of the year n will be 12 . p_n. Thus, a table as shown below can be constructed to show the number of chemists in service at the end of each year.

Year(n)	:	0	1	2	3	4	5	6	7	8	9	10
Probability (P_n)	:	1.00	0.95	0.64	0.44	0.37	0.32	0.27	0.21	0.13	0.03	0
Number of chemists (12. P_n)	:	12	11	8	5	4	4	3	2	2	0	0

This table shows that there are 3, 2, and 2 persons in service during 6th, 7th and 8th year, respectively. The total of such chemists is less than the number of senior posts, *i.e.,* 8. Hence, promotions of the new chemist must start by the end of the 5th year.

Example 17(c):

A certain piece of equipment is extremely difficult to adjust. During a period when no adjustment is made, the running cost increases linearly with time, at a rate of A rupees per-hour. The running cost immediately after an adjustment is not known precisely until the adjustment has been made. Before the adjustment, the resulting running cost x is seemed to be a random variable x with density function f(x). If each adjustment costs k rupees, when should the replacement be made?

Solution :

The running cost Rs. x is a random variable with density function f(x). Suppose that the maximun of x be X.

If the adjustment is made when running cost equals Z, then there can be two possibilities

(i) Z > X and (ii) Z < X.

Case 1: When Z > X : Let Rs. x be the running cost at time t = 0. If adjustment is made after time t, then the running cost at time t will be Rs. (x + bt), because running cost increases at the rate of Rs. b per hour. Obviously,

$$Z = x + bt \text{ or } t = \frac{(Z-x)}{b}$$

If C(Z) is the total cost incurred between the period of one adjustment to another adjustment, then

C(Z) = Cost of one adjustment + Total running cost from

t = 0 to t = (Z – x)/b

$$= k + \int_0^{(Z-x)/b} (x + bt)\, dt$$

$$= k + \left[\frac{(x+bt)^2}{2b}\right]_0^{(z-x)/b} = k + \frac{1}{2b}(Z^2 - x^2)$$

Therefore, the average cost per hour is given by

$$\text{Average cost per hour} = \frac{C(Z)}{t} = \frac{kb}{Z-x} + \frac{Z+x}{2}$$

Since the running cost x is random variable with density function, therefore, expected cost per hour is given by

$$E\{C(Z)\} = \int_0^x \left(\frac{kb}{Z-x} + \frac{Z+x}{2}\right) f(x)\, dx$$

The value of $\Sigma\{C(Z)\}$ will be minimum for some value of Z, for which

$$\frac{d}{dZ}[E\{C(Z)\}] = 0 \text{ and } \frac{d^2}{dZ^2}[E\{C(Z)\}] > 0$$

Now, $\frac{d}{dZ}[E\{C(Z)\}] = \frac{d}{dZ}\int_0^x \left(\frac{kb}{Z-x} + \frac{Z+x}{2}\right) f(x)\, dx$

$$= \int_0^x \frac{d}{dZ}\left(\frac{kb}{Z-x} + \frac{Z+x}{2}\right) f(x)\, dx$$

$$= \int_0^x \left\{\frac{1}{(Z-x)^2} + \frac{1}{2}\right\} f(x)\, dx$$

$$= \frac{1}{2} - kb \int_0^x \frac{f(x)}{(Z-x)^2}\, dx; \int_0^x f(x)\, dx = 1$$

For E{C(Z)} to be minimum, we must have

$$\frac{d}{dZ}[E\{C(Z)\}] = 0$$

which gives $\frac{1}{2} - kb \int_0^x \frac{f(x)}{(Z-x)^2}\, dx = 0$

or $\int_0^x \frac{f(x)}{(Z-x)^2}\, dx = \frac{1}{2kb}$

Hence, the value of Z can be determined with the help of Eqn. (23).

Case 2 : When Z < X : In this case, it can be shown that the minimum of Z cannot occur and therefore, its optimal value can only be determined in Case (i).

Example 18:

The cost of a lathe is Rs. 60,000. From the records and experience, the costs are found to be as following:

Year:	*1*	*2*	*3*	*4*	*5*	*6*	*7*	*8*
Operating cost: in thousands	*10*	*12*	*14*	*18*	*23*	*28*	*34*	*40*
Resale price: in thousands	*30*	*15*	*7.5*	*3.75*	*2*	*2*	*2*	*2*

When should machine be replaced?

Solution

The average cost per year during the life of machine is computed as given in Table.

Table

Year of Replacement (n)	Operating cost (R_n) '000 Rs.	Total operating cost (ΣR_n) '000 Rs.	Difference between initial price and resale price $C - S_n$ '000 Rs.	Total cost T_n $R_n + C - S_n$	Average cost $T_n/_n$
1	10	10	30	40	40
2	12	22	45	67	33.5
3	14	36	52.5	88.5	29.5
4	18	54	56.25	110.25	27.56
5	23	77	58	135	27*
6	28*	105	58	163	27.17
7	34	139	58	197	28.15
8	40	179	58	237	29.62

From Table, it may be observed that the machine should be replaced at the end of the 5th year, because the average total cost in the sixth year is more than the average cost for 5 years, *i.e.*, average cost per year will start increasing after the end of 5th year.

Example 19:

A firm is considering replacement of a machine, wnose cost price is Rs. 12,200, and the scrap value Rs. 200. The running (maintenance and operating) costs are found from experience to be as follows:

Year : 1 2 3 4 5 6 7 8

Running cost (Rs.) : 200 500 800 1,200 1,800 2,500 3,200 4,000

When should the machine be replaced?

Solution:

We are given the running cost, R (n), the scrap value S = Rs. 200 and the cost of the machine, C = Rs. 12,200. In order to determine the optimal time n when the machine should be replaced, first we calculate average cost per year during the life of the machine as shown in Table.

Table : Calculations of Average Running Cost

Year of Service n	*Running Cost (Rs.)* $R(n)$	*Cumulative Running Cost(Rs.)* $\Sigma R(n)$	*Depreciation Cost(Rs.)* $C-S$	*Total Cost (Rs.)* TC	*Average Cost (Rs.)* ATC_n
(1)	*(2)*	*(3)*	*(4)*	*(5)=(3)+(4)*	*(6)=(5)/(1)*
1.	200	200	12,000	12,200	12,000
2.	500	700	12,000	12,700	6,350
3.	800	1,500	12,000	13,500	4,500
4.	1,200	2,700	12,000	14,700	3,675
5.	1,800	4,500	12,000	16,500	3,300
6.	2,500	7,0,00	12,000	19,000	**3,167**
7.	3,200	10,200	12,000	22,200	3,171
8.	4,000	14,200	12,000	26,200	3.275

From Table it may be noted that the average cost per year, ATC_n is minimum in the sixth year (Rs. 3,167).

Also the average cost in seventh year (Rs. 3,171) is more than the cost in the sixth year. Hence, the machine should be replaced after every six years.

Example 20:

The data collected in running a machine, the cost of which is Rs. 60,000, are given below:

Year	:	*1*	*2*	*3*	*4*	*5*
Resale value (Rs.)	:	*42,000*	*30,000*	*20,400*	*14,400*	*9,650*
Cost of spares (Rs.)	:	*4,000*	*4,270*	*4,880*	*5,700*	*6,800*
Cost of labour(Rs.)	:	*14,000*	*16,000*	*18,000*	*21,000*	*25,000*

Determine the optimum period for replacement of the machine.

Solution:

The costs of spares and labour together determine running (operational or maintenance) cost. Tlius, the running costs and the resale price of the machine in successive years are as follows:

Year	:	1	2	3	4	5
Resale value (Rs.)	:	42,000	30,000	20,400	14,400	9,650
Running cost (Rs.)	:	18,000	20,270	22,880	26,700	31,800

The calculations of average running cost per year during the life of the machine are shown in Table.

Table : Calculations of Average Running Cost

Year of Service n	*Running Cost (Rs.) R(n)*	*Cumulative Running Cost (Rs.) ΣR(w)*	*Resale Value (Rs.) S*	*Depreciation Cost (Rs.) C–S*	*Total Cost (Rs.) TC*	*Average Cost (Rs.) ATC_n*
(1)	*(2)*	*W*	*W*	*(5)=60,000–(4)*	*(6)=(3)+(5)*	*(7)=(6)/(1)*
1.	18,000	18,000	42,000	18,000	36,000	36.000.00
2.	20,270	38,270	30,000	30,000	68,270	34,135.00
3.	22,880	61,150	20,400	39,600	1,00,750	33,583.30
4.	26,700	87,850	14,400	45,600	1,33,450	**33,362.50**
5.	31,800	1,19,650	9,650	50,350	1,70,000	34,000.00

The calculations in Table show that the average cost is lowest during the fourth year. Hence, the machine should be replaced after every fourth year, otherwise the average cost per year for running the machine would start increasing.

Example 21:

An industry has three lathe machines of purchase price Rs. 60,000 each and operating cost per year for each machine is same as in Example 4.1. Two of these lathes are 2 years old and the third is 1 year old. The industry is considering a new lathe of purchase price of Rs. 80,000 with 50% more capacity than one of the old ones. The estimate of the operating for new lathe are as follows:

Year:	*1*	*2*	*3*	*4*	*5*	*6*	*7*	*8*
Operating cost Rs. '000	*12*	*15*	*18*	*24*	*31*	*40*	*50*	*61*

Resale price Rs. '000	*40*	*20*	*10*	*0.5*	*0.3*	*0.3*	*0.3*	*0.3*

Assuming that sufficient work is available for the old 3 machines and loss of flexibility due to fewer machines is of no significance.

Solution

First the average yearly costs during the life of a new lathe are computed as for old machine It is observed that

$$40{,}000 > 35{,}400,$$

i.e., $R_6 > R_5\ (T_5/n)$.

Thus, decision would be to replace at the end of 5th year.

Now, the decision is to be made whether it is economically justified to replace smaller lathe by new larger one.

Since the new lathe possesses 50% more capacity than that of the old one, three old lathes would be equivalent to two new lathes. As a result, the lowest average cost would be of Rs. 35,400.

Table

Year of Replace-ment (n)	Operating cost (R_n) '000 Rs.	Total operating cost (ΣR_n) '000 Rs.	Difference between ini-tial price and resale price $C - S_n$ '000 Rs.	Total cost T_n $R_n + C - S_n$	Average cost T_n/n
1	12	12	40	52	52
2	15	27	60	87	43.5
3	18	45	70	115	38.33
4	24	69	75	144	36
5	31	100	77	177	35.40*
6	40*	140	77	217	36.16
7	50	190	77	267	38.14
8	61	251	77	328	41

Now, the decision is to be made that when to purchase a new lathe. Assuming that for uniformity, the replacement will involve two new lathes and all the three old lathes. The new lathe should be purchased when the cost for the next year of running the three old lathes exceeds the average yearly cost for two new lathes.

From Table it can be observed that total annual cost for one old machine is as follows:

Total cost during first year = 40,000

Total cost during second year = 67,000 – 40,000 = 27,000

Total cost during third year = 88,500 – 67,000 = 21,500

and similarly Rs. 21,750, Rs., 24,750, Rs. 28,000, Rs. 34,000, and Rs. 40,000 during 4th, 5th, 6th, 7th, and 8th year, respectively.

Hence, total cost next year for 2 old lathes aged 2 years and one aged 1 year would be

= 2 × 21,500 + 27,000 = 70,000.

Similarly,

Total cost during 2nd year = 2 × 21,750 + 21,500 = 65,000. Total cost during 3rd year = 2 × 24,750 + 21,750 = 71250.

Total cost during 4th year = 2 × 28,000 + 24,750 = 80,750.

But the minimum average cost for two new machines would be

= 2 × 35,400 = 70,800

Thus, it can be observed that cost (Rs. 65,000) for the old lathes will not exceed the cost (Rs. 70,800) for the new lathes until 3rd year (Rs. 71,250). Therefore, all the three old lathes should be replaced after 2 years before any one of them reaches the normal replacement age of 5 years (Table).

Example 22:

A manufacturer is offered 2 machines A and B. A is priced at Rs. 5,000, and running costs are estimated at Rs. 800 for each of the first 5 years, increasing by Rs. 200 per year in the 6th year and the subsequent years. Machine B, which has the same capacity as A, costs Rs. 2,500 but will have running costs of Rs. 1,200 per year for 6 years increasing by Rs. 200 per year thereafter. If the money is worth 10% per year, which machine should be purchased? Assume that the machines will eventually be sold for scrap at a negligible price.

Solution

In order to compare machines A and B, the present worth of the expenditure has to be computed on the two machines.

In the given problem, discount rate $d = 1/(1 + 0.10) = 0.909$.

The optimum replacement period N should satisfy the relationship

$$C_{N+1} > \frac{X + \sum_{i=1}^{N-1} C_i d^{N-1}}{1 + d + d^2 + \dots + d^{N-1}} > C_N$$

$$C_{N+1} > \frac{F_N}{\Sigma d^{N-1}}.$$

For the optimum replacement period *N*, required calculations are tabulated for machines *A* and *B*, in Table respectively.

From Table (a), it is observed that C_{10} = 1800 becomes greater than the weighted average cost Rs. 1752 for nine years.

Thus, it would be optimum to replace machine *A* after 9 years. Further, from the Table (b), the equivalent fixed payment for machine *A* is observed from last column as M_1 = weighted average for 9 years = Rs. 1752.

In a similar manner, optimum replacement period for machine *B* can be computed as given in Table.

Table (a): Replacement Costs for Machine A

Year N	Operating cost C_N	PWF d^{N-1}	$C_N d^{N-1}$	$X + \Sigma C_N d^{N-1}$	Σd^{N-1}	$F_N/\Sigma d^{N-1}$
1	800	1.000	800	5,800	1.000	5800
2	800	0.909	737	6,527	1.909	3419
3	800	0.826	661	7,188	2.7355	2628
4	800	0.751	601	7,889	3.487	2234
5	800	0.683	546	8,335	4.170	1999
6	1000	0.621	621	8,956	4.791	1896
7	1200	0.565	677	9,633	5.355	1799
8	1400	0.513	718	10,351	5.868	1764
9*	1600	0.466	746	11,097	6.335	1752*
10.	1800*	0.424	763	11,860	6.759	1752

Since C_B > weighted average for 8 years (1800 > 1680), it would be optimum to replace machine *B* after 8 years. The equivalent fixed annual payment for machine *B* is observed from Table as

M_2 = weighted average for 8 years = Rs. 1680.

Table (b): Replacement Costs for Machine B

Year N	Operating cost C_N	PWF d^{N-1}	$C_N d^{N-1}$	$X + \Sigma C_N d^{N-1}$	Σd^{N-1}	$F_N/\Sigma d^{N-1}$
1	1200	1.000	1200	3,700	1.000	3700
2	1200	0.909	1091	4,791	1.909	2510
3	1200	0.826	991	5,783	2.7355	2114
4	1200	0.751	902	6,684	3.487	1917
5	1200	0.683	820	7,504	4.170	1800
6	1200	0.621	745	8,249	4.791	1722
7	1400	0.565	790	9,039	5.355	1688*
8	1600	0.513	821	9,860	5.868	1680
9	1800	0.466	840	10,700	6.335	1689

Since $M_1 > M_2$, it would be preferred to procure machine *B* instead of *A*. Although, the average of actual payments (without considering money value) is Rs. 1578 for *A* and Rs. 1588 for *B*.

EXERCISES

1. The cost of maintenance of a machine is given as a function that the average annual cost will be minimized by replacing the machine when the average cost to date becomes equal to the current maintenance cost.
2. It is required to find the optimum replacement time of a certain type of equipment. The initial cost of equipment is C. Salvage value and repair costs are given by S(t) and R(t), respectively. The cost of capital is r per cent and T is the time period of replacement cycle.
   (i) Show that the present value of all future costs associated with a policy of equipment after T is
   $$\left(\frac{1}{1-e^{-rt}}\right)\left\{C - S(t)e^{-rt} + \int_0^T R(t)\, e^{-rt} dt\right\}$$
   (ii) The optimal value of T is given by, $R(t) - S'(T) + S(t)\, r = r^k/(1\_ e^{-rt})$

   where k is the present value of the cycle.
3. There are N lamps on a life test and the testing is terminated as soon as the rth failure occurs. Failed lamps are not replaced. Assume that life x of a lamp has the probability density function

$$f(x) = \frac{1}{\theta} e^{-t/\theta}, x . 0, \theta > 0$$

Show that the expected waiting time to the rth failure is : $\sum_{i=1}^{r}\left(\frac{1}{N-i+1}\right)$

4. A new item is placed in a system at time zero. The probability that the system again has a new item for the first time at time t is f(t). Certain costs are incurred during the interval 0 to t (called a cycle), the probabilities of which are known. Show that in the long run, the average cost per unit time is: $c/\bar{u}$ where c is expected cost over one cycle and $\bar{u}$ is expected duration of one cycle.

5. Assume that present value of one rupee to be spent in a year's time is Re 0.9 and C = Rs. 3,000, capital cost of equipment. Running costs are given in the table below:

Year :	1	2	3	4	5	6	7
Running cost (Rs.) :	500	600	800	1,000	1,300	1,600	2,000

When should the machine be replaced?

6. A manual stamper currently valued at Rs. 1,000 is -expected to last two years and costs Rs. 4,000 per year to operate. An automatic stamper which can be purchased for Rs. 3,000 will last four years and can be operated at an annual cost of Rs. 3,000. If money carries a rate of interest of 10 per cent per annum, determine which stamper should be purchased.

7. Suppose the life X of electric light bulbs follows the gamma distribution

$$P(x \le X < x + dx) = \frac{a^p}{\Gamma(p)} e^{-a\lambda} x^{p-1}dx \ (a > 0, 0 < x < \infty)$$

Determine the renewal rate for one point at the end of time period (0, t).

8. What is replacement? Describe some important replacement situations.

9. The cost of maintenance of a machine is given as a function increasing with time and its scrap value is constant.

   (a) If time is measured continuously, then the average annual cost will be minimized by replacing the machine when the average cost till date becomes equal to the current maintenance cost.

   (b) If time is measured in discrete units, then the average annual cost will be minimized by replacing the machine when the next period's maintenance cost becomes greater than the current average cost.

10. Describe the problem of replacement of items whose maintenance cost increase with time. Assume that the value of money remains constant.
11. What are situations which make the replacement of items necessary?
12. What are the three strategies of replacement of items which follow sudden failure mechanisms? Explain each of them with examples.
13. The cost of a machine is Rs. 6,100 and its scrap value is Rs. 100. The maintenance costs found from experience are as follows:

Year	:	1	2	3	4	5	6	7	8
Maintenance cost (Rs.)	:	100	250	400	600	900	1,200	1,600	2,000

When should the machine be replaced?

14. A truck owner finds from his past records that the maintenance costs per year of a truck whose purchase price is Rs. 8,000 are as given below:

Year	:	1	2	3	4	5	6	7	8
Maintenance cost (Rs.)	:	1,000	1,300	1,700	2,000	2,900	3,800	4,800	6,000
Resale price (Rs.)	:	4,000	2,000	1,200	600	500	400	400	400

Determine at which time it is profitable to replace the truck.

15. A fleet owner finds from his past records that the cost per year of running a vehicle, whose purchase price is Rs. 50,000, is

Year	:	1	2	3	4	5	6	7
Running cost (Rs.)	:	5,000	6,000	7,000	9,000	11,500	16,000	18,000
Resale value (Rs.)	:	30,000	15,000	7,500	3,750	2,000	2,000	2,000

Thereafter, running cost increases by Rs. 2,000, but resale value remains constant at Rs. 2,000. At what age is a replacement due?

16. On its production line the Bhalla Food Company uses a battery of 400 small sprinklers for cleaning fresh vegetables, fruits, etc., before they are prepared for canning. Failure of a sprinkler, which costs Rs. 50 per unit, does not disrupt production flow but may create quality control problem from insufficient cleaning.

    Such failures are reported by the line foreman for the maintenance department, which must disassemble the arc-shaped battery frame from the production line before replacing a sprinkler at the end of the shift or on weekends. Due to the high set-up cost for this task, management is considering a policy of group replacement. What replacement policy should the management adopt when the information regarding sprinkler breakdowns and cost is as given below?

Run time (months)	:	1	2	3	4	5	6
Probability of failure	:	0.05	0.05	0.10	0.10	0.30	0.40

Replacement Cost

	Purchase (Rs.)	*Installation (Rs.)*	*Per unit (Rs.)*
Individually	50	175	225
Group	50	25	75

17. A computer has 20,000 resistors. When any resistor fails, it is replaced. The cost of replacing a resistor individually is Re 1. If all the resistors are replaced at the same time the cost per resistor is reduced to Re 0.40. The per cent surviving at the end of month t, and the probability of failure during the month are given below:

		0	1	2	3	4	5	6
Per cent surviving at the end of t	:	100	96	90	65	35	20	0
Probability of failure during the month t	:	–	0.04	0.06	0.25	0.30	0.15	0.20

What is the optimum replacement plan?

18. Let p(t) be the probability that a machine in a group of 30 machines would break down in period t; the cost of repairing a broken machine is Rs. 200.00. Preventive maintenance is taken by servicing all the 36 machines. Find optimal T which will minimize the expected total cost per period of servicing, given that

$$P(t) = \begin{cases} 0.03 & \text{, for } t = 1 \\ p(t-1) + 0.01 & \text{, for } 1 = 2, 3, \ldots, 10 \\ 0.13 & \text{, for } t = 11, 12, 13, \ldots \end{cases}$$

19. Suppose a special purpose type of light bulb never lasts longer than two weeks. There is a chance of 0.3 that a bulb will fail at the end of the next week. There are 100 new bulbs initially. The cost per bulb for individual replacement is Re 1 and the cost per bulb for a group replacement is Re 0.50. Is it cheapest to replace all bulbs:

(i) initially, (ii) every week,

(iii) every second week, and (iv) every third week?

20. A company is considering to replace grinder X presently of worth Rs. 10,000 by a new grinder Y of Rs. 20,000 but will be economic in running expenditures. The expected life of grinder X is 5 years with running expenditure of Rs. 4,000 in first year and then additional increase of Rs. 400 per year for next four years. For the new grinder, the annual running cost is Rs. 1,000 per year and scrap value ofRs 2,000. As an advisor to the company, find

(a) The present value of the cost of old and new grinders considering 12 per cent normal rate interest.

(b) Suggest whether the old grinder be. replaced by the new grinder, assuming the life of new grinder to be 5 years.

21. An electric company which generates and distributes electricity conducted a study on the life of poles. The appropriate life data are given in the following table:

(a) If the company now installs 5,000 poles and follows a policy of replacing poles only when they fail, how many poles are expected to be replaced each year during the next ten years. To simplify the computation assume that failures occur and replacements are made only at the end of a year.

(b) If the cost of replacing individually is Rs. 160 per pole and if we have a common group replacement policy, it costs Rs. 80 per pole; find out the optimal period for group replacement.

22. A truck-owner finds from his past experience that the maintenance costs are Rs. 200 for the first year and then increase by Rs. 2000 every year. The cost of Truck Type A is Rs. 9,000. Determine the best age at which to replace the truck. If the optimum replacement is followed what will be the average yearly cost of owning and operating the truck? Truck Type B costs Rs. 20,000. Annual operating costs are Rs. 400 for the first year and then increase by Rs. 800 every year. The truck owner has now the Truck Type A which is one year old. Should it be replaced by B type, and if so, when?

23. (a) Machine A costs Rs. 9,000. Annual operating costs are Rs. 200 for the first year, and then increase by Rs. 2,000 every year. Determine the best age at which to replace the machine. If the optimum replacement policy is followed, what will be the average yearly cost of owning and operating the machine?

(b) Machine B costs Rs. 10,000. Annual operating costs are Rs. 400 for the first year, and then increase by Rs. 800 every year. You now have a machine of type A which is one year old. Should you replace it with B, if so, when?

24. A manufacturer is offered two machines A and B. Machine A is priced at Rs. 5,000 and running costs are estimated at Rs. 800 for each of the first five years increasing by Rs. 200 per year in the sixth and subsequent years. Machine B which has the same capacity as A, costs Rs. 2,500 but will have running costs of Rs. 1,200 per year for six years, increasing by Rs. 200 per year thereafter.

If money is worth 10 per cent per year, which machine should be purchased? (Assume that the machine will eventually be sold for scrap at a negligible price.)

25. Explain with examples the failure mechanism of items.
26. The maintenance cost increases with time and the money value decreases with constant rate, *i.e.*, depreciation value is given. Then obtain a mathematical result in order to support the following:
    (i) Replace if the next period's cost is greater than the weighted average of previous costs.
    (ii) Do not replace if the next period's cost is less than the weighted average of previous costs.
27. Find an optimal replacement policy which minimizes the total of all future discounted costs for an equipment which costs Rs. C and which needs maintenance costs of Rs. R_1, R_2 ..., R_n ($R_{n+1} > R_n$) during 1, 2,..., n years, respectively, and further d is the depreciation value per unit of money during a year.
28. Explain how the theory of replacement is used in the following problems,
    (i) Replacement of items whose maintenance cost varies with time.
    (ii) Replacement of items that fail completely.

3

Some Problems of Simulation

INTRODUCTION

In a number of problems, mathematical solution can be obtained through straight- forward techniques, such as *economic order quantity in inventory system, simplex technique to a linear programming, transportation technique, queueing models*, etc. However, in all these cases, certain assumptions are made to simplify the problem and to employ the appropriate mathematical techniques.

If all the problems have to be solved mathematically, situation has to be simplified for the solution sacrificing realism, which may lead to real trouble. For example, the assumption of normality in dealing with inventory distribution demand may be realistic, whereas assumption of linearity in a specific linear programming problem may not be realistic. Further, in many cases, the result, obtained from simplifying assumptions may not be suitable for decision maker.

Therefore, in some situations, the solutions obtained from simplifying assumptions are suitable for decision taking, whereas in many cases, the solutions are not suitable. Simulation proves to be an appropriate substitute for mathematical evolution of model in such a situation. Although, simulation also involves assumptions, they are manageable. The use of simulation provides an insight into many management problems where mathematical evaluation of a model is not possible.

These reasons of simulation's use can be classfied under the following three categories:

LIMITATIONS OF ANALYTICAL TECHNIQUES

Analytical techniques, employed in queueing theory, network models, dynamic programming, etc., may not be adequate to solve all the important problems requiring data analysis due to,

(a) Computation work is quite complex and difficult in the situation of state variables being large in dynamic programming and other models.

(b) Analytical techniques can solve only small-scale systems. However, while making a number of asumptions in relatively larger systems, the systems are simplified to such an extent that the results obtained may be only rough approximations.

LIMITATIONS OF SCIENTIFIC/MATHEMATICAL TECHNIQUES

(a) When the proceses cannot be observed or are difficult (very costly) to observe in real life situations (*e.g.*, space flight, plane designing, etc.), simulation may be the only available technique.

(b) The observed system is very complex and not possible to describe in terms of a set of mathematical equations.

(c) A straightforward analytical solution is not available for the formulated mathematical model to describe the system under study. For example, complex queueing problems, complicated stochastic models, multi-integral problems, etc.

(d) Performing the validating experiments on mathematical models may be either impossible or very costly.

Limitations of Iterative Techniques

(a) In linear programming models, data is assumed to be unchanged over the entire planning horizon, which is one-time decision process and, thus, assumes average values for the decision variables. If the planning horizon is long, say 20-years, the model may deal with the yearly averaged data. This will not take care of months and weeks and, thus, month to month and week to week operations are left implicit.

(b) Further, the iterative method assumed that data should be known with certainty. In many real life problems, the uncertainties about the data are so much that they cannot be overlooked. In case of uncertainties prevailing only in a few variables, the sensitivity analysis helps in determining its effect on the decision. But, sensitivity analysis is too cumbersome and computationally difficult in case of uncertainties prevailing in the entire model.

Therefore, whenever there is a combined situation of uncertainity, complexity, dynamic interaction between the decision and subsequent event need to develop detailed procedures, and finely divided intervals, the model becomes too complex to be solved by any of the usual techniques of operations research. In such situations, some other quantitative technique should be used to yield quite accurate and reliable results. Simulation technique, in geneal, is a dependable tool in such cases.

SIMULATION DEFINED

Simulation is by no means a recent operations research technique. Simulation is one of the oldest analysis tool known to man—that is, the representation of the real world by numbers and other symbols that can be readily manipulated. To gain a better grasp of the real world, games such as chess to simulate battles, backgammon to simulate racing, and other games to simulate hunting and diplomacy were already invented in antiquity.

Today, a modem game like monopoly simulates the competitive arena of real estate. Many have played baseball with a deck of cards which has hits, strikeouts and walks with a cardboard, diamond and plastic chips as runners. The distribution of hits, runs and outs, etc., in a deck of cards serves as a realistic reflection of the overall average with which each will occur in real life. Other games people play, generate experiences, understanding and gain knowledge which is basically what we will be trying to do through simulation.

What is new in modem simulation? It is the availability of computers which make it possible for us to deal with an extraordinarily large quantity of details which can be incorporated into a model and the ability to manipulate the model over many 'experiments' (*i.e.,* replicating all the possibilities that may be imbedded in the external world, and events would seem to recur). The modem use of the word simulation can be traced to the mathematicians Von Neumann and Ulam in the late 1940's when they developed the term '*Monte Carlo Analysis*' while trying first to 'break' the Casino at Monte Carlo (which they did not succeed!) and subsequently, applying it to the solution of nuclear shielding problems that were either too expensive for physical experimentation, or too complicated for treatment by known mathematical techniques.

An agreed definition for the world simulation has not been reached so far, however a few definitions are stated as:

- *A simulation of a system or an organism is the operation of a model or simulator which is a representation of the system or organism. The model is amenable to manipulation which would be impossible, too expensive or unpractical to perform on the entity it portrays. The operation of the model can be studied and for it, properties concerning the behaviour of the actual system can be inferred.*

  This definition is broad enough to be applied equally to military war games, business games, economic models, etc. In this view simulation involves logical and mathematical constructs that can be manipulated on a digital computer using iterations or successive trials.

- *Simulation is the process of designing a model of a real system and conducting experiments with this model for the purpose of understanding the behaviour (within the limits imposed by a criterion or set of criteria) for the operation of the system.*
- *Simulation is a numerical technique for conducting experiments on a digital computer, which involves certain types of mathematical and logical relationships necessary to describe the behaviour and structure of a complex real-world system over extended periods of time.*

Few other definitions of simulation are as under:

- *'X simulated Y' is true if and only if,*
  - *(i) X and Y are formal systems,*
  - *(ii) V is taken to be the real system,*
  - *(m) X is taken to be an approximation to the real system, and*
  - *(iv) The rules of validity in X are non-error-free, otherwise X will become the real system.*
- *Simulation is the use of a system model that has the designed characteristics of reality in order to produce the essence of actual operation.*

For operations research, simulation is a problem solving technique which uses a computer-aided experimental approach to study problems that cannot be analysed using direct and formal analytical methods. As a result simulation can be thought of as a last resort technique.

Table 1.1 : Simulation—What it is/not

It is	*It is not*
• a technique which uses computers.	• an analytical technique which provides exact solution.
• an approach for reproducing the processes by which events of chance and change are created in a computer.	• a programming language but it could be prograammed into a set of commands which can form a language to facilitate the programming of simulation.
• a procedure for testing and experimenting on models to answer what if.... then so and so ... types of questions.	

It is not a technique which should be applied in all cases. However, Table 1.1 highlights what simulation is and what it is not.

APPLICATIONS OF SIMULATION

There is a wide range of applications of computer-based simulation models because it is an approach rather than an application of specific techniques.

The major use of computer-based *Monte-Carlo simulation model* has been in the solution of complex queuing problems.

A number of job shop simulation programmes have been developed involving deterministic times for the individual operations of a given order. Due to different processing times for similar operations and different order operations sequences, it is difficult to predict the waiting time for a particular job at any given work centre. For better scheduling, orders must be scheduled with a provision of waiting at the various work centres they will pass through. Simulation can help in estimating accurately such waiting times.

A good deal of work has been done in the development of inventory simulation models such as determination of optimal reorder level and lot size under conditions of probabilistic demand and lead time, optimal review period and ordering policy for continuous review inventory models.

A number of network simulation models have also been developed. For example, with a randomly selected activity times the critical path can be evaluated. Repeating this process many times, the probability distribution of project completion time can be obtained as well as the probability that each given activity is on the critical path.

A variety of other problems which could be solved by simulation include:

(i) Military studies of logistics, support planning and weapon systems effectiveness.

(ii) Studies of individual and group behaviour.

(iii) Financial studies involving risky investments.

(iv) Testing of decision rules for hospital admission and operating policies.

STEPS OF SIMULATION PROCESS

The process of simulating a system consists of following steps:

Step 1. Identify the Problem

If any inventory system is being simulated, then the problem may concern the determination of the size of order (number of units to be ordered) when inventory level falls up to the reorder level (point).

Step 2. (a) Identify the decision variables

(b) Decide the performance criterion (objective) and decision rules.

In the context of the above defined inventory problem, the demand (consumption rate), lead time and safety stock are identified as decision variables. These variables shall be responsible to measure the performance of the system in terms of total inventory cost under the decision rule—when to order.

Step 3. Construct a Numerical Model

A numerical model is constructed to be analysed on the computer. Sometimes the model is written in a particular simulation language which is suited for the problem under analysis.

Step 4. Validate the Model

Validation of the model is necessary to ensure whether it is truly representing the system being analysed and the results will be reliable.

Step 5. Design the Experiments

Conduct experiments with the simulation model by listing specific values of variables to be tested (*i.e.*, list courses of action for testing) at each trial (run).

Step 6. Run the Simulation Model

Run the model on the computer to get the results in the form of operating characteristics.

Step 7. Examine the Results

Examine the results of problem as well as their reliability and correctness. If the simulation process is complete, then select the best course of action (or alternative) otherwise make desired changes in model decision variables, parameters or design, and return to Step 3.

EXAMPLES OF HAND COMPUTED SIMULATION

Inventory Control Simulation

In order to provide an efficient service to the customers, it is required to select the reorder point with due consideration of demand during lead time. If the demand of inventory per unit time and lead time both are random variables, the simulation method can be used to find the effect of alternate inventory policies on a stochastic inventory system (*e.g.*, different combinations of reorder point and order quantity). The two basic steps involved in the process would be as follows:

(i) Find the probability distribution of the input and output functions of the past data.

(ii) Run the inventory system artificially by generating the future observation on the assumption of same distribution.

The technique is explained with the help of the following inventory problem.

SIMULATION OF QUEUEING PROBLEM

Some queueing problems, which cannot be solved by analytical methods, can be solved only through simulation technique.

Application to Capital Budgeting

An important decision of financial analysis is to determine the best alternative among different policies of capital investment along with the evaluation of risk involved associated with the given decision. The basic objective of determining the risk is to obtain the effect of various factors, such as market growth rate, market size, selling policy, etc., on financial parameters. The samples from the frequency (probability) distributions of different factors involved can be drawn and analyzed to compute the rate of return on investment.

Danial Hertz (1964) has proposed a method for simulation of capital budgeting problem as described below:

(1) The probability distributions are drawn on the basis of assessment of likely outcomes. To evaluate an investment proposal, following factors are considered.

 (a) Selling price,

 (b) Share of market,

 (c) Market size,

 (d) Growth rate of market,

 (e) Investment needed,

 (f) Residual value of investment,

 (g) Cost of operations,

 (h) Fixed costs,

 (i) Useful life of facilities.

(2) A set of random numbers is generated and to each factor in the system, probability distributions are assigned as to compute the expected values of the factors involved.

(3) The step-2 is repeated several times to simulate a clear picture of investment risk. The following example will illustrate the method clearly.

PERT/COST, DECISION CPM, PRECEDENCE NETWORKING AND GENERAL REMARKS

PERT/Cost

The PERT/Cost system was developed in 1962, by the U.S. Department of Defence and the National Aeronautics and Space Administration; and was published in a U.S. Government manual, 'DOD and NASA Guide; PERT Cost System Design.' The basic concept of PERT and CPM cost system or simply PERT/Cost is that costs are measured and controlled on a project basis, rather than according to functional organisation of the firm. Instead of departments of the organisation, it is the activities or work packages (groups of activities), which form the basis of project control, in the PERT/Cost system. PERT/Cost integrates the time data, the cost data and the work accomplished. The essence of PERT/Cost system is that the responsibility for expenditure should coincide with the responsibility of managing the associated work. In this process, PERT/Cost aims at achieving a more realistic estimate of the project cost and to have a better control of costs when the project is in progress. Cost overruns are easily Y defected and corrective actions readily taken by controlling the activities responsible for over-runs.

Work Packages

As discussed above, the basic idea of PERT/Cost system is that the activities, which form the basis for project planning and scheduling. Should also form the basis for the measurement and control of costs. The activities are the result of work breakdown structure, which could be either end-oriented or functionally oriented, that is organisationally structured. The size of an activity depends upon the level of work breakdown, which further depends upon a number of factors. In many cases, the activities into which a project is broken down, may be essential for the purpose of detailed planning and scheduling, but may be too small for the purpose of cost accounting and control. In such a case, the activities generally falling on a continuous path and related to each other are grouped together to form a cost work package or simply work package. The work package which may comprise of a single activity or a group of activities, represents a particular unit of work, for which the responsibility of execution and cost control can clearly be defined, and which is manageable for planning and control purposes. It has a clear starting and terminating event and is preferably single functional. The formation of work packages from a detailed network. While forming a work, package care should be taken that the activities being grouped arc related to each other from the accounts point of view as well as from the execution point of view, that is the precedence of activities should be taken in to consideration. A work package in PERT/Cost system is identified by a charge account number in the cost chart and is generally the responsibility of one individual.

The level of accuracy in PERT/cost estimates depends to a large extent no the size of work packages, which in turn depends upon a large number of parameters, such as size and complexity of the project, type of industry, the detail obtained in W.B.S. and the stage of the project. When the project is of huge size, the work packages are also generally large. When a project is blown up into greater details, the work packages arc comparatively small in size. At certain stages of project, more detailed information i.e., smaller work packages may be required. The type of industry to which the project belongs also affects the size of the work packages. Work packages may be large in the aero-space craft and ship building industry, as compared to those in an electronic industry.

Though, the factors discussed above affect the size of the work packages, work are no specific rules or guide lines which can be used in the formation of work packages in a project. The analyst is required to look into the various aspects of the project, the structure of the organisation, the level of management and make best use of his judgement, while grouping the activities into work packages.

The DOD and NASA Guide, written primarily for the aero-space industry, suggests the value of a work package to be no more than $ 1,00,000 and of duration no more than 3 months. On the other hand in a project on the development of Boeing 707, none of the work package required more than 1,000 man-hours and none required more than 15 weeks execution time.

ROLE OF COMPUTERS IN SIMULATION

Without a computer, it is quite difficult (if not impossible) to perform simulation, particularly in case of simulation period and other variable being larger in number. Therefore, real simulations are generally carried out on computers.

A simulation computer program can be written in one of the conventional computer languages, *i.e., FORTRAN, COBOL, ALGOL*, etc. However, an extensive programming experience is required. There are many simulation languages, which have been developed to reduce considerably the program, preparation time, and cost. These can be designed with special features suitable for different types of models and systems.

The important special purpose languages developed are *GPSS, SIMSCRIPT, SIMPAC, DYNAMO, SIMULATE* and *CSL* (for different types of problem). The basic objective of these languages is to speed up the conversion of simulation model to computer program. Among the languages, *GPSS, SIMSCRIPT and DYNAMO* are more popular which give automatic instructions for time keeping and other general simulation operations. *GPSS* (General purpose system simulation) has been developed as a queueing simulation tool. *SIMSCRIPT* is more flexible than *GPSS,* but requires the knowledge of *FORTRAN*. This is also well suited to queueing problems.

The *DYNAMO* is similar to *SIMSCRIPT* except that the former simulates continuous type models, rather than models involving individual events. Hence *DYNAMO* seems to be more applicable to "Macro" simulations.

The role of computers in simulation is vital. They are used to generate random numbers, simulate the given problem with varying values of variables in few-minutes and help the decision-maker to prepare reports which enable him to make decisions quickly as well as draw valid conclusions.

Computer languages available to help the simulation process can be divided into two categories:

General Purpose Programming Languages

The general purpose programming languages include FORTRAN, BASIC, COBOL, PL/I, Pascal, etc. To use these languages for simulation process an extensive programming experience is required. As can be seen, even in a simple queuing problem, many tedious details are involved in a simulation model.

Special Purpose Simulation Languages

Special simulation languages have a few advantages such as:

(i) They reduce programme preparation time and cost with features specially designed for simulation model. Such features generally include a master sequencing routine to automatically maintain an event sequence and to keep track of simulated time sub-routines to handle arrivals and departures in a queuing system;

(ii) They have the capability to readily generate different types of random variates automatic generation of certain types of statistical tables, and various other features,

(iii) They require little or no prior programming knowledge for use. Major special purpose simulation languages are

(i) *GPSS (General Purpose System Simulation) :* Usually, it does not-require programme writing. The system model is constructed via block diagrams.using block commands. The third version of this language, *i.e.,* GPSS III consists of two parts. The first part is an assembly programme which converts the system descriptors into input for the second part that performs the simulation. This language was developed by IBM in early 1960s.

(ii) *SIMSCRIPT :* This language neither depends on any predefined coding forms nor on any intermediate language such as FORTRAN for its implementation. This language was developed by RAND Corporation in early 1960s.

(iii) *DYNAMO :* It is a computer programme which is capable of taking input in the form of a set of equations describing the system. These equations are evaluated continuously for each time interval to understand the behaviour of the system. This language was developed at MIT in 1959 and is best suited for econometric modelling of industrial complexes, urban, social and world systems planning.

The choice of a simulation package depends mainly on the specific purpose, the availability of simulation languages on a particular computer, the training and experience in simulation modelling and programming, and the availability of experienced programmers.

WHAT IS SIMULATION?

The real life situations may be so complex (due to complexity in problem formulation, stochastic nature of problem, or the conflicting informations required to describe the given problem in a proper manner) that mathematical solution is not possible. Under such situations, when all other techniques fail, *Simulation Technique* offers a good alternative. Thus, simulation is generally viewed as a "method of last resort".

Often, we do not find a mathematical technique that can solve a model which has been constructed with great difficulties. Also, often it does seem possible to simplify the model in any way without destroyingits acceptability as a reasonable representation of 'reality'. Consequently, the model cannot be manipulated to formulate a decision strategy or to obtain some appreciation of potential responses when the model is subjected to various situations or assumptions. However, a model once constructed may permit us to predict what will be the consequences of taking a certain action. In particular, we could 'experiment' on the model by 'trying' alternative actions or parameters and compare their consequences. This 'experimentation' allows us to answer 'what if' questions relating the effects of your assumptions on the model response.

For example, suppose that we have built a model for some problem, but we neither have the means nor the knowhow to solve it. The model could still be used by simply substituting and comparing the consequences of using various parameters into the model. Analyzing a model in this way is referred to as *simulating* the model.

As the complexity of a model increases, simulation is often the only remaining tool for analysis. This is the case for problems which exhibit many sources of uncertainty. For such problems, simulation seeks to replicate the uncertainty in the model and to assess the model's response to events made to occur (*i.e.,* simulated) with a frequency characterized by pre-specified probabilities.

Where is simulation used? As implied earlier, it is used in almost all conceivable fields, restricted only by our imagination and our ability to translate such imagination into a set of computer directives. The following are some simple examples which will make us appreciate what simulation is and what we can do with it.

Location of ambulances In such studies, it is not known exactly where the demand for ambulance services will arise and, therefore, simulation is required to test alternative scheduling rules of the ambulances, their locations (in a geographical area), the response time to an emergency call and, of course, the overall service quality and the costs incurred if ambulances were to be configured in a certain way (in types, quantity, location, scheduling and staffing).

Design of Optimal Replenishment Policy : In inventory control, the problem of optimal replenishment policy arises due to the probabilistic (stochastic) nature of demand and lead time. Thus, instead of manually trying out an appropriate replenishment alternative for each level of demand and lead time for a specific period and then selecting the best one, we process data (called *experiment*) on the computer and obtain the results in a very short time at a very small cost.

Design of a Queuing System : In queuing theory, the problem of balancing the cost of waiting against the cost of idle time of service facilities in the system arises due to the probabilistic nature of the inter-arrival times of customers and the time taken to complete the service to the customer. Thus, instead of trying out in actual manually with data to design a queuing system, we process the data on computers and obtain the expected value of various characteristics of the queuing system such as idle time of servers, average waiting time, queue length, etc.

Design of Computer Systems : In general, it is difficult to specify future needs. Even the best forecasts are just that, forecasts! Simulation is then useful to highlight the basic characteristics of a computer system configuration (its speed, size, computing qualities, memory and so on.) in terms of the equipment used, the management of the computer system, the costs of such configurations and the resulting computational service which it provides to users.

Shop Floor Management : The management of modem shop floor factories is extremely complex, involving many persons, machines, products parts, robots, material handling systems, Television and computer aided vision and inspection systems. Even if we were able to manage some specific aspects of the shop floor, integrating it into a simple mathematical model is simply very difficult, provided we can construct a model (however complex it may be) of the shop floor. Simulation is very useful to assess its behaviour and how it responds to certain policies (such as scheduling jobs to be performed on the basis of their due-dates, with earliest dates jobs performed first, by comparing alternative configurations and routing control policies, and so on). It can also be used to test alternative work flows, the introduction of a new machinery, and in some cases the use of completely new manufacturing and management technologies (such as in testing 'Japanese approaches' Just-in-Time manufacturing, flexible manufacturing, etc.). In such cases, simulation is a proper framework which provides insights regarding the 'new' shop floor before it is implemented. It can, thereby, provide an experience and a learning tool which will give us greater confidence in the productivity and the management of the future system, at a relatively small cost.

Other problems, such as aircraft management and routing, scheduling of bank tellers and location of bank branches, the deployment of fire stations, routing and dispatching when roads are not secured (where materials sent might not, potentially, reach their destination), the location and the utilization of recreational facilities (such as parks, public swimming pools, etc.), and many other problems have been studied,or could be studied through simulation.

Simulation refers to a representative model for real situation, *i.e.,* it is a quantitative technique, which describes an operation/process by developing a model of that operation/process followed by carrying out a series of designed experiments to predict the behaviour of the real system over a time. Consequently, observing experiments is quite identical to observing the actual operation/process. For example, testing of an aircraft model in a wind tunnel from which the performance of the real aircraft is obtained for being fit under real operating conditions. The designer can solve different equations describing the aerodynamics of the plane. If the equations are difficult and complex, scale model can be constructed and its behaviour observed in wind tunnel. Therefore, simulation may be considered as the representation of reality being either in physical form or in a mathematical equation form. In order to find the reaction to certain changes in the real system, the changes can be made in the model and then simulate the reaction of the real system to those changes.

Few more definitions of *simulation* can be considered as following:

(1) Simulation may be referred to as a representation of reality through the use of model or other device responding in the same manner as real situation under a given set of conditions.

(2) Simulation may be considered as the use of a system model having designed characteristics of real situation so that the essence of actual operation is obtained.

(3) According to Donald G. Malcoln, a simulated model is considered as one, which represents the working of a large-scale system (of men, machines, materials, and information) operating over a period of time in a simulated environment of the real situation.

(4) According to Naylor and others, simulation is referred to as a numerical technique for carrying out experiments on a digital computer involving specific types of mathematical and logical relationships, which are required to describe the behaviour and structure of complex real situation over extended periods of time.

In simulation, mathematical models which cannot be solved, are run on sample data to simulate the behaviour of the system. Therefore, simulation involves carrying out experiments on the model of the system. Simulation analysis may be considered as a natural and logical extension to the analytical and mathematical techniques in operations research. Simulation determines the effect of alternate choices without disturbing the real system.

The first important application of simulation was perhaps made by John Von Neumann and Stanislaw Ulam for determining the complicated behaviour of neutrons in a nuclear shielding problem. This was very complex for mathematical analysis. The remarkable success in this field led to the use of simulation in business and industry problems. The development of digital computers aided the rapid progress in the simulation techniques and presently simulation is readily available to most of the professionals engaged in operations research projects.

Recent developments and advances in simulation techniques, availability of softwares, and technical developments have made simulation as one of the most commonly used and accepted technique in *Operations Research* and

Systems Analysis. It helps in obtaining the best decision with the prior assurances for benefits to the organization.

As regarding the use, simulation may be considered as one of the easiest techniques of management science, but perhaps it is one of the hardest to apply properly and may be most difficult for drawing the accurate conclusions. However, inspite of these drawbacks, simulation is a useful technique particularly suitable for complicated situations.

PROJECT COST SCHEDULE

The cost schedule of a project is prepared by adding the cost of work packages, period by period, according to the activity time schedule. The activity time schedule may be based on the early start or laic start of the activities, or on any other feasible activity schedule. While computing the project schedule from period to period, it is assumed that the expenditure on a work package is made at a constant rate over the duration of the work package. In some cases, this assumption may be very severe. Such work packages should be divided into sub-work packages, each of which has a relatively constant expenditure rate.

Table 2

Activity or Work Package	*Duration (Weeks)*	*Early Start Time*	*Late Start Time*	*Total Cost (Rs.)*	*Cost Per Week (Rs.)*
1-2	4	0	0	4,000	1.000
1-3	3	0	8	4,500	1,500
2-4	5	4	11	6,000	1,200
2-5	3	4	4	4,500	1,500
3-4	5	3	11	2,000	400
4-6	2	9	16	1,00	800
5-6	7	7	11	7,000	1,000
5-7	5	7	7	6,000	1,200
6-8	2	14	18	1,000	500
7-8	8	12	12	12,800	1,600
7-9	6	12	16	4,200	700
8-9	2	20	20	2,000	1,000

The early start times, the late start times, activity or work package durations and total cost per week of the work-packages are given in Table 2. The scheduled completion time for the project has been taken to be equal to the earliest completion time which is 22 weeks. The same network is drawn in Fig. 4.8 as a schedule graph. Two schedule networks are drawn, one for the early start schedule and the other for the late start schedule. The cost per week has been computed for each week, by adding the cost of works 10 be carried in that week. For example, in the first weak of early start schedule, activities 1-2 and 1-3 are to be carried out at a cost of Rs. (1.000 + 1,500) = Rs. 2,500, while in the 8th week of the same schedule, four activities 5-7, 5-6, 2-4 and 3-4 are active, giving the cost for that week as Rs. 3,800 [Rs. (13.00 + 1.000 + 1,200 + 400)]. Along with the cost per month, the cumulative-costs have also been given find two schedules.

The cumulative costs for the early son and late start schedules have been illustrated graphically. The area between the two curves represents a range of feasible project cost schedules. This graphical representation gives a clear idea of the budget implications of the early start and late start schedules. From the budgetary point of view, the cumulative project cost should follow a relatively straight line *i.e.*, the expenditure should not vary much from period to period.

PROJECT MONITORING AND COST CONTROL

An essential requirement of project management is the mechanism for continuous comparisons of actual expenditure made to the emanated expenditure.

The PERT/Cost System Acts as Such a Mechanism

In addition to comparison of costs, it provides a means for comparing work scheduled and the work accomplished. As the project progresses, at various points in time, which we may call milestones, the management would like to check the slate of the project, that is whether it is on schedule, what is the new expected completion time, the cost incurred on the project *vis-a* the estimated cost, the work accomplished, delays and overruns—their causes and sources and the like. This detailed information helps the management to initiate, appropriate action to control the performance and cost of the project The state of the project can more easily be maintained by graphic aids, as shown in Fig. 4.10 Curve I depicts the budgeted cost of the project obtained during the planning phase. This curve corresponds to the accepted feasible schedule between the early start and late start schedules. The actual cost incurred in the execution of the project is shown by curve II in the figure. A simple comparison of the expected and actual cost curves can not reveal overrun or short runs, i.e. whether the actual expenditure is over or short of the estimated. It depends upon the extent of work; accomplished by that date.

The value of work done is given by curve III. Let us check the state of the project at the end of 8th week. The estimated project cost is Rs. 20,600, while the actual cost as given by curve is Rs. 25,000. This .gives the impression that the expenditure made on a project upto this dale is more than required (estimated).

How the Networks (PERT/CPM) Help Management

1. The networks clearly designate the responsibilities of different supervisors. Supervisor of an activity knows his time schedule precisely and also the supervisors of other activities with whom be has to co-ordinate.
2. These techniques help the management in achieving the objective with minimum of time and least cost and also in predicting the probable duration and the associated cost.
3. The networks provide a number of checks and safeguards against going astray in developing the plan for the project and thus there are little chances of oversight of certain activities and events.
4. The flexibility of the networks permits the management to make the necessary alterations and refinements as and when needed. These allocations may be made during deployment of resources or reviewing.
5. The network techniques help the management in planning the complicated projects, controlling the implementation of the plan and keeping the plan up-to-date. They also help in locating the potential trouble spots and in taking corrective measures.
6. Application of network techniques has resulted in better managerial control, improved utilisation of resources, improved communication and progress reporting and better decision making.
7. Applications of PERT and CPM have resulted in saving of time which directly results in saving of cost. Saving in time or early completion of the project results in earlier return of revenue and introduction of the project or process ahead of the competitors resulting in increased profits.

Few Comments on the Assumptions of PERT and CPM

1. It is not always possible to sort out completely identifiable activities and their start and finish times.
2. Cost-time trade-offs used for finding the cost curve slopes are also subjective and a great effort and expertise is required to estimate them.

3. Beta distribution may not always be applicable.
4. Time estimates have an element of subjectiveness in them.
5. In calculating the S.D. of the critical path, independence of activities is assumed. Limitations of resources may invalidate this independence of activities.
6. The formulae for the expected duration and standard deviation are simplifications. In certain cases the errors, due to these assumptions, may even be of the order of 33%.

Difficulties in Using Network Methods

Following are some of the problems faced in the managerial use of network methods:

1. The planning and implementation of networks require personnel trained in the network methodology. Managements are reluctant to spare the existing staff to learn these techniques or to recruit trained personnel.
2. Determination of the level of network detail is another troublesome area. The level of detail varies from planner to planner and depends upon the judgement and experience.
3. Difficulty in securing the realistic urne estimates. In the case of new and non-repetitive type projects, the time estimates produced are often mere guesses.
4. Developing a clear logical network is also troublesome. This depends upon the data input and thus, the plan can be no better than the personnel who provides the data.
5. The natural tendency to oppose changes results in the difficulty of persuading the management to accept these techniques.

BASIC STEPS IN THE SIMULATION PROCESS

In general, all effective simulations need a great deal of planning and organization. Though, simulations vary in complexity from case to case, following are the basic steps to be followed in simulation:

(1) The problem/system to be simulated is defined.

(2) The model, intended to be used, is formulated.

(3) The model is tested by comparing its behaviour with the behaviour in the acutal situation.

(4) Required data on the variables are identified and collected to compute probabilities associated with the variables. The data collected on a

variable are presented in such a manner as to give a frequency distribution for the variable.

(5) Frequency distribution is converted to cumulative probability distribution.

(6) Random numbers 00 to 99 are assigned to each of the values of the variable which are allocated to a particular value of the variable being directly proportional to the cumulative probability.

(7) *'n'* sets of random numbers are selected from random number table and the value of each of the variables is assigned to each random number.

(8) The simulated data are processed to generate the required information.

(9) The data is summarized and analyzed for interpretation.

(10) If desired, the solution, to be evaluated, is changed.

(11) Simulation is carried out to test the new solution.

(12) Simulation is validated with increased chances of inferences about the real situation.

APPLICATIONS OF NETWORK TECHNIQUES

The list containing PERT and CPM applications is very large and the applications arc expanding to many new areas. Following are a few typical areas in which these techniques are widely accepted :

1. *Administration :* Networks have been used by the administration for straitening paperwork system, for making major administrative system revisions, for long range planning and developing staffing plans, etc.
2. *Marketing :* Networks have been used for advertising programmes for development and launching of new projects and for planning their distribution.
3. *Construction Industry :* It is one of the largest areas in which the network techniques of project management have found application.
4. *Research and Development :* R and D has been the most extensive area where PERT has been used for development of new products, processes and systems.
5. *Inventory Planning :* Installation of production and inventory control, acquisition of spare parts, etc. have been greatly helped by network techniques.
6. *Maintenance Planning :* Shutdown and Maintenance of power plants, chemical plants, steel furnaces and overhauling of large machines have been carried out by using PERT.

7. *Manufacturing :* The design, development, and testing of new machines, installing machines and plant layouts are a few examples of how it can be applied to the manufacturing function of a firm.

ADVANTAGES AND DISADVANTAGES OF SIMULATION

The simulation technique possesses the following advantages over mathematical and other analysis techniques.

(i) The simulation technique is simple and easier than mathematical ones and hence, assumed to be superior over mathematical analysis.

(ii) Simulation models are relatively more flexible and can also be modified to incorporate the variation in the environments of real system.

(iii) Simulation gives the solution by carrying out experiments with a system's model without disturbing the real system. As a result, complex mathematical analysis can be by-passed.

(iv) The dificulties and problems arising due to addition of new equipment/ machine/process can be foreseen and, thus, simulation eliminates the requirement of costly trial and errors to study the new concept on real systems.

(v) Simulated exercise can be developed to train the people on simulated models before they are put to work on costly real systems. This makes the people more confident and familiar with data processing on computer.

(vi) Since simulation technique is relatively free from complicated mathematics, the technique can be understood by even non-technical staff.

(vii) The performance a of system over many years and involving huge calculation work, can be compressed by computer simulation, into a few minutes of computer running time.

Advantages

1. Simulation experiments are done with the model, not on the system itself. It also allows to include additional information during analysis that most quantitative models do not permit. In other words, simulation can be used to 'experiment' on a model of a real situation without incurring the costs of operating on the system.

2. This approach is suitable to analyse large and complex real-life problems which cannot be solved by usual quantitative methods.

3. It is useful for sensitivity analysis of complex systems. In other words, it allows the decision-maker to study the interactive system variables

and the effect of changes in these variables on the system performance in order to determine the desired one.

5. Simulation can be used as a pre-service test to try out new policies and decision rules for operating a system before running the risk of experimentation in the real system.

Disadvantages

1. The simulation model does not produce answers by itself. The user has to provide all the constraints for the solutions which he wants to examine.)
2. It is the trial and error approach that produces different solutions in repeated runs. This means it does not generate optimal solutions to problems.
3. Each application of simulation is ad hoc to a great extent.
4. The only 'remaining tool' when all other techniques become intractable or fail.
5. Sometimes simulation models are expensive and take a long time to develop. For example, a corporate planning model may take a long time to develop and prove expensive also.

LIMITATIONS OF SIMULATION TECHNIQUES

Since the use of simulation, in place of other techniques, involves a trade-off and, hence, when the problems are large and complex, simulation may also suffer the similar drawbacks as other models. The limitations of simulation approach can be briefly given as follows:

(i) Since the simulation deals mostly with uncertainties, the results are only reliable approximations involving statistical errors. Thus, simulation is not precise and is not optimization. It does not give answer, rather provides merely a set of system's responses to different operating conditions. In many situations, this lack of precision may not be possible to measure.

(ii) In many cases, quantification of all the variables affecting the behaviour of the system is not possible.

(iii) Simulation generates a way of evaluating solutions but does not generate solution themselves, and thus, solutions are to be generated for test.

(iv) Since simulation requires the use of computer, a good simulation model may be quite expensive as well as time consuming. Sometimes, it takes years to develop a usable corporate planning model.

(v) Each situation cannot be evaluated by simulation. Situations involving uncertainty are the only ones for which simulation is applicable. Without a random component, same answer will be obtained by simulated experiments.

(vi) In the situation of problem being very large and complex, computer program becomes difficult due to large number of variables and the involved inter-relationships among them.

METHODS OF SIMULATION

Following three methods are based on simulation:

(i) Monte Carlo Method, (ii) Operational Gaming Method, and

(iii) System Simulation Method.

Among the above three methods, the Monte Carlo Method is the most flexible and is commonly used. "Monte Carlo" simulation technique is developed by Von Neumann and S.M. Ulam to solve problems, which are too complicated for mathematical technique and are too expensive for experimental solution.

Though, in simple situations, simulation can be performed by hand, usually a computer is required to speed up process.

ELEMENTS OF SIMULATION

Random Events

Random events are those events which can occur with equal probability and only chance determines their occurrence.

Random Variable

It is real valued function defined over a sample space associated with the outcome of a conceptual chance experiment. Random variables may be classified depending upon their probability density function.

A Random Number

A random number refers to a uniform random variable or a numerical value assigned to a random variable following uniform probability density function (*i.e.,* Poisson, normal, exponential, etc.). In other words, it is the number in a sequence of numbers, which can appear with equal probability.

Pseudo Random Numbers

These are the random numbers, when they are generated by some deterministic process but they qualify the pre-determined statistical test for randomness.

RESOURCES LEVELLING

The analysis aiming at stabilization of rate of resources utilization by various activities at different times without changing the project duration is called resources levelling.

In order to stabilize the use of existing level of resources that total float of non-critical activities is used. By shifting a non-critical activity between its earliest start time and latest allowable time, project manager may be able to lower the maximum resources requirement.

The following two general rules are normally used in scheduling non-critical activities:

(i) If the total float of non-critical activity is equal to its free float, then it can be scheduled anywhere between its earliest start and latest completion times.

(ii) If the total float of non-critical activity is more than its free float, then its starting time can be delayed relative to its free float, then its starting time can be delayed relative to its earliest start time by no more than the amount of its float without affecting the scheduling of its immediately succeeding activities.

RESOURCES SMOOTHING

The analysis aiming to reduce peak demand for resources and re-allocating among activities of a project in a manner so that the total projects duration remains shortest is known as resources smoothing (or loading).

The procedure of carrying out resource smoothing can be summarized in the following steps:

Step I. Calculate the earliest start and latest finish times of each activity and then draw a time scaled version of the network. In this network critical path is drawn along straight line and non-critical activities on both sides of the line. Resource requirement of each activity is given along the arrows.

Step II. Draw the resource histogram by taking earliest start times or latest start times of activities on the x-axis and cumulative resources required on y-axis.

Step III. Shift start time of non-critical activities from having largest float in order to smoothen the resources.

STOCHASTIC SIMULATION AND RANDOM NUMBERS

In simulation, probability distributions are used to define numerically outcomes in a sample space by assigning a probability to each of possible outcomes. For example, if you flip a coin, the sample space (H, T) is the set of possible outcomes. Each outcome can occur with some probability, reflecting the element of chance. A random variable assigns a number to this element of chance. In statistics, these numbers are estimated to assess the uncertainty inherent in the model, but in simulation these variables are controlled numerically and used to mimic these elements of uncertainty which are defined in a model. This is done by generating (using the computer) outcomes with same frequency as those encountered in the process being mimicked (simulated). In this manner many experiments (also called *simulation runs*) can be performed, and leading to a collection of outcomes that have a frequency (probability) distribution similar to that of the model you wish to study.

To use simulation, it is first necessary that you learn how to generate the sample random events that make up complex models. Once this is done, it is possible to use the computer to reproduce the process through which chance is generated in real life. In this manner a problem can be evaluated that involves many interrelationships for their aggregate behaviour and assess this behaviour as a function of a set of given parameters. Thus process generation (simulating chance processes) and modelling are the two fundamental techniques that we need in simulation.

The most elementary and important type of process is the random process, which requires for its simulation the selection of samples (or events) drawn from a given distribution so that repetition of this selection process will yield a frequency distribution of sample values that faithfully matches the original distribution. When these samples are generated through some mechanical or electronic means, they are *pseudo random numbers* (for they are not really random since they are generated by a machine). Alternately it is possible to use table of random numbers where the selection of number in any consistent manner will yield numbers that behave as if they were drawn from a uniform distribution.

There are several ways of generating random numbers such as: Random numbers generator (which are inbuilt feature of spread sheets and many computer languages), a roulette wheel, etc.

Random numbers between 00 and 99 are used to obtain values of random variables that have a known discrete probability distribution in which the random variable of interest can assume one of a finite number of different values.

In some applications, however, the random variables are continuous, that is, they can assume any real value according to a continuous probability distribution. For example, in queuing theory applications, the amount of time a server spends with a customer is such a random variable which might follow an exponential distribution.

RANDOM NUMBERS OF GENERATION

Monte Carlo simulation technique requires the generation of a sequence of random numbers. These numbers constitute an integral part of the simulation method and also help in obtaining random observations from the probability distribution. Random numbers are assigned in such a way that their proportion is exactly equal to the probability distribution. The random numbers may be selected by computer, random tables, or manually. In manual method, the random numbers are obtained by drawing numbered chips (0-9), from box or roulette wheel, dice rolling, etc. The manual method is time consuming and cannot be used in practice.

The most common method to obtain random numbers is to generate them by computer program. These numbers lie between *0* and *1* (*0* and 100%) in representing cumulative probability distribution of a random variable, including 0, but not 1.

In literature, many tables of random numbers are available. These numbers are considered to be truely random numbers since these were generated using some random physical process.

While selecting the random numbers from the table, the starting point is not important, (*i.e.,* the first random number can be taken from any place in the random number table), but subsequent ones have to be taken proceeding sequentially either in a horizontal (same row) or vertical (same column) direction. The random numbers may be selected in sets of single digit, 2 digit, or 3 digit numbers depending upon the number of digits required. In order to simulate data for more than one variable and to reduce requirements of random numbers, the first 2 digits and last 2 digits can be chosen to give a pair of 2 digit-random numbers.

Further, while selecting random numbers for more than one concerned variable, different list of numbers for each variable should be used, otherwise, same random numbers would mean dependence among different variables. In other words generation of rendom numbers.

Monte Carlo simulation requires the generation of a sequence of random numbers. This sequence of random numbers help in choosing random observations (samples) from the probability distribution.

(a) *Arithmetic Computation :* The nth random number r_n consisting of A-digits generated by using multiplicative congruential method is given by

$$r_n \equiv p.r_{n-1} \text{ (modulo m)}$$

where, p and m are positive integers, p < m, r_{n-1} is a k-digit number and modulo m means that r_n is the remainder when $p.r_{n-1}$ is divided by m. This means, r_n and $p.r_{n-1}$ differ by an integer multiple of m. To start the process of generating random numbers, the first random number (also called *seed*) r_n is specified by the user. Then using above recurrence Jelation a sequence of A-digit random number with period h < m at which point the number r_0 occurs again can be generated.

For illustration, let = 35, m = 100 and arbitrarily start with $r_0 = 57$. Since m – 1 = 99 is the 2-digit number, therefore, it will generate 2-digit random numbers:

$$r_1 = pr_0 \text{ (modulo m)} \quad = 35 \times 57 \text{ (modulo 100)}$$
$$= 1{,}995/100 = 95, \text{ remainder}$$
$$r_2 = p\ r_1 \text{ (modulo m)} \quad = 35 \times 95 \text{ (modulo 100)}$$
$$= 3{,}325/100 = 25, \text{ remainder}$$
$$r_3 = p\ r_2 \text{ (modulo m)} \quad = 35 \times 25 \text{ (modulo 100)}$$
$$= 875/100 = 75, \text{ remainder.}$$

The choice of r_0 and p for any given value of m require great care, and the method used is also not a random process because sequence of numbers generated is determined by the input data for the method. Thus, the numbers generated through this process are *pseudo random numbers* because these' are reproducible and hence, not random.

The above defined recurrence relation can also be used to generate random numbers as decimal fraction between 0 and 1 with a desired number of digits. For this, the recurrence relation $u_n = r_n/m$ is used to generate uniformly distributed decimal fraction between 0 and 1.

(b) *Computer Generator* : The random numbers that are generated by using computer software are uniformly distributed decimal fractions between 0 and 1. The software works on the concept of cumulative *distribution function* for the random variables for which we are seeking to generate random numbers.

For example, for the negative exponential function with density function $f(x) = \lambda^{e-\lambda x}$, $0 < x < \infty$, the cumulative distribution function is given by:

or $\qquad e^{-\lambda x} = 1 - F(x)$

Taking logarithm on both sides, we have

$$-\lambda x = \log[1 - F(x)]$$

or $$x = -(1/\lambda) \log [1 - F(x)]$$

If r = F(x) is a uniformly distributed random decimal fraction between 0 and 1, then the exponential variable associated with r is given by

$$x_n = -(1/\lambda) \log (1 - r) = (1/\lambda) \log r.$$

This is an exponential process generator since 1 – r is a random number and can be replaced by r.

Remark : While picking up random numbers from the random number table, the starting point on the table is immaterial. That is, we may start with any number in any column or row, and proceed in the same column or row to the next number, but a consistent, unvaried (*i.e.,* we should not jump from one number to another indiscriminately) pattern should be followed in drawing random numbers. If random numbers are to be taken for more than one concerned variables, then different random numbers for each variable should be used because same random numbers could imply dependence among different variables.

COMPLEXITIES OF PROJECT SCHEDULING WITH LIMITED RESOURCES

The process of load smoothening and load levelling have been demonstrated with the help of a small project comprising of only 11 activities, and a resource of only one type. The activities were shifted from high-load periods to low-load periods just arbitrarily to smooth or level the resource requirement. In this small network, the juggling of activities was possible. From this example, we observe that in levelling of load to which we resort in case of limited resources, the job start are constrained not only by their precedence relationship, but also by the availability of the resource in the levelled network, generally, there is no critical path from the activity duration point of view. Thus, the concepts of slack and criticality lose their normal meanings.

In a real life project, a number of resources are required in the form of men, machines and materials, and many of these are available only in limited quantities. The problem of scheduling a project with multiple of limited resources is a very different task, even for a project of moderate size. A very large number of feasible schedules are possible in such a project. To determine all these schedules and then to find the best out of these, by the method of juggling activities, is just impossible such a problem, where a large number of feasible combinations of job start times are possible, is called a *combinational problem.* No mathematical technique is yet available to solve such a problem of resource scheduling. Integer Programming (I.P.) has been employed by some O.R. analysts, but with a limited success, only to small projects. For large projects the I.P. also becomes computationally impracticable. Only the *heuristic methods* have been found helpful in such large combinatorial problems. The heuristics, which in simple terms is just a set of rules, may not lead to an optimal solution, but definitely lead to a practical solution close to optimal and with a moderate effort on the part of the analyst.

A heuristic a collection of rules for solving a problem, is not an analytical technique, but a sort of guide for accomplishing the objectives. In a small problem, manual application of the heuristic technique may be possible, but the large projects require the employment of computers. A heuristic procedure put in the form of a computer program is called *heuristic program*. A number of such programs for project scheduling with limited resources have been developed by different persons. Here we will discuss the heuristic program for resource levelling, when there is no constraint on project duration. The object is to find the shortest project schedule subject to the constraint on resource availability. This may be called a *resource allocation problem*.

HEURISTIC PROGRAMMES FOR RESOURCE ALLOCATION

The best method of illustrating the heuristic programmes is with the help of some examples.

Consider the project the required data for which is given in Table 4.2. After determining the critical path, the project has been drawn as a squared network using early start schedule . Only one type of resource, the manpower required for executing different activities, has been considered in this case. The daily manpower required for each activity has been shown along the activity arrow. The daily manpower required for executing the project according to the early start schedule has also been shown below the squared network. Now, there let be 10 men available for the project. The project will have to be rescheduled, so that the demand on men is always less than or equal to 10, and at same time the project duration is extended to the minimum possible. This is the case of load levelling. A number of heuristic procedures are available for tackling such problems a common on being the day-by day scheduling. This program is based on the following rules (heuristic):

1. Starting with day one, allocate resource serially in time.
2. When a number of activities complete for the same resource assign priority according to the criticality of the job, job with least slack is taken up first.
3. Reschedule non-critical jobs, if possible, when resources are required fir critical or non-slack jobs.

4. Jobs once started are not interrupted.

Table

Activity	:	*A*	*B*	*C*	*D*	*E*	*F*	*G*	*H*	*I*	*J*	*K*	*L*	*M*
Duration	:	1	2	3	4	4	4	2	4	1	2	3	2	3
Manpower required (MPR)	:	8	5	4	5	4	6	1	2	2	4	6	3	6

Day 1 : There is only one activity A, which require 8 men and thus there is no problem in its starting.

Day 2 : Three activities B, C and D are due to start on day 2, requiring 14 men, but we have only 10 men available. Apply rule 2.

Schedule activity C, slack = 0, 4 men required, 6 remain.

Activities B and D have equal slack of 1 day, any of these can be taken up first.

Schedule activity B, slack = 1, 5 men required, 1 remains.

Postpone activity D, slack = 1, 5 men required.

Day 3 : Activities C and B are in progress.

Continue activity C, slack = 0, 4 men required.

Continue activity B, slack = 1, 5 men required.

Postpone activity D, slack = 0.

At this stage activity D has become critical, and none of the activities B and C can be postponed. This will increase the project duration by one day.

Day 4 : Activity C already in progress.

Continue activity C, slack = 0, 4 men required.

Schedule activity D, slack = 0, 5 men required.

No other job is due to start on fourth day.

Day 5 : Activities E, F and D are the candidates for the resources. D is already in progress.

Continue activity D, slack = 0, 5 men required.

Activity F, slack = 0, required 6 men, while only 5 men are available. Check if rule 3 can be applied. Activity D which is active, is already non-slack activity. Therefore postpone activity F, this will delay the project completion also.

Day 6 : Activities E and D continue, F is postponed.

Day 7 : Activities E and D continue, F is postponed.

Day 8 : Activities E, F, G and H are the candidates for the resource allocation.

Continue activity E, slack = 4, 4 men required

Schedule activity F, slack = 0, 6 men required.

Postpone activity G, slack = 2.

Postpone activity H, slack = 7.

Day 9 : Activities E, F, G and H are the candidates for consideration.

Continue activity F, slack = 0, 6 men required.

Schedule activity G, slack = 1,1 men required.

Schedule activity I, slack = 4,2 men required.

Postpone activity H, slack = 6.

Day 10 : Continue activity F, slack = 0, 6 men required.

Continue activity G, slack = 1, 1 men required.

Schedule activity H, slack = 5, 2 men required.

Day 11 : Activities F and H continue, 8 men required.

Day 12 : Activities J, K and H are the candidates for the resource allocation.

Continue activity H, slack = 5, 2 men required.

Schedule activity J, slack = 0, 4 men required.

Postpone activity K, slack = 1.

Day 13 : Activity K also becomes critical at this stage. Check if any of the active activities can be rescheduled. Activity H has a slack of 5 days and can be rescheduled.

Re-scheduled activity H, no men allocated.

Continue activity J, slack = 0, 4 men required.

Schedule activity K, slack = 0, 6 men required.

This process continues till the last job is completed. The summary for the remaining days is given below.

Day 14 : Activities L and K active, postpone H, 9 men required.

Day 15 : Activities L and K active, postpone H, 9 men required.

Day 16 : Schedule activities M and H, 8 men required.

Day 17 : Activities M and H Active, 8 men required.

Day 18 : Activities M and H Active, 8 men required.

Day 19 : Activity H active, 2 men required.

Day 20 : Activity H active, 2 men required.

MONTE CARLO SIMULATION

Since Monte Carlo simulation has become almost an integral part of simulation models, the term is considered to be synonymous. However, it remains to be a special technique of simulation, which involves the selection of random observations within the simulation model. The technique is based on the principle of replacement of actual statistical environment by another environment described by some assumed probability distribution, followed by sampling from this theoretical population by means of random numbers. This simulation technique is applicable only to systems involving random numbers to solve deterministic and stochastic problems.

In fact, the process consists of generation of random variables explainable in sample terms. Random variables can be obtained by standard probability density function.

The principle behind the Monte Carlo simulation technique is representative of the given system under analysis by a system described by some known probability distribution and then drawing random samples from probability distribution by means of random numbers. In case it is not possible to describe a system in terms of standard probability distribution such as normal, Poisson, exponential, gamma, etc., an empirical probability distribution can be constructed.

The Monte Carlo simulation technique consists of following steps:

(i) Setting up a probability distribution for variables to be analysed.

(ii) Building a cumulative probability distribution for each random variable.

(iii) Generate random numbers. Assign an appropriate set of random numbers to represent value or range (interval) of values for each random variable.

(iv) Conduct the simulation experiment by means of random sampling.

(v) The required number of simulation runs has been generated.

(vi) Design and implement a course of action and maintain control.

SOLVED EXAMPLES

Example 1:

In a manufacturing firm, if the number of sales per day is Poisson with mean 5, generate 15 days of sales by Monte Carlo Technique.

Solution:

To calculate the cumulative distribution of sales, first the probabilities for different demands (0,1,2,.....) are computed.

The probability for sales is given by,

$$P_s = \frac{e^{-m}\, m^s}{s!}, \text{ when } m = s \text{ (given) or } P_s = \frac{e^{-5}\, 5^s}{s!}, (s = 0, 1, 2,...)$$

The cumulative probabilities for s = 0, 1, 2, ... are computed as given in Table 1.

Table 1

Value of s	*Cumulative Probability (%)*	*Random Numbers Allotted*
0	1	–
1	4	1 - 3
2	12	4 - 11
3	26	12 - 25
4	44	26 - 43
5	62	44 - 61
6	76	62 - 75
7	87	76 - 86
8	93	87 - 92
9	97	93 - 96
10	98	97 - 97
11	99	98 - 98
12 or more	100	99 - 99

Now, 15 two digit random numbers are taken from random number tables and the corresponding values of sales *s* are tabulated as in Table 2.

Table 2

Random No.	*Sales (s)*	*Random No.*	*Sales (s)*	*Random No.*	*Sales (s)*
39	4	16	3	06	2
85	7	59	5	61	5
75	6	46	5	12	3
26	4	06	2	20	3
95	9	35	4	47	5

Example 2:

A firm has a single channel service station with the following arrival and service time probability distributions:

Inter-Arrival Time (minutes)	*Probability*	*Service Time (minutes)*	*Probability*
10	*0.10*	*5*	*0.08*
15	*0.25*	*10*	*0.14*
20	*0.30*	*15*	*0.18*
25	*0.25*	*20*	*0.24*
30	*0.10*	*25*	*0.22*
		30	*0.14*

The customer's arrival at the service station is a random phenomenon and the time between the arrivals varies from 10 minutes to 30 minutes. The service time varies from 5 minutes to 30 minutes. The queuing process begins at 10 A.M. and proceeds for nearly 8 hours. An arrival goes to the service facility immediately, if it is free. Otherwise it will wait in a queue. The queue discipline is first-come First-served. If the attendant's wages are Rs. 10 per hour and the customer's waiting time costs Rs. 15 per hourS then would it be an economical proposition to engage a second attendant? Answer using Monte Carlo simulation technique.

Solution:

The cumulative probability distributions and random number interval both for inter-arrival time and service time are shown in Tables 1 and 2, respectively.

Table 1

Inter-arrival Time (minutes)	*Probability*	*Cumulative Probability*	*Random Number Interval*
10	0.10	0.10	00.09
15	0.25	0.35	10.34
20	0.30	0.65	35.64
25	0.25	0.90	65.89
30	0.10	1.00	90.99

Table 2

Inter-arrival Time (minutes)	*Probability*	*Cumulative Probability*	*Random Number Interval*
5	0.08	0.08	00.07
10	0.14	0.22	08.21
15	0.18	0.40	22.39
20	0.24	0.64	40.63
25	0.22	0.86	64.85
30	0.14	1.00	86.99

The simulation worksheet developed to the given problem is shown in Table 3.

Table 3 : Single Server Queuing Simulation for 15 Arrivals

Arrival Number	*Random Number*	*Arrival Interval*	*Arrival Time*	*Service Time*	*Waiting Time*	*Random Number*	*Service Time*	*Exit Time*	*Time in System*
1.	20	15	15	15	0	26	15	30	15
2.	73	25	40	40	0	43	20	60	20
3.	30	15	55	60	5	98	30	90	35
4.	99	30	85	90	5	87	30	120	35
5.	66	25	110	120	10	58	20	140	30
6.	83	25	135	140	5	90	30	170	35
7.	32	15	150	170	20	84	25	195	45
8.	75	25	175	195	20	60	20	215	40
9.	04	10	185	215	30	08	10	225	40
10.	15	15	200	225	25	50	20	245	45
11.	29	15	215	245	30	37	15	260	45
12.	62	20	235	260	25	42	20	280	45
13.	37	20	255	280	25	28	15	295	40
14.	68	25	280	295	15	84	25	320	40
15.	94	30	310	320	10	65	25	345	35

From the 15 samples of waiting time, 225 minutes and the time spent 545 minutes by the customer in the system, we compute all average waiting time in the system and average service time as follows:

Average waiting time = 225/15 =15 minutes.

Average service time = 545/15 = 36.33 minutes

Thus, the average cost of waiting and service is given by

Cost of waiting = 15 × (15/60) = Rs. 3.75 per hour

Cost of service = 10 × (36.33/60) = Rs. 6.05 per hour.

Since average cost of service per hour is more than the average cost of waiting per hour, therefore, it would not be an economical proposition to engage a second attendant.

Example 3:

The resource requirement (man-days) and the range of permissible crew size for the activities of a project are given in Table. Any crew size with in the permissible range may be employed to carry out the job, subject to the condition that the total number of men employed on any day should not exceed 16. Schedule the project to minimise the project duration.

Table

Job	*Immediate Predecessor*	*Resource Required*	*Range of Permissible Crew Size*	
	(Man-days)		*Minimum*	*Maximum*
a	–	45	5	15
b	*a*	24	2	6
c	*a*	96	4	12
d	*a*	50	2	10
e	*d*	30	2	10
f	*c*	60	4	12
g	*c*	12	1	6
h	*b*	35	5	7
i	*f*	42	3	14
j	*g, e*	24	3	8
k	*i, j*	20	2	10

Solution:

It may be started with a network based on maximum crew size and then expanding the activities while allocating the resources or with a network based on minimum crew size and crashing the jobs during allocation of resources.

Since the normal times are not given the following procedure has been used to find the pseduo-normal durations of jobs.

Total man-days required in the project are 438. Since 16 men are to be employed, length of the critical path should be a minimum of 438/16 $\simeq$ 28 days. The network, based on largest crew size (minimum activity duration) gives a critical path of 21 days.

Thus each activity on the critical path be increased by multiplying the minimum duration by 23/21 and then rounding it off to the nearest acceptable whole number. For example, the duration of job A can be 45/5 = 9, 45/ 9 = 5, 45/15 = 3 days and can not be 3 × 28/21 = 4 days. Acceptable duration will the 5 days (crew size of 5). Similarly, for activity C, the normal duration 96 × 28/21 = 10.6 can be rounded to the nearest acceptable duration of 12 days (crew size of 8).

The network is then drawn using those normalised durations for the critical activities. Activities on the non-critical paths are then expanded to fill the slack. The slack on a path is distributed between the contending activities in the ratio of their durations. The schedule graph with activities expanded. Now the day-by-day resource scheduling resorted to.

Day 1	:	There is only one activity A, and the same can be scheduled at the maximum crew size of 15 men.
Days 2 and 3	:	Activity A with 15 men is continued.
Day 4	:	Activities B, C and D can start. The load as computed is 15 men. The remaining one man should also be allocated if possible. Starting with critical activities, addition of one man to C is not possible, neither is it possible to add one man to D. It can be added to allocated manpower of B to make it 3 (activity duration 8 days).
Days 5 to 11	:	Continue with the schedule of day 4.
Day 12	:	Priority is given to jobs already in progress. Continue activity C with 8 men. Continue activity D with 5 men. Activity H can be started with the remaining 3 men. Since H has slack, it can be postponed.
Day 13	:	Continue C and d with 13 men postpone H.
Day 14	:	Continue activity C with 8 men. Schedule critical activity E with 3 men. Since H can not be scheduled with remaining 3 men, postpone it. Now check, if the remaining three men can be allocated to jobs C and E. Since, the next crew size of C is 12, none can be added to the present crew size of 8. Crew size of activity E can be increased to 6 to reduce its duration to 5 days.
Day 15	:	Continue jobs C and E with 14 men.
Day 16	:	Continuing the job E, already in progress with 6 men, activities F, G and H are due to start on this day. Activities F and G are critical and require 13 (10 + 3) men. One of these will have to be extended. Next possible crew size for F is 6. After allocating 6 men to E, 6 to F and 3 to G, one man remains. With one man, H can not stand, postpone it and add one man to the crew of activity G.
Days 17 to 18	:	Continue the jobs E, F and G with 16 men, and postpone H.
Day 19	:	Continue job F with 6 men.

		Schedule job J with 3 men.
		Schedule job H with 5 men.
		Out of the remaining 2 men, none can be allocated 10 F and only one can be added to the crew of J. The remaining one can not be added to the crew of H and will thus remain idle.
Days 20 to 24	:	Continue with the schedule of day 19th. Continue F with 6 men and H with 5 men.
		No other activity is due for scheduling on this day.
Day 26	:	There is only one activity I, requiring a maximum of 16 men. Schedule it
Day 27 & 28	:	Job I is continued.
Day 29	:	There is only one activity K. Schedule it employing the maximum permissible crew size of 10.
Day 30	:	Job K is continued.

The project duration is 30 days. Now the amount of idle man-days can be computed by summing up the idle man-days for the entire project duration of 30 days which comes to 42 man-days.

Example 4(a):

The activities, their durations and skilled and unskilled men required their execution are given below.

Activity	:	*A*	*B*	*C*	*D*	*E*	*F*	*G*	*H*	*I*	*J*
Duration (days)	:	*1*	*4*	*3*	*1*	*2*	*2*	*2*	*3*	*1*	*3*
Skilled men reqd. day	:	*7*	*1*	*4*	*3*	*5*	*3*	*2*	*6*	*7*	*10*
Unskilled men reqd. day	:	*12*	*3*	*9*	*6*	*10*	*8*	*4*	*10*	*14*	*15*

Solution:

The precedence relationships are : B, C, D, E, F > B; G > C; H > D; I > G, H; J > I, E.

The project is to be scheduled for the case when only 10 skilled and 20 unskilled men arc available throughout the project duration.

The values along the activity arrows represent the daily resource requirement as skilled/unskilled men required. For this schedule. The day to day manpower requirements arc given below the network. For allocating the limited resources day-by-day scheduling heuristics can be applied.

Day 1 : Activity which can start on this day is A.

S.M.R (skilled men required) are 7 and

U.M.R (unskilled men required) arc 12.

Schedule activity A.

Day 2 : Activities B, C, D and E arc candidates for the resources, and no activity is already in progress.

Priority order of these activities according to slack is C, D, B and E.

Schedule C, slack = 0, S.M.R. = 4, U.M.X. = 9.

Scheme D, slack = 0, S.M.R. = 3, U.M.K. = 6.

Schedule B, stack = 3, S.M.R. = 1, U.M.R. = 3.

Activity E, slack = 4, S.M.R. = 5, postpone to next day.

Day 3 : Same as for day 2.

Day 4 : Activities C and B are already in progress.

Continue C. slack = 0. S.M.R. = 4, U.M.R. = 9.

Continue B. slack = 3. S.M.R. = 1, U.M.R. = 3.

Activity H. slack = 0, S.M.R. = 6 and U.M.R. = 10 is a critical activity. Its stan is possible only if the non-critical activity B is rescheduled.

Day 9 : On this day activities F and I are candidates for the resources. I is critical, while F has a slack of one day. Though, skilled men required by Fand I are 10, the limit on unskilled men is exceeded. Therefore, schedule activity I and postpone F.

Example 4(b):

In an engineering firm, tools are issued at a centrally located tool crib. The workmen, wishing to exchange/return/receive the tools, approach the tool crib. The clerk, working at tool crib, accepts and issues the tools on "First in first out" (FIFO) basis. The workmen arrive at the tool crib at random intervals of time and the service is rendered according to the idividuals, requirements, and, thus, servicing time is also random.

The interarrival time frequency distribution of 100 arrivals is given as following:

Interarrival time in minutes	*1*	*2*	*3*	*4*	*5*	*6*	*7*	*8*	*9*	*10*
Frequency	*5*	*5*	*10*	*15*	*25*	*20*	*10*	*4*	*4*	*2*

Further, service time study for the above 100 arrivals give the following service time frequency distribution.

Servicing time (Minutes)	*1*	*2*	*3*	*4*	*5*
Frequency	*10*	*20*	*30*	*25*	*15*

Using the random numbers from the simulate a sample of 20 workers and compute the average % customer waiting time and the average percent crib clerk's idle time.

Solution:

Taking the following random numbers:

17051, 49669, 75239, 29179, 34002, 69127, 08442, 99918, 78329, 19495, 33374, 21969, 52793, 48542, 434534, 70547, 00985, 44409, 42900, 04920

The following distribution for the interarrival time and service time are converted to cumulative probability distribution and random numbers assigned in Tables (a) and (b).

Table (a) : Interarrival Time and Cumulative Probability

Interarrival Time (Min.)	*Frequency*	*Cumulative Probability (%)*	*Random Number Allotted*
1	5	5	00 - 04
2	5	10	05 - 09
3	10	20	10 - 19
4	15	35	20 - 34
5	25	60	35 - 59
6	20	80	60 - 79
7	10	90	80 - 89
8	5	95	90 - 94
9	4	99	95 - 98
10	1	100	99

Table (b) : Servicing Time and Cumulative Probability

Service Time (Min.)	*Frequency*	*Cumulative Probability (%)*	*Random Number Allotted*
1	10	10	00 - 09
2	20	30	10 - 29
3	30	60	30 - 59
4	25	85	60 - 84
5	15	100	85 - 99

Now, interarrival time and service time are sampled for each of the random numbers of 20 sets of random numbers given (Table c). Simulated data are then processed into waiting time of customers and idle time of crib-clerk.

The results so obtained are finally summarized and interpreted to compute the percent waiting time of customers and percent idle time of crib-clerk.

From Table 3, it is found that

(i) Time spent by the crib-clerk at his working place = 88 minutes.
Idle time for the crib-clerk = 29 minutes
Therefore, time spent by the clerk in rendering service = 85-25 = 60
Hence % utilization of the crib-clerk = 60/85 = 70.6%

(ii) Total waiting time of workmen in queue = 14 minutes.
Average waiting time per workman = 14/20 = 0.70 minute.

Table (c) : Computation for Simulation

Work man	*Arrival Time*		*Service Time*		*Time of arrival*	*Time of start of service*	*Time to finish service*	*Workman*	*Waiting Time Minutes Crib Clerk*
	Random-Nos. first 2 digits	*Inter-arrival time min.*	*Random Nos. Last 2 digits*	*Service time in minutes*					
1	17	3	51	3	3	03	06	–	3
2	49	5	69	4	8	08	12	–	2
3	75	6	39	3	14	14	17	–	2
4	29	4	79	4	18	18	22	–	1
5	34	4	02	1	22	22	23	–	–
6	69	6	27	2	28	28	30	–	5
7	08	2	42	3	30	30	33	–	2
8	99	1	18	2	31	35	37	–	–
9	78	6	29	2	37	37	39	–	–
10	19	3	95	5	40	40	45	–	1
11	33	4	74	4	44	45	49	1	–
12	21	3	69	4	47	49	53	2	–
13	45	5	93	5	52	53	58	1	–
14	48	5	42	3	57	58	61	1	–
15	43	5	34	3	62	62	65	–	1
16	70	6	47	3	68	68	71	–	3
17	00	1	85	5	69	71	76	2	–
18	44	5	09	1	74	76	77	2	–
19	92	8	00	1	82	82	83	–	5
20	04	1	20	2	83	83	85	–	–
		Total	60	–	–	85	14	25	

Example 4(c):

An investment firm desires to study the investment proposals based on following three factors:

(a) Market demand (in units).

(b) Profit per unit, and

(c) Investment required.

The above factors are considered to be independent of each other. In the analysis of a new product, the firm estimates the following probability distribution (Table a).

Table (a) : Probability Distribution of Demand, Profit and Investment

Market Demand (Annual)		*Profit per Unit (Price–Cost)*		*Investment Required*	
Units '000	*Probability*	*Rs.*	*Probability*	*Rs. '000*	*Probability*
10	*0.10*	*10*	*0.10*	*2000*	*0.3*
15	*0.15*	*12*	*0.30*	*2500*	*0.5*
20	*0.20*	*14*	*0.25*	*3000*	*0.2*
25	*0.25*	*16*	*0.25*		
30	*0.15*	*20*	*0.10*		
35	*0.10*				
40	*0.05*				

Employ the simulation technique and repeat the trial 10 times. Determine the return on investment for each trial considering the above given three factors. Also compute the most likely return.

Solution:

$$\text{The yearly return (R)} = \frac{\text{Profit} \times \text{units demand per year}}{\text{Investment}}$$

A cumulative probability distribution corresponding to each of the three factors is computed by assigning an appropriate set of random numbers representing each factor as given in Tables (b) to (c).

Table (b) : Random Numbers Assigned to Probability of Demand

Market Demand per year '000	*Probability*	*Cumulative Probability*	*Random Numbers Assigned*
10	0.10	0.10	00 - 09
15	0.15	0.25	10 - 24
20	0.20	0.45	25 - 44
25	0.25	0.70	45 - 69
30	0.15	0.85	70 - 84
35	0.10	0.95	85 - 94
40	0.05	1.00	95 - 99

Table (c) : Random Numbers Assigned to Probability of Profit

Profit per Unit (Rs.)	*Probability*	*Cumulative Probability*	*Random Numbers Assigned*
10	0.10	0.10	00 - 09
12	0.30	0.40	10 - 39
14	0.25	0.65	40 - 64
16	0.25	0.90	65 - 89
20	0.10	1.00	90 - 99

Table (d) : Random Numbers Assigned to Probability of Investment

Investment Required '000	*Probability*	*Cumulative Probability*	*Random Numbers Assigned*
2000	0.30	0.30	00 - 29
2500	0.50	0.80	30 - 79
3000	0.20	1.00	80 - 99

Now the simulation work sheet is prepared for 10 trials. The simulated return (R) is also computed by using the formula for R. The results of simulation are presented in Table (e).

Table (e) : Simulation Results

Trials	*Random No. of demand*	*Simulated Demand '000*	*Random No. for profit*	*Simulated Profit Rs.*	*Random No. for Investment*	*Simulated Investment '000*	*Simulated Return (R) %*
1	15	15	81	16	96	3000	8
2	09	10	28	12	82	3000	4
3	41	20	12	12	56	2500	9.6
4	74	30	57	14	68	2500	16.8
5	00	10	99	20	58	2500	8
6	72	30	45	14	40	2500	16.8
7	67	25	49	14	82	2500	14
8	55	25	03	10	11	2000	12.5
9	71	30	64	14	34	2500	16.8
10	35	20	93	20	23	2000	20

According to Table, the highest likely return is 20% corresponding to the yearly demand of 20,000 units, resulting in a profit of Rs. 20 per unit and the investment required would be Rs. 20,00,000.

Example 4(d):

Using random numbers to simulate a sample, find the probability that a packet of 6 products does not contain any defective product, when the production line produces 10 per cent defective products. Compare your answer with the expected probability.

Solution:

Given that 10 per cent of the total production is defective and 90 per cent is non-defective. If we have 100 random numbers (0 to 99), then 90 (or 90 per cent) of them represent non-defective products and remaining 10 (or 10 per cent) of them represent defective products.

Thus, the random numbers 00 to 89 are assigned to variables representing non-defective products and 90 to 100 are assigned to variables representing defective products.

If we choose a set of 2-digit random numbers in the range 00 to 99 to represent a packet of 6 products as shown below, then we would expect that 90 per cent of the time they would fall in the range 00 to 89.

Sample Number	Random Number					
A	86	02	22	57	51	68
B	39	77	32	77	09	79
C	28	06	24	25	93	22
D	97	66	63	99	61	80
E	69	30	16	09	05	53
F	33	63	99	19	87	26
G	.87	14	77	43	96	43
H	99	53	93	61	28	52
1	93	86	52	77	65	15
J	18	46	23	34	25	85

Here, it may be noted that out of ten simulated samples 6 contain one or more defectives and 4 contain no defectives. Thus, the expected percentage of non-defective products is 40 per cent. However, theoretically the probability that a packet of 6 products containing no defective product is (0.9)6 = 0.53144 = 53.14%.

Example 4(e):

A bakery keeps stock of a popular brand of cake. Previous experience shows the daily demand pattern for the item with associated probabilities, as given below:

Daily demand (number)	:	*0*	*10*	*20*	*30*	*40*
Probability	:	*0.01*	*020*	*0.15*	*0.50*	*0.12.*

Use the following sequence of random numbers to simulate the demand for next 10 days.

Random numbers : 25, 39, 65, 76, 12, 05, 73, 89, 19, 49.

Also estimate the daily average demand for the cakes on the basis of simulated data.

Solution:

Using the daily demand distribution, we obtain a probability distribution as shown in Table (a).

Table (a) : Daily Demand Distribution

Daily Demand	*Probability*	*Cumulative Probability*	*Random Number Interval*
0	0.01	0.01	00
10	0.20	0.21	01-20
20	0.15	0.36	21-35
30	0.50	0.86	36-85
40	0.12	0.98	86-97
50	0.02	1.00	98-99

Conduct the simulation experiment for demand by taking a sample of 10 random numbers from a table of random numbers, which represent the sequence of 10 samples. Each random sample number here is a sample of demand.

The simulation calculations for a period of 10 days are given in Table (b).

Table (b) : Simulation Experiments

Days	*Random Number*	*Demand*	
1	40	30	because $0.36 < 0.40 < 0.85$
2	19	10	because $0.01 < 0.19 < 0.20$,
3	87	40	and so on
4	83	30	
5	73	30	
6	84	30	
7	29	20	
8	09	10	
9	02	10	
10	20	10	
		Total = 220	

Expected demand = 220/10 = 22 units per day.

Example 5:

A book store wishes to carry a particular book in stock. Demand is probabilistic and replenishment of stock takes 2 days (i.e., if an order is placed-on March 1, it will be delivered at the end of the day on March 3). The probabilities of demand are given below:

Demand (daily) :	*0*	*1*	*2*	*3*	*4*
Probability :	*0.05*	*0.10*	*0.30*	*0.45*	*0.10*

Each time an order is placed, the store incurs an ordering cost of Rs. 10 per order. The store also incurs a carrying cost of Re 0.05 per book per day. The inventory carrying cost is calculated on the basis of stock at the end of each day. The manager of the book store wishes to compare two options for his inventory decision.

A : Order 5 books when the inventory at the beginning of the day plus orders outstanding is less than 8 books.

B : Order 8 books when the inventory at the beginning of the day plus orders outstanding is less than 8.

Currently (beginning of 1 st day) the store has a stock of 8 books plus 6 books ordered two days ago and expected to arrive next day. Using Monte Carlo simulation for 10 cycles, recommend which option the manager should choose.

The two digit random numbers are : 89, 34, 78, 63, 61, 81, 39, 16, 13, 73.

Solution:

Using the daily demand distribution, we obtain a probability distribution as shown in Table 1.

Table 1 : Daily Demand Distribution

Daily Demand	***Probability***	***Cumulative Probability***	***Random Number Interval***
0	0.05	0.05	00-04
1	0.10	0.15	05-14
2	0.30	0.45	15-44
3	0.45	0.90	45-89
4	0.10	1.00	90-99

Given that stock in hand is of 8 books and stock on order is 5 books (expected next day).

Table 2 : Option A

Random Number	*Demand Daily*	*Closing Stock in Hand*	*Receipt*	*Opening Stock in Hand*	*Stock on Order*	*Order Quantity*	*Closing Stock*
89	3	8	–	8 – 3 = 5	6	–	6
34	2	5	6	6 + 5 – 2 = 9	–	–	–
78	3	9	–	9 – 3 = 6	–	5	5
63	3	6	–	6 – 3 = 3	5	–	5
61	3	3	–	3 – 3 = 0	5	5	10
81	3	0	5	5 – 3 = 2	5	5	10
39	2	2	–	2 – 2 = 0	10	–	10
16	2	0	5	5 – 2 = 3	5	–	5
13	1	3	5	5 + 3 – 1 = 7	0	5	5
73	3	7	–	7 – 3 = 4	5	–	5

Since 5 books have been ordered four times as shown in Table 2, therefore, total ordering cost is Rs. (4 × 10) = Rs. 40.

Closing stock of 10 days is of 39 (= 5 + 9 + 6 + 3 + 2 + 3 + 7 + 4) books. Therefore, the holding cost at the rate of Re 0.5 per book per day is Rs. (39 × 0.5) = Rs. 19.5.

Total cost for 10 days = Ordering cost + Holding cost

= Rs. (40 + 19.5) = Rs. 59.5.

Table 3 : Option B

Random Number	*Demand Daily*	*Closing Stock in Hand*	*Receipt*	*Opening Stock in Hand*	*Stock on Order*	*Order Quantity*	*Closing Stock*
89	3	8	–	8 – 3 = 5	6	–	6
34	2	5	6	6 + 5 – 2 = 9	–	–	–
78	3	9	–	9 – 3 = 6	–	8	8
63	3	6	–	6 – 3 = 3	8		8
61	3	3	–	3 – 3 = 0	8	–	8
81	3	0	8	8 + 0 – 3 = 5	–	8	8
39	2	5	–	5 – 2 = 3	8	–	8
16	2	3	–	3 – 2 = 1	8	–	8
13	1	1	8	8 + 1 – 1 = 8	–	–	–
73	3	8	–	8 – 3 = 5	–	8	8

Since 8 books have been ordered three times as shown in Table 3, when the inventory of books at the beginning of the day plus orders outstanding is less than 8. Therefore, total ordering cost is: Rs. (3 × 10) = Rs. 30.

Closing stock of 10 days is of 45 (= 5 + 9 + 6 + 3 + 5 + 3 + 1 + 8 + 5) books. Therefore, holding cost, Re 0.5 per book per day is Rs. (45 × 0.5) = Rs. 22.50. Total cost for 10 days = Ordering cost + Holding cost = Rs. 52.50. Sinre option B has lower total cost than option A, therefore, manager should choose option B.

Example 6:

A firm dealing in TVs wishes to carry TVs in stock. The firm utilizes reorder level system to replenish stock, i.e., a fresh order is placed when the stock of TVs falls or approaches its pre-fixed level (re-order level). The past records of weekly demand of TVs costing Rs. 10,400 has the following distribution:

Demand (weekly)	*0*	*1*	*2*	*3*	*4*	*5*	*6*
Probability (in %)	*2*	*8*	*22*	*34*	*18*	*9*	*7.*

When an order is placed to replenish stock, there is delivery lag with the following distribution:

Lead time (weeks)	*1*	*2*	*3*	*4*	*5*
Probability (in%)	*22*	*34*	*20*	*18*	*6.*

The re-order level is fixed at 15 units and re-order quantity is optimized at 20 units. The inventory carrying cost and procurement cost are 20% of the average inventory investment per year and Rs. 400 per order, respectively. Simulate the average cost (inventory carrying cost, procurement cost) for 10 weeks.

39911, 85595, 75467, 26435, 95726, 16894, 59780, 46215, 06831, 35905.

Assume that closing stock at the end of the week is 25 number of TVs.

Solution:

(i) Frequecny distribution for demand and lead time are converted to cumulative probability distribution as given in Tables 1 and 2.

(2) Random numbers 00–99 assigned to each of the value of the demand and lead time (the range of the random numbers allocated is proportional to cumulative probability).

(3) 10 sets of random numbers are selected from given random number table, and the demand and lead time are sampled for each of the random numbers (Table-3). Random numbers for demand and lead time are formed by picking up the first 2 numbers and last 2 numbers, respectively, from the random number table.

Table 1

Weekly Demand (Units)	*Probability %*	*Cumulative Probability %*	*Random No. Allocated*
0	2	2	00 - 01
1	8	10	02 - 09
2	22	32	10 - 31
3	34	66	32 - 65
4	18	84	66 - 83
5	9	93	84 - 92
6	7	100	93 - 99

Table 2

Lead time (Weeks)	*Probability %*	*Cumulative Probability %*	*Random No. Allocated*
1	22	22	00 - 21
2	34	56	22 - 55
3	20	76	56 - 75
4	18	94	76 - 93
5	6	100	94 - 99

Table 3 : Results of Simulation Process

Week	*Demand*		*Lead time*		*Opening*	*Receipt*	*Closing*	*Ordering of*	*Stock*
No.	*Random no.*	*Demand (units)*	*Random no.*	*Lead time weeks*	*Stock in the beginning of the week*	*During the week*	*Stock at the end of the week*	*Quantity*	*To receive at the end of the week*
0	-	-	-	-	-	-	25	-	-
1.	39	3	11	1	25	-	22	-	-
2.	85	5	95	5	22	-	17	-	-
3.	75	4	67	3	17	-	13	20	6th week
4.	26	2	35	2	13	-	11	-	-
5.	95	6	26	2	11	-	5	-	-
6.	16	2	94	5	5	20	23	-	-
7.	59	3	80	4	23	-	20	-	-
8.	46	3	15	1	20	-	17	-	-
9.	06	1	31	2	17	-	16	-	-
10.	35	3	05	1	16	-	13	20	11th week

(4) The simulated data is then processed into average inventory per week and number of orders executed during the simulation period as shown in columns 6-10 of Table 3.

(5) The results are summarized and interpreted to obtain the average cost per week. Table 4 represents the summary data extracted from Table 3.

Table 4 :Summary of the Results to Compute Average Cost per Week

Week No.	*Opening Stock OS*	*Closing Stock CS*	*Average Inventory* *OS + CS/2*	*Inventory Carrying Cost (ICC) per week Average Inventory × price × ICC/52*	*Procurement Cost per Order*
1.	25	22	23.5	940	-
2.	22	17	19.5	780	-
3.	17	13	15	600	400
4.	13	11	12	480	-
5.	11	5	8	320	-
6.	5	23	14	560	-
7.	23	20	21.5	860	-
8.	20	17	18.5	740	-
9.	17	16	16.5	660	-
10.	16	13	14.5	580	400
			Total	6520	800

Therefore, inventory carrying cost for 10 weeks = 6520

Procurement cost for 10 weeks = 800

Total cost for 10 weeks = 6520 + 800 = 7320

Average cost per week = 7320/10 = 732.

The opening stock is assumed and different set of random numbers is used, the average cost per week may be quite different. However, if the simulation is carried out for large number of random numbers, the results obtained may not be much different.

Example 7:

The manager of a warehouse is interested in designing an inventory control system for one of the products in stock. The demand for the product comes from numerous retail outlets and orders arrive on a weekly basis. The warehouse receives its stock from the factory but the lead time is not constant.

The manager wants to determine the best time to release orders io the factory so that stockouts are minimized, yet inventory holding costs are at acceptable levels. Any order from retailers not supplied on a given day constitute lost demand. Based on a sampling study, the following data are available.

Demand per Week (in thousand)	*Probability*	*Lead Time*	*Probability*
0	0.20	2	0.30
1	0.40	3	0.40
2	0.30	4	0.30
3	0.10		

The manager of the warehouse has determined the following cost parameters: Ordering cost (C_0) per order equals Rs. 50, carrying cost (C_h) equals Rs. 2 per thousand units per week, and shortage cost (C) equals Rs. 10 per thousand units.

The objective of inventory analysis is to determine the optimal size of an order and the best time to place an order. The following ordering policy has been suggested.

Policy : Whenever the inventory level becomes less than or equal to 2,000 units (reorder level), an order equal to the difference between current inventory balance and the specified maximum replenishment level is equal to 4,000 units is placed.

Simulate the policy for a week's period assuming that the (i) beginning inventory is 3,000 units, (ii) no back orders are permitted, (iii) each order is placed at the beginning of the week as soon as inventory level is less than or equal to the reorder level, and (iv) the replenishment orders are received at the beginning of the week.

Solution:

Using weekly demand and lead time distributions, assign an appropriate set of random numbers to represent value (range) of variables as shown in Tables 1 and 2, respectively.

The simulation experiment conducted for 10 weeks period . The simulation process begins with an inventory level of 3,000 units. The following four steps occur in the simulation process.

1. Begin each simulation week by checking whether any order has just arrived. If it has, increase the beginning (current) stock (inventory) by the quantity received.

2. Generate a weekly demand from the demand probability distribution by selection of a random number. This random number is recorded in column 4. The demand simulated is recorded in column 5.

Table 1 : Probabilities and Random Number Interval for Weekly Demand

Weekly Demand (in thousand)	*Probability*	*Cumulative Probability*	*Random Number Interval*
0	0.20	0.20	00-19
1	0.40	0.60	20-59
2	0.30	0.90	60-89
3	0.10	1.00	90-99

Table 2 : Probabilities and Random Number Interval for Lead Time

Lead Time (weeks)	*Probability*	*Cumulative Probability*	*Random Number Interval*
2	0.30	0.30	00-29
3	0.40	0.70	30-69
4	0.30	1.00	70-99

The random number 31 generates a demand of 1,000 units when it is subtracted from the initial inventory level value of 3,000 units, yields an ending inventory of 2,000 units at the end of the first week.

3. Compute the ending inventory every week and record it in column 7.

   Ending inventory = Beginning inventory – Demand.

   = 3,000 – 1,000 = 2,000.

   If on hand inventory is not sufficient to meet the week's demand, then record the number of units short in column 6.

4. Determine whether the week's ending inventory has reached the reorder level. If it has, and if there is no outstanding (back orders), then place an order.

   Since ending inventory of 2,000 units is equal to the reorder level, therefore, an order for 4,000 – 2,000 = 2,000 units is placed.

Example 8:

XYZ spare parts company wishes to determine the levels of stock it should carry for the items in its range. Demand is not certain and there is a lead time for stock replenishment. For one item X, the following information is obtained:

Demand (units/day)	:	*3*	*4*	*5*	*6*	*7*
Probability	:	*0.10*	*0.20*	*0.30*	*0.30*	*0.10*
Carrying cost (per unit/day)	:	*Rs. 2*				
Ordering cost (per order)	:	*Rs. 50*				
Lead time for replenishment	:	*3 days.*				

Stock on hand at the beginning of the simulation exercise was 20 units.

Carry out a simulation run over a period of 10 days with the objective of evaluating the inventory rule: Order 15 units when present inventory plus any outstanding order falls below 15 units.

The sequence of random numbers to be used is:

0, 9, 1, 1, 5, 1, 8, 6, 3, 5, 7, 1, 2, 9

using the first number for day one.

Solution:

Let us begin simulation by assuming that

(i) orders are placed at the end of the day and received after 3 days at the end of the day.

(ii) back orders are accumulated in case of short supply and are supplied when stock is available.

The cumulative probability distribution and the random number range for daily demand is shown in Table 1.

Table 1 : Daily Demand Distribution

Daily Demand	*Probability*	*Cumulative Probability*	*Random Number Range*
3	0.10	0.10	00
4	0.20	0.30	01-02
5	0.30	0.60	03-05
6	0.30	0.90	06-08
7	0.10	1.00	09

The results of the simulation experiment conducted are shown in Table 2.

Table 2 : Simulation Experiments

Days	*Opening Stock*	*Random Number*	*Resulting Demand*	*Closing Stock*	*Order Placed*	*Order Delivered*	*Average Stock in the Evening*
1	20	0	3	17	–	–	18.5
2	17	9	7	10	15	–	13.5
3	10	1	4	6	–	–	8
4	6	1	4	2	–	–	4
5	2	5	5	0 (–3)	15	15	1
6	12	1	4	8	–	–	10
7	8	8	6	2	–	–	6
8	2	6	6	0 (–4)	15	15	1
9	11	3	5	6	–	–	8.5
10	6	5	5'	1	–	–	3.5

Average ending stock = 78/10 = 7.8 units/day

Daily ordering cost = (Cost of placing one order) × (Number of orders placed per day)

= 50 × 3 = Rs. 150.

Daily carrying cost = (Cost of carrying one unit for one day) × (Average ending stock)

= 2 × 7.8 = Rs. 15.60.

Total daily inventory cost = Daily ordering cost + Daily carrying cost = 150 + 15.60 = Rs. 165.60.

Example 9:

A dentist schedules all his patients for 30-minute appointments. Some of the patients take more or less than 30 minutes depending on the type of dental work to be done. The following surpmary shows the various categories of work, their probabilities and time actually needed to complete the work:

Category of Service	*Time Required (minutes)*	*Probability of Category*
Filling	*45*	*0.40*
Crown	*60*	*0.15*
Cleaning	*15*	*0.15*
Extraction	*45*	*0.10*
Checkup	*15*	*0.20*

Simulate the dentist's clinic for four hours and determine the average waiting time for the patients as well as the idleness of the doctor. Assume that all the patients show up at the clinic at exactly their scheduled arrival time starting at 8.00 a.m. Use the following random numbers for handling the above problem:

40 82 11 34 25 66 17 79.

Solution:

The cumulative probability distribution and random number interval for service time are shown in Table 1.

Table 1

Category of Service	*Service Time Required (minutes)*	*Probability Probability*	*Cumulative Interval*	*Random Number*
Filling	45	0.40	0.40	00-39
Crown	60	0.15	0.55	40-54
Cleaning	15	0.15	0.70	55-69
Extraction	45	0.10	0.80	70-79
Checkup	15	0.20	1.00	80-99

The various parameters of a queuing system such as arrival pattern of customers, service time, waiting time in the context of the given problem are shown in Tables 2 to 3.

Table 2 : Arrival Pattern and Nature of Service

Patient Number	*Scheduled Arrival*	*Random Number*	*Category of Service*	*Service Time (minutes)*
1	8.00	40	Crown	60
2	8.30	82	Checkup	15
3	9.00	11	Filling	45
4	9.30	34	Filling	45
5	10.00	25	Filling	45
6	10.30	66	Cleaning	15
7	11.00	17	Filling	45
8	11.30	79	Extraction	45

Table 3 : Computation of Arrivals, Departures and Waiting of Patients

Time	*Event (Patient Number)*	*Patient Number (Time to Exit)*	*Waiting (Patient Number)*
8.00	1 arrive	1 (60)	–
8.30	2 arrive	1 (.30)	2
9.00	1 departs; 3 arrive	2(15)	3
9.15	2 depart	3(45)	—
9,30	4 arrive	3(30}	4
10.00	3 depart; 5 arrive	4(45)	5
10.30	6 arrive	4(15)	5, 6
10.45	4 depart	5 (45)	6
11.00	7 arrive	5 (30)	6,7
11.30	5 depart; 8 arrive	6(15)	7, 8
11.45	6 depart	7(45)	8
12.00	End	7(30)	8

The dentist was not idle during the entire simulated period. The waiting times for the patients were as follows:

Table 4 : Computation of Average Waiting Time

Patient	*Arrival Time*	*Service Starts at*	*Waiting Time (minutes)*
1	8.00	8.00	0
2	8.30	9.00	30
3	9.00	9.15	15
4	9.30	10.00	30
5	10.00	10.45	45
6	10.30	11.30	60
7	11.00	11.45	45
8	11.30	12.30	60
			280

The average waiting time = 280/8 = 35 minutes.

EXERCISES

1 An owner of a petrol pump with a single attendant wishes to perform a simulation of his operations to see whether any improvement is possible. He studied the system and found that an average of 6 customers arrive for service with random arrival times and form a queue, and the attendant provides service for exactly 9 minutes. For simulating the arrival times of customers, he has selected 10 random numbers with expected length of interval equal to one as:

3.62, 1.78, 1.84, 1.31, 1.27 0.14, 1.71, 0.77, 0.97, 1.32

Find:

(a) The total idle time for the attendant

(b) Total waiting time for the customers; and

(c) Maximum queue length during this period.

If the service time is reduced to 6 minutes what is the quality of the service?

2. Explain how simulation can be applied in the case of inventory control where the demand is probabilistic and lead time is random.

3. What types of problems can be solved more easily by quantitative techniques other than simulation?

4. State the considerations involved in trading-off costs with reliability in designing a simulation experiment.

5. Do you think the application of simulation will increase strongly in the next ten years? Why?

6. What types of problems can be solved more easily by quantitative techniques other than simulation?

7. Why would an analyst ever prefer a general purpose language such as FORTRAN or BASIC in a simulation when there are advantages of using special purpose languages such as GPSS or S1MSCRIPT?

8. "Simulation typically is nothing more or less than the technique of performing sampling experiments on the model of the system". Discuss.

9. Define simulation. Why is simulation used? Give one application area when this technique is used in practice.

10. '... simulation is a quantitative technique developed for studying alternative courses of action by building a model of that system and

then conducting a series of repeated trial and error experiments to predict the behaviour of the system over a period of time.' Discuss.

11. Why is a computer necessary in conducting a real-world simulation?
12. State two major reasons for using simulation. Explain the basic steps of Monte Carlo simulation. Briefly describe the application in Finance and Accounting.
13. Explain what factors must be considered when designing a simulation experiment.
14. Draw a flow chart to describe the simulation of a simple system.
15. Bharat Transport Company is considering discontinuing its leasing of 12 pickups and delivery trucks. If it does this, it will have to buy 12 trucks right away and then buy replacement trucks in the future, one by one, as the old ones wear out. The question that the Bharat Transport Company's manager wants to answer is how many trucks will they have to buy during the next five years (including the initial 12 trucks) in order to keep 12 trucks in operation all the time. At the moment, they are not concerned with the fact that at the end of five years they will have 12 trucks in hand, some of which will be relatively new and some of which will be old. The only question is how many will have to be purchased so they can plan their cash requirements accordingly. The following table shows a history of truck life:

Truck life (months) :	12	15	18	21	24	27	30
Percentage of trucks which have worn out :	5	10	20	25	30	5	5.

16. Distinguish between solutions derived from simulation models and solutions derived from analytical models?
17. What are random numbers? Why are random numbers useful in simulation models and solutions derived from analytical models?
18. 'Monte Carlo Technique has been used to tackle a variety of problems involving stochastic situations and mathematical problems which cannot be solved with mathematical techniques and where physical experimentation with the actual system is impracticable." Discuss.
19. "When it becomes difficult to use an optimization technique for solving a problem, one has to resort to simulation technique". Discuss.
20. XYZ Company operates an automatic car-wash facility in a city. The manager is concerned about the long lines of cars that build up waiting

for service. The service time for the system is machine paced and thus constant, and the manager has the opportunity to decrease the service time by increasing the speed of the conveyor that pulls the cars through the system. Of course, the quicker the pace, the lower is the quality of the car-wash. The manager wants to study the effects of setting the system for a 2-minute car-wash. The following data on customer arrivals have been gathered.

Inter-arrival time (minutes)	:	1	3	3	4	5
Number of occurrences	:	136	34	102	51	17

(a) Compare the traffic density for a service rate of 2 minutes per car.

(b) Simulate the arrival of 20 customers. The doors open at 8.00 a.m.

Compute the average waiting time per customer, the average time spent in the system, the percentage of time the system is ideal, and the maximum queue length.

21. (a) What are the advantages and limitations of simulation models?

    (b) What are the advantages and disadvantages of simulation over the use of analytical models? Is the use of computers in simulation absolutely essential?

22. What is Monte Carlo Simulation? Describe the idea of experimentation (Random sampling) in simulation.

23. The materials manager of a company is interested in determining the reorder point for an item, the pattern of demand for which is as given below:

No. of units per day	: 0	1	2	3	4	5
No. of days on which the demands occurred	: 5	9	16	38	23	9

Past experience indicates that there are fluctuations in the lead time for procurement of items. The following data are available from the records for the last 30 orders:

Lead time (weeks)	: 1	2	3
No. of times the specified lead time occurred	: 18	7	5

The management policy is to ensure that the proportion of stockouts should not exceed 5 per cent. Illustrate how the simulation approach can be used to determine the reorder point. (Analysis for 20 orders is adequate).

24. A company trading in motor vehicle spares wishes to determine the level of stock it should carry for the items in its range. Demand is not certain and there is a lead time for stock replenishment for one item X. The following information is obtained:

Demand (units/day) :	3	4	5	6	7
Probability :	0.10	0.20	0.30	0.30	0.10

Carrying cost (per unit per day) = 20 paise.

Ordering cost (per order) = Rs. 5

Lead time for replenishment = 3 days.

Stock in hand at the beginning of the simulation exercise was 20 units.

You are required to carry out a simulation run over a period often days with the-objective of evaluating the following inventory rule: Order 15 units'when present inventory plus any outstanding order falls below 15 units.

The sequence of random numbers used is: 0, 9, 1, 1, 5, 1, 8, 6, 3, 5, 7, 1, 2, 9, using the first number for day one.

Your calculation should include the total cost of operating this inventory rule for 10 days.

25. A company manufactures 200 motor cycles per day. Depending upon the availability of raw materials and other conditions, the daily production has been varying from 196 motor cycles to 204 motor cycles, whose probability distribution is as given below:

Production/day :	196	197	198	199	200	201	202	203	204
Probability :	0.05	0.09	0.12	0.14	0.20	0.15	0.11	0.08	0.06

The motor cycles are transported in a specially designed three-storeyed lorry that can accommodate only 200 motor cycles. Using the following random numbers: 82, 89, 78, 24, 52, 53, 61, 18, 45, 04, 23, 50, 77, 27, 54, 10, simulate the process to find out:

(a) The average number of motor cycles waiting in the factory?

(b) The average number of empty spaces on the lorry?

26. A confectioner sells confectionary items. Past data of demand per week (in hundred kilograms) with frequency is given below:

Demand/week	:	0	5	10	15	20	25
Frequency	:	2	11	8	21	5	3

Using the following sequence of random numbers, generate the demand for the next 10 weeks. Also find the average demand per week: 35, 52, 90, 13, 23, 73, 34, 57, 35, 83, 94, 56, 67, 66, 60.

27. Describe the kind of problems for which Monte Carlo will be an appropriate method of solution.

28. Explain what factors must be considered when designing a simulation experiment.

4

Basic Simplex Algorithm

INTRODUCTION

This chapter contains a rigorous discussion on the mathematical method called the *simplex method* developed by *G.B. Dantzig* in 1947 for solving LP problems. The simplex method is an *iterative procedure* and refers to the idea of moving from one extreme (comer) point to another of the solution space or feasible region (convex polyhedron) that is formed by the constraints and non-negativity conditions of the linear programming problem. Since the number of extreme points (corners or vertices) of a solution space is finite, the method leads to the optimal extreme point (optimal solution) in a finite number of steps or indicates that there exist an unbounded solution. It was observed in the graphical approach to the solution of L.P.P. that in a given situation the set of constraints determines the feasible region and objective function gives the optimal point, the one that minimizes or maximizes, as the case may be.

The graphical method suffers from a great limitation that it can handle problems involving only two decision variables. Whereas in real world situations, we frequently encounter such problems where more than two variables are involved. Fundamental theorem of linear programming makes it easy to find an optimal solution because it deals with basic feasible solutions only. But, it is also not easy job to enumerate all the B.F.S. even for small values of m (number of constraints) and n (number of variables). The simplex method is an iterative procedure, for finding, in a systematic manner the optimal solution to a linear programming problem.

SIMPLEX ALGORITHM NO TATIONS

Some notations and definitions which are extremely useful in the discussion of simplex algorithm.

Consider a linear programming problem which after introducing slack and surplus variables is as follows:

$$\text{Max. } Z = c_1 x_1 + c_2 x_2 + \dots + c_n x_n + 0x_{n+1} + 0x_{n+2} + \dots + 0x_{n+m}$$

$$\text{subject to } a_{11} x_1 + a_{12} x_2 + \dots + a_{1j} x_j + \dots + a_{1n} x_n + x_{n+1} = b_1$$

$$a_{21} x_1 + a_{22} x_2 + \dots + a_{2j} x_j + \dots + a_{2n} x_n + x_{n+2} = b_2$$

$$\dots \quad \dots \quad \dots \quad \dots \quad \dots \quad \dots \quad \dots$$

$$\dots \quad \dots \quad \dots \quad \dots \quad \dots \quad \dots \quad \dots$$

$$a_{m1} x_1 + a_{m2} x_2 + \dots + a_{mj} x_j + \dots + a_{mn} x_n + x_{n+m} = b_m,$$

$x_i \geq 0$ for all $i = 1, 2, \dots ,N$, where $N = n + m$

$b_1, b_2, \dots ,bm$ are all positive.

The above linear programming problem can be easily converted to matrix form

$$\text{Max. } Z = c\,x$$

subject to $A\,x = b$, $x \geq 0$

where $A = [a_{ij}]_{m \times N}$ is the coefficient matrix of order $m \times N$,

$x = [x_1, x_2, x_3, \dots ,x_n, \dots ,x_N]$,

$c = [c_1, c_2, \dots ,c_n, 0, 0, \dots ,0]_{1 \times N}$

and $b = [b_1, b_2, \dots ,b_m]$,

where x and b are column vectors of order $N \times 1$ and $m \times 1$ respectively.

For convenience, we shall represent column vectors by row vectors without using transpose symbol. There should be no confusion in understanding scalar multiplication of two vectors c and x.

If we denote the jth column of the matıix A by a_j, $j = 1, 2, \dots ,N$, we can write

$$A = [\alpha_1, \alpha_2, \dots ,\alpha_N].$$

Form a non-singular sub-matrix B of order $m \times m$ whose column vectors are m number of linearly independent columns selected from A. If we denote these columns by $\beta_1, \beta_2, \dots ,\beta_m$ then

$$B = [\beta_1, \beta_2, \dots ,\beta_m].$$

B is called the *basis matrix.*

Since the vectors $\beta_1, \beta_2, \dots \beta_m$ are linearly independent they form a basis for E^m.

Therefore each $\alpha_j \in A \subset E^m$ can be expressed as a linear combination of vectors of B. Thus we can write

$$\alpha_j = \beta_1 y_{1j} + \beta_2 y_{2j} + \dots + \beta_m y_{mj}$$

$$= (\beta_1, \beta_2, ..., \beta_m) \begin{bmatrix} y_{1j} \\ y_{2j} \\ \vdots \\ y_{mj} \end{bmatrix}$$

or $$\alpha_j = BY_j, \text{ where } Y_j = \begin{bmatrix} y_{1j} \\ y_{2j} \\ \vdots \\ y_{mj} \end{bmatrix}_{m \times 1},$$

$y_{1j}, y_{2j}, ... ,y_{mj}$ are the scalars required to express α_j in such a form.

Also $\alpha_j = BY \Rightarrow Y_j = B^{-1} a_j$.

The vector Yj will change if the columns of A forming B change.

Any basis matrix B will provide a *basic solution* to A x = b.

The variables corresponding to $\beta_1, \beta_2, ... ,\beta_m$ are denoted by $x_{B1}, x_{B2}, ... ,x_{Bm}$ respectively and are called *basis variables.*

We denote the column vector of these m basic variables by x_B

$\therefore$ $x_B = [x_{B1}, x_{B2}, ... ,x_{Bm}]$

and $x_B = B^{-1}$ b.

This is called the basic feasible solution (B.F.S.) of the L.P.P.

Since $x_{B1}, x_{B2}, ... ,x_{Bm}$ are the basic variables, the remaining n variables belonging to x are called non-basic variables.

We shall denote the coefficients of basic variables $x_{B1}, x_{B2}, ... ,x_{Bm}$ in the objective function Z by $c_{B1}, c_{B2}, ... ,c_{Bm}$.

Corresponding to any x_B, c_B will represent the row vector contain the constants $c_{B1}, c_{B2}, ... ,c_{Bm}$.

$\therefore$ $c_B = (c_{B1}, c_{B2}, ... ,c_{Bm})$.

Since for any basic feasible solution all non-basic variables are zero therefore the objective function Z becomes

$$Z = c_{B1} x_{B1} + c_{B2} x_{B2} + ... + c_{Bm} x_{Bm} + 0$$
$$= (c_{B1}, c_{B2}, ... ,c_{Bm}) (x_{B1}, x_{B2}, ... ,x_{Bm})$$
$$= c^B x_B.$$

Finally, we introduce a new variables Z_j , given by

$$Z_j = y_j c_{B1} + y_{2j} c_{B2} + ... + y_{mj} c_{Bm}$$
$$= (c_{B1}, c_{B2}, ... c_{Bm}) (y_{1j}, y_{2j}, ... ,y_{mj})$$

$= c_B\, y_j.$

Therefore exists Z_j for each α_j and it changes as the columns of A forming B change.

LINEAR PROGRAMMING FUNDAMENTAL THEOREM

Theorem:

If a linear programming problem

max $Z = c\,x$ *subject to* $A\,x = b,\ x \geq 0,$

where A is an $m \times N$, $(N = m + n)$ *matrix of coefficients given by* $A = (\alpha_1, \alpha_2, \ldots, \alpha_N)$ *has an optimal feasible solution then at least one basic feasible solution must be optimal.*

Proof:

Let $x^* = [x_1, x_2, \ldots, x_N]$

be an optimal feasible solution of the given linear programming problem and

$$Z^* = \sum_{i=1}^{N} c_i x_i$$

be the corresponding optimum value of the objective function.

Also suppose that k $(k \leq N)$ variables in x^* are non-zero and the remaining $N - k$ variables are zero. For the sake of convenience we can assume that the first k variables of x^* are non-zero.

Thus $x^* = (x_1, x_2, \ldots, x_k, 0, 0, \ldots, 0)$.

$$\therefore \qquad \sum_{i=1}^{k} x_i \alpha_i = b \qquad \ldots(1)$$

$$\text{and} \qquad Z^* = \sum_{i=1}^{k} c_i x_i. \qquad \ldots(2)$$

Now two possibilities may arise:

The vectors $\alpha_1, \alpha_2, \ldots, \alpha_k$ may be either linearly independent or dependent.

Case 1. If $\alpha_1, \alpha_2, \ldots, \alpha_k$ are linearly independent.

Any feasible solution for which the vectors a_i, $i = 1, \ldots, k$ associated with non-zero variables x_i, $i = 1, \ldots, k$ are L.I. is called a basic feasible solution. Thus x^* is a B.F.S. which is also optimal.

Hence the result of the theorem is true.

The solution x is degenerate if $k < m$ and non-degenerate if $k = m$.

Case 2. If $\alpha_1, \alpha_2, \ldots, \alpha_k$ are linearly dependent and $k > m$.

In this case we shall reduce the number of non-zero variables step by step by step until we obtain a B.F.S. from feasible solution.

Since $\alpha_1, \alpha_2, \ldots, \alpha_k$ are linearly dependent therefore there exist scalars $\lambda_1, \alpha_2, \ldots, \lambda_k$ such that

$$\lambda_1 \alpha_1 + \lambda_2 \alpha_2 + \ldots + \lambda_k \alpha_k = 0$$

or $$\sum_{i=1}^{k} \lambda_i \alpha_i = 0 \qquad \ldots(3)$$

and at least one $\lambda_i \neq 0$.

We can assume that at least one li is positive because if none is positive then we can multiply the equation (3) by –1 and get positive li.

Now, suppose $$v = \max_{1 \le i \le k} \left(\frac{\lambda_i}{x_i} \right). \qquad \ldots(4)$$

Obviously v is positive since $x_i \geq 0$, i = 1, 2, ..., k and at least one λ_i is positive.

Multiplying both sides of (3) by 1/v and subtracting from (1), we get

$$\sum_{i=1}^{k} \left(x_i - \frac{\lambda_i}{v} \right) \alpha_i = b. \qquad \ldots(5)$$

(5) gives

$$x' = \left[x_1 - \frac{\lambda_1}{v}, x_2 - \frac{\lambda_2}{v}, \ldots, x_k - \frac{\lambda_k}{v}, 0, 0, \ldots, 0 \right]$$

a new solution of the matrix equation A x = b.

Also from (4) for i = 1, 2, ... ,k, we have

$$\Rightarrow \qquad v \geq \frac{\lambda_i}{x_i} \text{ or } x_i \geq \frac{\lambda_i}{v}$$

$$\Rightarrow \qquad x_i - \frac{\lambda_i}{v} \geq 0.$$

Since all the components of x' are non-negative therefore x' is a feasible solution to the given L.P.P.

Also $v = \frac{\lambda_i}{x_i}$, for at least one i

i.e., $v - \frac{\lambda_i}{x_i} = 0$ therefore the new feasible solution x' cannot have more than k – 1 non-zero variables.

In this way we have derived a new feasible solution from the given optimal feasible solution which contains less number of non-zero variables. This solution is B.F.S. if the column vectors associated to non-zero variables in this new solution are L.I. If these associated vectors are not L.I., we shall repeat the whole reduction procedure as explained above. Continuing in this way for finite number of times we will derive a solution in which columns corresponding to positive variables are L.I. *i.e.,* we will obtain a B.F.S. of the system.

Now it remains to prove that x' is also an optimal solution.

Let Z' be the new value of the objective function corresponding to the new solution x'.

Then $$Z' = \sum_{i=1}^{k} c_i\left(x_i + \frac{\lambda_i}{v}\right) = \sum_{i=1}^{k} c_i x_i - \frac{1}{v}\sum_{i=1}^{1} c_i \lambda_i$$

$$\Rightarrow \quad Z' = Z^* - \frac{1}{v}\sum_{i=1}^{k} c_i \lambda_i \text{, from (2)} \qquad ...(6)$$

Now for optimality, we must have

$$Z' = Z^*$$

i.e., x' will be optimal solution only if

$$\sum_{i=1}^{k} c_i \lambda_i = 0. \qquad ...(7)$$

We shall prove this result by contradiction.

If possible let us assume that

$$\sum_{i=1}^{k} c_i \lambda_i \neq 0.$$

Then either $$\sum_{i=1}^{k} c_i \lambda_i < 0 \qquad ...(A)$$

$$\Rightarrow \quad \sum_{i=1}^{k} c_i \lambda_i > 0. \qquad ...(B)$$

In either of these two cases, we can find a real number r such that

$$r \sum_{i=1}^{k} c_i \lambda_i > 0$$ [in case (A) r will be negative and in case (B) r will be positive]

$$\Rightarrow \quad \sum_{i=1}^{k} c_i (r\lambda_i) > 0$$

$$\Rightarrow \quad \sum_{i=1}^{k} c_i (r\lambda_i) - \sum_{i=1}^{k} c_i x_i > \sum_{i=1}^{k} c_i x_i$$

$$\Rightarrow \qquad \sum_{i=1}^{k} c_i (x_i + r\lambda_i) > Z^*, \text{ from (2).} \qquad ...(8)$$

Multiplying equation (3) by r and adding to (1), we get

$$\sum_{i=1}^{k} x_i \alpha_i + \sum_{i=1}^{k} r\lambda_i \alpha_i = b$$

$$\Rightarrow \qquad \sum_{i=1}^{k} (x_i + r\lambda_i)\alpha_i = b.$$

Obviously $[x_1 + r\lambda_1, x_2 + r\lambda_2, ... ,x_k + r\lambda_k, 0, 0, ... ,0]$ is also a solution of the matrix equation $A\,x = b$ for all values of r.

Furthermore, we can choose r in infinitely many ways for which the above solution also satisfies the non-negative restrictions.

Let us choose r such that

$$x_i + r\lambda_i \geq 0, \; i = 1, ... ,k$$

or $\quad r\lambda_i \geq - x_i$

$$\therefore \qquad r \geq -\frac{x_i}{\lambda_i} \text{ if } \lambda_i > 0,$$

$$r \leq -\frac{x_i}{\lambda_i} \text{ if } \lambda_i < 0$$

and r is unrestricted if $\lambda_i = 0$.

Thus $x_i + r\lambda_i \geq 0$ for $i = 1, 2, ... ,k$ if we select r such that

$$\max_{\substack{i \\ (\lambda_i > 0)}} \left(-\frac{x_i}{\lambda_i}\right) \leq r \leq \min_{\substack{i \\ (\lambda_i < 0)}} \left(-\frac{x_i}{\lambda_i}\right) \qquad ...(9)$$

which means that interval given by (9) is non-empty.

Thus, r lies in the non-empty interval given in (9).

Consequently, an infinite number of solution given by

$$[x_1 + r\lambda_1, x_2 + r\lambda_2, ..., x_k + x_k + r\lambda_k, 0, 0, ..., 0]$$

satisfy the non-negative restrictions as well.

Now, returning to result (8) we king that $\sum_{i=1}^{k} c_i (c_i + r\lambda_i)$ yields the value of the objective function which is strictly greater than the greatest value (or optimal value) Z^* of objective function, which is impossible.

$\therefore$ we must have $\sum_{i=1}^{k} c_i \lambda_i = 0$

or $Z' = Z^*$.

Hence $x' = \left[x_i - \frac{\lambda_1}{v}, x_2 - \frac{\lambda_2}{v}, \ldots, x_k - \frac{\lambda_k}{v}, 0, 0, \ldots, 0 \right]$

is also an optimal solution.

This proves the theorem.

INCONSISTENCY AND REDUNDANCY IN CONSTRAINT EQUATIONS

Redundancy is constraint equations.

By redundancy in constraint equations we mean that the system has more than enough number of constraint equations, in other words it has more constraint equations than the number of variables.

This is the situation when

$$r(A) = r(A\,b) = k \leq n < m.$$

In this case there will be $(m - k)$ redundant equations.

The Inconsistency

As already defined, the set of constraints (linear equations) is said to be inconsistent if

$$r(A) \neq r(Ab).$$

Before solving a LP. problem by simplex method, we should have $r(A) = r(Ab)$ *i.e.*, the constraint aquariums (after introducing the slack and artificial variables) shows be consistent. Since in simplex method we always have

$$r(A) = r(A \times b) = m.$$

If the system $A\,x = b$ involves artificial variables, then we cannot say whether this system is consistent or there is any redundancy. Below we give the cases to decide about the consistency and redundancy in such systems.

Case I. If at least one artificial vector appears in the basis B at a positive level *i.e.*, the value of at least one artificial variables corresponding to artificial vector in B is non-zero and the optimality condition is satisfied (at any iteration), then there exists no feasible solution of the problem.

Case II. If the basis B contains no artificial vector and the optimality condition is satisfied (at any iteration) then the current solution is a B.F.S. of the problem.

Case III. If one or more artificial vector appears in the basis B at a zero level *i.e.*, the value of the artificial variables corresponding to artificial vectors in B are zero and the optimality condition is satisfied (at any iteration) then the system is consistent. Furthermore if $y_{ij} = 0 \ \forall \ j$ and $x_{Br} = 0$ and r corresponds to the row containing an artificial vector, then the rth constraint equation is redundant.

TO DETERMINE IMPROVED B.F.S. FROM A GIVEN B.F.S.

Theorem:

Let $x_B = B^{-1} b$ be a B.F.S. of a linear programming problem with $Z = c_B x_B$ as the value of the objective function. If for any column aj in A, but not in B, the condition $c_j - Z_j > 0$ or $Z_j - c_j < 0$ holds and if at least one $y_{ij} > 0$, $i = 1, 2, \ldots, m$, then it is possible to obtain a new B.F.S. by replacing one of the columns in B by α_j and if Z' is the new value of objective function then $Z' \geq Z$.

If the initial B.F.S. $x_B = B^{-1} b$ is non-degenerate then $Z' > Z$.

Proof:

Consider the L.P.P.

$$\text{Max. } Z = cx, \text{ s.t. } Ax = b, x \geq 0,$$

where $A = (\alpha_1, \alpha_2, \ldots, \alpha_N)$, $N = m + n$,

Basis matrix $B = (\beta_1, \beta_2, \ldots, \beta_m)$.

Let $x_B (x_{B1}, x_{B2}, \ldots, x_{Bm})$ be a B.F.S. of the given L.P.P.

Since the vectors $\beta_1, \beta_2, \ldots, \beta_m$ are in the basis of A, therefore we can express α_j as a linear combination of b's.

$$\therefore \quad \alpha_j = \sum_{i=1}^{m} y_{ij}\beta_i = y_{1j}\beta_1 + y_{2j}\beta_2 + \ldots + y_{mj}\beta_m. \qquad \ldots(1)$$

If $y_{rj} \neq 0$ then α_j can replace br in B and B is still a basis matrix.

Let $y_{rj} \neq 0$ then from (1), we have

$$\Rightarrow \quad \beta_r = \frac{1}{y_{rj}}\alpha_j - \frac{y_{1j}}{y_{rj}}\beta_1 - \ldots - \frac{y_{(r+1)j}}{y_{rj}}\beta_{r+1} - \ldots - \frac{y_{mj}}{y_{rj}}\beta_m$$

$$\Rightarrow \quad \beta_r = \frac{1}{y_{rj}}\alpha_j - \sum_{i=1}^{m}\frac{y_{ij}}{y_{rj}}\beta_i. \qquad \ldots(2)$$

Now, we have

$$\Rightarrow \quad Bx_B = b$$

$$\Rightarrow \quad (\beta_1, \beta_2, \ldots, \beta_r, \ldots, \beta_m)\,(x_{B1}, x_{B2}, \ldots, x_{Br}, \ldots, x_{Bm}) = b$$

$$\Rightarrow \quad \beta_1 x_{B1} + \beta_2 x_{B2} + \ldots + \beta_r x_{Br} + \ldots + \beta_m x_{Bm} = b$$

$$\Rightarrow \quad \sum_{i=1}^{m} \beta_i x_{Bi} + \beta_r x_{Br} = b \qquad \ldots(3)$$

Putting for br from (2) in (3), we get

$$\Rightarrow \quad \sum_{i=1}^{m} \beta_i \left[x_{Bi} - \frac{y_{ij}}{y_{rj}} x_{Br} \right] + \frac{x_{Br}}{y_{rj}} \alpha_j = b \qquad \ldots(4)$$

$$\Rightarrow \quad \sum_{i=1}^{m} x_{Bi}'\beta_i + x_{Br}'\alpha j = b, \qquad \ldots(5)$$

where $x_{Bi}' = x\!-\! - x_{Br} \dfrac{y_{ij}}{y_{rj}}$, $i = 1, 2, \ldots, m, i \neq r$

$$x_{Br}' = \frac{x_{Br}}{y_{rj}}, \; i = r$$

Comparing (3) and (5), we observe that new basic solution of A x = b is given by

$$x'_B = (x'_{Bi}, x'_{Br}), \; i = 1, 2, \ldots, m, \; i \neq r$$

where the values of x'_{Bi}, x'_{Br} are given by (6).

This basic solution will be feasible if we have

$$x_{Bi} - \frac{y_{ij}}{y_{rj}} x_{Br} \geq 0, \; i = 1, 2, \ldots m, \; i \neq r$$

and $\dfrac{x_{Br}}{y_{rj}} \geq 0$, $i = r$. ...(7)

Since x_B is the initial B.F.S. we have

$$x_{Br} \geq 0, \; r = 1, 2, \ldots, m.$$

Thus we observe that (7) will hold only if

$$y_{rj} > 0 \text{ and } y_{ij} \leq 0, \; i = 1, 2, \ldots, m, \; i \neq r.$$

If $y_{rj} > 0$ and $y_{ij} > 0$, then (7) is satisfied only if

$$\Rightarrow \quad \frac{x_{Bi}}{y_{ij}} - \frac{x_{Br}}{y_{rj}} \geq 0$$

$$\Rightarrow \quad \frac{x_{Br}}{y_{rj}} \leq \frac{x_{Bi}}{y_{ij}}$$

$$\Rightarrow \qquad \frac{x_{Br}}{y_{rj}} = \min_{i}\left\{\frac{x_{Bi}}{y_{ij}}, y_{ij} > 0\right\} = v. \qquad \text{...(8)}$$

Thus, a new B.F.S. can be obtained from the initial B.F.S. by removing the column vector br of the basis matrix B by a_j if r is to be selected such that

$$v = \frac{x_{Br}}{y_{rj}} = \min_{i}\left\{\frac{x_{Bi}}{y_{ij}}, y_{ij} < 0\right\}.$$

If we have v = 0, which is possible only when $x_{Br} = 0$ then it means that the initial B.F.S. is degenerate.

Now we shall prove $Z' \geq Z$.

The value of the objective function for the initial B.F.S. x_B is

$$Z = c_B x_B$$

$$= (c_{B1}, c_{B2}, \dots, c_{Bm})(x_{B1}, x_{B2}, \dots, x_{Bm}) = \sum_{i=1}^{m} c_{Bi} x_{Bi}$$

Corresponding to the new B.F.S. x'_B, the value of the objective function is Z', so we have

$$Z' = \sum_{i=1}^{m} c'_{Bi} x'_{Bi}, \qquad \text{...(9)}$$

where c_{Bi}' are the coefficients of the basic variables x_{Bi}' (i = 1, 2, ... ,m) in the objective function.

Obviously, $c_{Bi}' = c_{Bi}$, i = 1, 2, ... , m, $i \neq r$

and $c_{Br}' = c_j$.

$\therefore$ we can write

$$Z' = \sum_{i=1}^{m} c_{Bi} x'_{Bi} + c_j x'_{Br}. \qquad \text{...(10)}$$

Substituting for x_{Bi}', x_{Br}' from (6) in (10), we get

$$Z' = \sum_{i=1}^{m} c_{Bi}\left(x_{Bi} - x_{Br}\frac{y_{ij}}{y_{rj}}\right) + c_j \frac{x_{Br}}{y_{rj}}$$

$$= \sum_{i=1}^{m} c_{Bi}\left(x_{Bi} - x_{Br}\frac{y_{ij}}{y_{rj}}\right) + c_j \frac{x_{Br}}{y_{rj}}$$

Since the term $c_{Bi}\left(x_{Bi} - x_{Br}\frac{y_{ij}}{y_{rj}}\right) = 0$ when i = r therefore it can be included in the summation without changing the value of Z'.

$$\therefore \quad Z' = \sum_{i=1}^{m} c_{Bi} x_{Bi} - \frac{x_{Br}}{y_{rj}} \sum_{i=1}^{m} c_{Bi} y_{ij} + \frac{x_{Br}}{y_{rj}} c_j$$

$$= Z + \frac{x_{Br}}{y_{rj}} (c_j - Z_j), \text{ where } Z_j = \sum_{i=1}^{m} c_{Bi} y_{ij}$$

$$= Z + v\,(c_j - Z_j), \text{ from (8).} \qquad \text{...(11)}$$

From (11), we observe that the new value of the objective function is equal to the original value of the objective function plus the quantity $v\,(c_j - Z_j)$.

We have $Z' \geq Z$ if $v\,(c_j - Z_j) \geq 0$.

Since $v \geq 0$ therefore $Z' \geq Z$ only if $c_j - Z_j \geq 0$.

Hence by choosing the vector α_j for which $c_j - Z_j > 0$ and at least one $y_{ij} > 0$, we obtain a new improved value of the objective function.

If the initial B.F.S. is non-degenerate then $v > 0$ and in that case $Z' > Z$.

CONDITIONS FOR THE EXISTENCE OF UNBOUNDED SOLUTIONS

Now, we have proved that if for any column aj in A but not in B the condition $c_j - Z_j > 0$ holds and if at least one $y_{ij} > 0$, $i = 1, 2, \ldots, m$ then it is possible to find an improved B.F.S. Now the question arises : what will be the implication if for at least one a_j all $y_{ij} \leq 0$, $i = 1, 2, \ldots, m$.

To get the answer of this question we shall prove the following theorem.

Theorem:

If for any basic feasible solution $x_B = B^{-1} b$ to $A x = b$ there is some column α_j in A but not in B for which $c_j - Z_j > 0$ and $y_{ij} \leq 0$, $i = 1, 2, \ldots, m$ then if the objective function is to be maximized, the problem has an unbounded solution.

Proof:

Consider the linear programming problem

Max. $Z = c\,x$ s.t. $A\,x = b$, $x \geq 0$,

where $A = (\alpha_1, \alpha_2, \ldots \alpha_N)$. $N = m + n$,

basis matrix $B = (\beta_1, \beta_2, \ldots, \beta_m)$.

Let $x_B = (x_{B1}, x_{B2}, \ldots, x_{Bm})$ be a B.F.S. of the given L.P.P. Then we have

$$Bx_B = b \text{ or } \sum_{i=1}^{m} x_{Bi} \beta_i = b \qquad \text{...(1)}$$

and the corresponding value of the objective function is

$$Z = c_B x_B = \sum_{i=1}^{m} c_{Bi} x_{Bi} \quad ...(2)$$

Adding and subtracting $\lambda\alpha_j$ in (1), we get

$$\sum_{i=1}^{m} x_{Bi}\beta_i - \lambda\alpha_j + \lambda\alpha_j = b, \quad ...(3)$$

where l is some scalar.

Let $\alpha_j \in A$ s.t. $\alpha_j \notin B$.

Since the vectors $\beta_1, \beta_2, ..., \beta_m$ are in the basis of A therefore we can express α_j as the linear combination of b's

$$\therefore \quad \alpha j = \sum_{i=1}^{m} y_{ij}\beta_i$$

$$\Rightarrow \quad -la_j = -l \sum_{i=1}^{m} y_{ij}\beta_i .$$

Substituting the above value of $-\lambda\alpha_j$ in (3), we get

$$\Rightarrow \quad \sum_{i=1}^{m} x_{Bi}\beta_i - \lambda \sum_{i=1}^{m} y_{ij}\beta_i + \lambda\alpha_j = b$$

$$\Rightarrow \quad \sum_{i=1}^{m} (x_{Bi} - \lambda y_{ij})\beta_i + \lambda\alpha_j = b$$

Thus we obtain a new solution

$$x'_B = (x_{B1}', x_{B2}', ... ,x_{Bm}', \lambda) \quad ...(4)$$

where $x_{Bi}' = x_{Bi} - \lambda y_{ij}$, $i = 1, 2, ..., m$.

When $\lambda > 0$, $x_{Bi} - \lambda y_{ij} \geq 0$ since $y_{ij} \leq 0$, $i = 1, 2, ... ,m$ therefore (4) gives the feasible solution in which the number of positive variables is less than or equal to $(m + 1)$. It may be less than $(m + 1)$ because some $x_{Bi} - \lambda y_{ij}$ may be zero for some i. In case the number of positive variables in this solution is equal to $(m + 1)$ then this solution will be non-basic feasible solution.

If Z' is the new value of the objective function corresponding to this new solution, then we have

$$\Rightarrow \quad Z' = \sum_{i=1}^{m} c_{Bi}(x_{Bi} - \lambda y_{ij}) + c_j\lambda$$

$$\Rightarrow \quad Z' = \sum_{i=1}^{m} c_{Bi}x_{Bi} + \lambda(c_j - c_{Bi}y_{ij}) = Z + \lambda\,(c_j - Z_j).$$

Since $c_j - Z_j > 0$ (given) therefore Z' can be made as large as we please by giving sufficiently large values to l. We know that a L.P.P. has an unbounded solution if the value of its objective function can be increased or decreased arbitrarily.

Hence the given L.P.P. has an unbounded solution.

ARTIFICIAL VARIABLES TECHNIQUE

(a) **Big-M Method :** Sometimes in linear programming problems constraints may also have ≥ and = signs after ensuring that all bi ≥ 0. In such problems we first introduce *surplus variables* to convert inequalities into equations. In such cases basis matrix is not obtained as an identity matrix in the starting simplex table. To overcome this difficulty we introduce new variables, called, the *artificial variables* to each of such constraints. These variables are fictitious and cannot have any physical meaning.

The artificial variables are introduced for the limited purpose of obtaining an *initial solution.* It is not relevant whether the objective function is of the maximization or minimization type. Since artificial variables do not represent any quantity relating to the decision problem they must be driven out of the system and must not be present in the final solution. Keeping this in mind a method known as *big-M method or Cranes M-method* was developed. It we suggestedby A. Cranes that a very high penalty can be paid for introducing the artificial variables in the constraints of a given problem by assigning an extremely high negative cost (penalty) to them.

∴ the objective function can be written as

$$Z = c\,x + 0.x_{slack} + 0.x_{surplus} - M.x_{art}.$$

It is significant to note that the initial solution obtained using the artificial variables is not a feasible solution to the given problem. It only gives the starting point and the artificial variables are driven out in he normal course of applying simplex method to the problem.

Note: A solution to the problem which does not contain an artificial variables in the basic, represents a feasible solution to the problem.

BASIC FEASIBLE SOLUTION TO BECOME OPTIMAL

Theorem:

Let us $x_B = B^{-1} b$ be the basic (degenerate or non-degenerate) feasible solution of the L.P.P. $Z = c\,x$ s.t. $A\,x = b$, $x \geq 0$. Let $Z^* = c_B\, x_B$ be the value of the objective function at any iteration of simplex method. If $c_j - Z_j \leq 0$

for every column α_j in A but not in B then Z* is the optimum value of the objective function Z and x_B is an optimal basic feasible solution.

Proof:

Suppose $x_B = (x_{B1}, x_{B2}, \dots, x_{Bm})$ is the B.F.S. of the given L.P.P. We have,

$A = (\alpha_1, \alpha_2, \dots, \alpha_N)$, $N = m + n$

and the basis matrix $B = (\beta_1, \beta_2, \dots, \beta_m)$.

$\therefore \quad B_{mB} = b$ or $x_B = B^{-1} b$. ...(1)

The value of the objective function for the B.F.S. xB is

$$Z^* = c_B\, x_B = \sum_{i=1}^{m} c_{Bi} x_{Bi}\,. \quad ...(2)$$

Also, we are given that $c_j - Z_j \le 0$ for every column α_j in A but not in B.

Let 'x' = $[x_1', x_2', \dots, x_N']$ be any feasible solution and Z' be the value of the objective function for this solution.

Then we have $A\,x' = b$ ...(3)

and $$Z' = c\,x' = \sum_{j=1}^{N} c_j x_j' \quad ...(4)$$

Now Z* will be the optimum value of the objective function if we have $Z^* \ge Z'$. To prove $Z^* \ge Z'$ we proceed in the following manner.

We have $x_B = B^{-1} b = B^{-1} (A\,x')$, from (3)

$= (B^{-1} A)\, x'$

$= Y\,x'$, where $Y = [Y_1, Y_2, \dots, Y_N]$

$= [Y_1, Y_2, \dots, Y_N]\,[x_1', x_2', \dots, x_N']$

$$= \begin{bmatrix} y_{11} & y_{12} & \cdots & y_{1j} & \cdots & y_{1N} \\ y_{21} & y_{22} & \cdots & y_{2j} & \cdots & y_{2N} \\ \cdots & \cdots & \cdots & \cdots & \cdots & \cdots \\ \cdots & \cdots & \cdots & \cdots & \cdots & \cdots \\ y_{m1} & y_{m2} & \cdots & y_{mj} & \cdots & y_{mN} \end{bmatrix} \begin{Bmatrix} x_1' \\ x_2' \\ \vdots \\ x_j' \\ \vdots \\ x_N' \end{Bmatrix}$$

$$\Rightarrow \quad [x_{B1}, x_{B2}, \dots, x_{Bi}, \dots, x_{Bm}]$$

$$= \left[\sum_{j=1}^{N} y_{1j} x_j', \sum_{j=1}^{N} y_{2j} x_j', \dots, \sum_{j=1}^{N} y_{ij} x_j', \dots, \sum_{j=1}^{N} y_{mj} x_j' \right]$$

Equating ith component on both sides, we get,

$$x_{Bi} = \sum_{j=1}^{N} y_{ij} x_j' . \qquad ...(5)$$

We have $c_j - Z_j \le 0$ for all j for which α_j is not in B.

If this inequality also holds for all those j for which α_j is in B then $c_j - Z_j \le 0$ for all j for which α_j also belong to B.

Now if $\alpha_j = B_i$, then

$$\alpha_j = \beta_i = 0.\beta_1 + 0.\beta_2 + ... + 0.\beta_{i-1} + 1.\beta_i + ... + 0.\beta_m$$

which shows that $Y_j = e_i$, a vector whose ith component is unity.

Again $\alpha_j = \beta_i$ gives $c_j = c_{Bi}$

$$\therefore \quad c_j - Z_j = c_j - c_B Y_j = c_j - c_B e_i = c_j - c_{Bi} = 0$$

Thus $c_j - Z_j = 0$ for all those j for which $\alpha_j \in B$.

$$\therefore \quad c_j - Z_j \le 0 \text{ for all } \alpha_j \text{ in A}$$

$$\Rightarrow \quad c_j \le Z_j$$

$$\Rightarrow \quad c_j x_j' \le Z_j x_j', \because x_j' \ge 0$$

$$\Rightarrow \quad \sum_{i=1}^{N} c_j x_j' \le \sum_{j=1}^{N} Z_j x_j'$$

$$\Rightarrow \quad Z' \le \sum_{j=1}^{N} x_j'(c_B Y_j), \text{ from (4)}$$

$$= \sum_{j=1}^{N} x_j' \left(\sum_{i=1}^{m} c_{Bi} y_{ij} \right)$$

$$= \sum_{i=1}^{m} c_{Bi} \left(\sum_{j=1}^{N} x_j' y_{ij} \right)$$

$$= \sum_{i=1}^{m} c_{Bi} x_{Bi}, \text{ from (5)} \qquad \therefore$$

$$Z' \le Z^*.$$

Hence Z^* is the optimum value of the objective function.

THE ALTERNATIVE OPTIMAL SOLUTIONS

The given linear programming problem is said to possess an alternative optimal solution if the set of variables giving the optimal value of the objective function is not unique.

Theorem:

(Conditions for Alternative Optimum Solution)

Suppose there exists an optimum B.F.S. to a L.P.P. and

(i) if for some a_j in A but not in B, $c_j - Z_j = 0$ and y_{ij} £ 0 for all $i = 1, 2, ..., m$ then a non-basic alternative solution will exist.

(ii) if for some a_j in A but not in B, $c_j - Z_j = 0$ and $y_{ij} > 0$ for all least one i then an alternative basic optimum solution will exist.

Proof:

(i) We have discussed in 6 that if we introduce the column vector a_j in B where a_j is in A but not in B and $y_{ij} \leq 0$ for all $i = 1, 2, ..., m$ then a non-basic feasible solution x_B' with $(m + 1)$ number of positive variables is given by

$$\Rightarrow \qquad x_B' = [x_{B1}', x_{B2}', ..., x_{Bm}', l]$$

where
$$x_{Bi}' = x_{Bi} - \lambda y_{ij}, \ i = 1, 2, ..., m, \ l > 0$$

and the value of the objective function for this new F.S. is given by

$$Z' = Z + l\,(c_j - Z_j).$$

If
$$c_j - Z_j = 0, \text{ then } Z' = Z$$

i.e., the value of the objective function for this new non-basic F.S. is also equal to Z (optimal value). Hence this new non-basic F.S. is an alternative optimal solution of the given L.P.P.

(ii) We have shown in theorem of 5 that if $y_{ij} > 0$ for at least one $i = 1, 2, ..., m$ then by palpation one column br in B by the column aj which is in A but not in B, we obtain a new B.F.S. x_B' given by

$$x_B' = [x_{B1}', x_{B2}', ..., x_{Bm}']$$

$$\text{where } x_{Bi}' = x_{Bi} - \frac{y_{ij}}{y_{rj}} x_{Br}, \ i = 1, 2, ..., m, \ i \geq r$$

$$x_{Br}' = \frac{x_{Br}}{y_{rj}}, \ i = r$$

$$\text{and } \frac{x_{Br}}{y_{rj}} = \underset{i}{\text{Mini}} \left(\frac{x_{Bi}}{y_{ij}}, y_{ij} > 0 \right).$$

The value of objective function for this new B.F.S. is given by

$$Z' = Z + \frac{x_{Br}}{y_{rj}} (c_j - Z_j)$$

i.e., the value of the objective function for this new B.F.S. is also equal to Z' (optimal value).

Hence this new B.F.S. is an alternative optimal F.F.S.

TO DETERMINE STARTING B.F.S.

In this article we are going to discuss a method for finding a most convenient initial B.F.S. to a linear programming problem .

In the constraints of a general linear programming problem three may be any of the three signs $\leq = \geq$. Let us assume that the requirement vector $b \geq 0$ (if any of the b_i's is negative, multiply the corresponding constraint by -1.)

Case I. To find initial B.F.S. when at the original constraints have $\leq$ sign. To convert all the constraints into equations we insert slack variables only .the equations obtained are as follows.

$$a_{11}x_1 + a_{12}x_2 + \ldots + a_{1n}x_n + 1.x_{n+1} = b_1$$

$$a_{21}x_1 + a_{22}x_2 + \ldots + a_{2n}x_n + 1.x_{n+2} = b_2$$

$$\ldots \quad \ldots \quad \ldots \quad \ldots \quad \ldots \quad \ldots$$

$$\ldots \quad \ldots \quad \ldots \quad \ldots \quad \ldots \quad \ldots$$

$$a_{m1}x_1 + a_{m2}x_2 + \ldots + a_{mn}x_n + \ldots + 1.x_{n+m} = b_m$$

Here $\quad x_{n+1}, x- = 2, \ldots, x_{n+m}$ are slack variables.

In matrix from these equations can be written as

$$\begin{bmatrix} a_{11} & a_{12} & \ldots & a_{1n} & 1 & 0 & \ldots & 0 \\ a_{21} & a_{22} & \ldots & a_{2n} & 0 & 1 & \ldots & 0 \\ \ldots & \ldots & \ldots & \ldots & \ldots & & \ldots & \\ \ldots & \ldots & \ldots & \ldots & \ldots & & \ldots & \\ a_{m1} & a_{m2} & \ldots & a_{mn} & 0 & 0 & \ldots & 1 \end{bmatrix} \begin{bmatrix} x_1 \\ x_2 \\ \vdots \\ x_n \\ x_{n+1} \\ \vdots \\ x_{n+m} \end{bmatrix} = \begin{bmatrix} b_1 \\ b_2 \\ \vdots \\ b_m \end{bmatrix}$$

Taking the initial basis matrix

$$B = I_m, \text{ (unit matrix of order } m \times m).$$

$\therefore$ the initial basic solution is given by $x_B = B^{-1}b = I_m b = b \geq 0$

Thus the initial B.F.S. is

$$x_{n+1} = x_{B1} = b_1, x_{n+2} = x_{B2} = b_2, \ldots, x_{n+m} = x_{Bm} = b_m,$$

which can be obtained by writing all the non-basic variables (*i.e.,* given variables) $x_1, x_2, \ldots x_n$ equal to zero and solving the equations for the remaining variables (*i.e.,* slack variables) $x_{n+1}, x_{n+2}, \ldots, x_{n+m}$.

Case II. To find initial B.F.S. when all the original constraints have $\geq$ sign. First we convert all the constraints into equations by inserting surplus variables. The equations obtained are as follows:

$$a_{11}x_1 + a_{12}x_2 + \dots + a_{1n}x_n - x_{n+1} = b_1$$
$$a_{21}x_1 + a_{22}x_2 + \dots + a_{2n}x_n - x_{n+2} = b_2$$
$$\dots \quad \dots \quad \dots \quad \dots \quad \dots \quad \dots$$
$$\dots \quad \dots \quad \dots \quad \dots \quad \dots \quad \dots$$
$$a_{m1}x_1 + a_{m2}x_2 + \dots + a_{mn}x_n - x_{n+m} = b_m$$

Here $x_{n+1}, x_{n+2}, \dots, x_{n+m}$ are surplus variables.

In matrix form, these equations can be writing as

$$\begin{bmatrix} a_{11} & a_{12} & \dots & a_{1n} & -1 & 0 & \dots & 0 \\ a_{21} & a_{22} & \dots & a_{2n} & 0 & -1 & \dots & 0 \\ \dots & \dots & & & \dots & \dots & & \dots \\ \dots & \dots & & & \dots & \dots & & \dots \\ a_{m1} & a_{m2} & 0 & 0 & \dots & & \dots & -1 \end{bmatrix} \begin{bmatrix} x_1 \\ x_2 \\ \vdots \\ x_n \\ x_{n+1} \\ \vdots \\ x_{n+m} \end{bmatrix} = \begin{bmatrix} b_1 \\ b_2 \\ \vdots \\ b_m \end{bmatrix}$$

If we take the initial basis matrix $B = -I_m$,

we have $x_B = B^{-1}b = = -I_m$,

$b = -b \le 0$, which is not a B.F.S.

To avoid this difficulty we add one more variable to each constraint. These variables are called *"Artificial Variables"*.

Adding surplus and artificial variables, the constraints of the given L.P.P. change to the following equations.

$$a_{11}x_1 + a_{12}x_2 + \dots + a_{1n}x_n - x_{n+1} + x_{n+m+1} = b_1$$
$$a_{21}x_1 + a_{22}x_2 + \dots + a_{2n}x_n - x_{n+2} + x_{n+m+2} = b_2$$
$$\dots \quad \dots \quad \dots \quad \dots \quad \dots \quad \dots \quad \dots$$
$$\dots \quad \dots \quad \dots \quad \dots \quad \dots \quad \dots \quad \dots$$
$$a_{m1}x_1 + a_{m2}x_2 + \dots + a_{mn}x_n - x_{n+m} + m_{n+m+m} = b_m$$

Here $x_{n+m+1}, x_{n+m+2}, \dots, x_{n+m+m}$ are the artificial variables.

In matrix, these equations can be written as

$$\begin{bmatrix} A_{11} & a_{12} & \dots & a_{1n} & -1 & 0 & \dots & 0 & 1 & 0 & \dots & 0 \\ a_{21} & a_{22} & \dots & a_{2n} & 0 & -1 & \dots & 0 & 0 & 1 & \dots & 0 \\ \dots & \dots & \dots & \dots & \dots & \dots & \dots & \dots & \dots & \dots & \dots & \dots \\ \dots & \dots & \dots & \dots & \dots & \dots & \dots & \dots & \dots & \dots & \dots & \dots \\ a_{m1} & a_{m2} & \dots & a_{mn} & 0 & 0 & \dots & -1 & 0 & 0 & \dots & 1 \end{bmatrix}$$

$$\begin{bmatrix} x_1 \\ x_2 \\ \vdots \\ x_n \\ x_{n+1} \\ \vdots \\ x_{n+m} \\ x_{n+m+1} \\ \vdots \\ x_{n+m+m} \end{bmatrix} = \begin{bmatrix} b_1 \\ b_2 \\ \vdots \\ b_m \end{bmatrix}$$

Now taking the basis matrix $B = I_m$.

$$\therefore \qquad x_B = B^{-1}\, b = I_m\, b = b \geq 0,$$

which is a basic feasible solution.

$\therefore$ the B.F.S. is $x_{n+m+1} = x_{B1} = b_1$, $x_{n+m+2} = x_{B2} = b_2$, ... ,$x_{n+m+m} = x_{Bm} = b_m$, which can be obtained by writing all the non basic variables (*i.e.,* given variables and surplus variables) $x_1, x_2, \ldots, x_n; x_{n+1}, x_{n+2}, \ldots, x_{n+m}$ equal to zero and solving the equations for the remaining basic variables (*i.e.,* artificial variables) $x_{n+m+1}, x_{n+m+2}, \ldots, x_{n+m+m}$.

Case III. To find initial B.F.S. when the constraints have '≤', '≥' and '=' signs. In this case we convert the constraint into equations by inserting slack, surplus and artificial variables. Here the basis matrix $B = I_m$ is obtained by introducing unit column vectors corresponding to the slack and artificial variables. To obtain the initial B.F.S. we put the non-basic variables equal to zero and solve for remaining basic variables. Here also the initial B.F.S. $x_B = b \geq 0$.

COMPUTATIONAL PROCEDURE OF THE SIMPLEX METHOD

Step 1. Find the initial B.F.S. follow the method discussed in 10 to find the initial B.F.S. If artificial variables are introduced in the L.P.P. then follow the two-method for Big M-method for solving such prob lems.

Step 2. Construct the initial simplex table (starting simplex table).

It should be remembered that the values of non-basic variables are always zero at each iteration

Step 3. Test the initial B.F.S. for optimality.

Compute the net evaluation Δ_j for each variables x_j by using the formula $\Delta_j = c_j - c_B\, Y_j$.

Step 4. If the given problem is of minimization, convert it into the maximization problem.

For this, multiply both sides of the objective function by –1 and put $-Z = Z'$.

If v is the maximum value of Z' then –v will be the minimum value of Z.

Step 5. Make all the b_i's non-negative.

The R.H.S. of each of the constraints should be non-negative. If the L.P.P. has a constraint for which a negative b_i is given, it should be converted into positive value by multiplying both sides of the constraint by –1.

Step 6. Convert inequalities of constraints into equations.

For this introduce slack or surplus variables. The coefficients of slack or surplus variables in the objective function are zero. Introduce artificial variables, if necessary.

OPTIMAL TEST

(a) If $\Delta_j \leq 0$ for all j, the solution under consideration is optimal.

Alternative optimal solution will exist if any non-basic Δ_j is also zero.

(b) If $\Delta_j > 0$ for any j *i.e.*, if at least one Δ_j is positive the solution under test is not optimal, we must proceed to improve the solution (step 7).

(c) If corresponding to maximum positive D_j, all elements of the column Y_j are negative or zero, the solution under test will be unbounded.

(d) If optimality condition is satisfied but the value of at least one artificial variables present in the basis is non-zero, the problem will have no feasible solution.

Step 1. *Select the entering (incoming) vector and departing (outgoing) vector.*

To improve the initial B.F.S. we select the vector entering the basis matrix and the vector to be removed from the basis matrix.

Incoming Vector. The incoming vector α_k is always selected corresponding to the largest positive value of Δ_j.

If maximum value of Δ_j occurs for more than one α_j then we can select any of these vectors as incoming vector.

Outgoing Vector. The departing vector β_r is selected corresponding to that value of r for which

$$\frac{x_{Br}}{y_{rk}} = \min_{i} \left\{ \frac{x_{Bi}}{y_{ik}}, y_{ik} > 0 \right\},$$

is α_r is the incoming vector.

Step 2. If α_k is the entering vector and β_r is the outgoing vector then the element yrk which lies at the intersection of minimum ration arrow (←) and incoming vector arrow ↑ is called the pivot element (key element).

We put this element in □.

In order to bring b_r in place of incoming vector Y_k, unity must occupy the place □. In other words key element y_{rk} should be 1. If it is not so then divide all the elements of this row by the key element y_{rk}. Then subtract suitable multiples of the row containing the key element from all other rows and obtain zero at all other positions of this column Y_k. Now bring br in place of α_r and construct the revised simplex table.

Thus, we get improve basic feasible solution.

Step 3. Test the improved B.F.S. for optimality.

If it is not optimum, repeat steps 7 and 8 until we obtain an optimums solution.

Note: If the above mentioned minimum value is not unique then more than one variable will vanish in the next solution. As a result the next solution will be a degenerate B.F.S. for which the outgoing vector is selected in a different way.

COMPUTE THE INVERSE OF A MATRIX WHOSE ONE COLUMN IS DIFFERENT FORM OF A MATRIX WHOSE INVERSE IS KNOWN

$B = (\beta_1, \beta_2, \ldots, \beta_n)$ is the given non-singular matrix whose inverse is known.

Consider a matrix $B_\alpha = (\beta_1, \beta_2, \ldots, \beta_{r-1}, \alpha, \beta_{r+1}, \ldots, \beta_n)$.

We have obtained the matrix Ba by replacing the rth column of matrix B by the column vector a.

If we have $\alpha = \sum_{i=1}^{n} y_i \beta_i$,

Ba will be non-singular iff $y_r \neq 0$.

Using components of the vector $Y = B^{-1}\alpha$, we introduce a new matrix E where E is a square matrix of order n which differs from identity matrix In the rth column only. To obtain the rth column of matrix E we proceed in the following manner:

We have $\alpha = y_1\beta_1 + y_2\beta_2 + \ldots + y_r\beta_r + \ldots + y_m\beta_m$.

Transposing yr br to the left and a to the right, we get

Phase I.

Step 1. To convert each of the constraints into equations, subtract a surplus variable and add an artificial variables.

Step 2. Assign zero coefficients to each of the primary variables and surplus variables and the coefficient (–1) to each of the artificial variables in the objective function. As a result the objective function changes to Z = – (sum of the artificial variables)

Step 3. Solve the problem formed in step 2 by applying the simplex method. If the original problem has a feasible solution then this problem shall have an optimal solution with optimal value of the objective function equal to zero as each of the artificial variables will be equal to zero.

If max $Z < 0$ and at least one artificial variables appears in the optimum basis at a positive level then the given problem does not possess any feasible solution.

If max $Z = 0$ and at least one artificial variable appears in the optimum basis at zero level, we proceed to phase II.

If max $Z = 0$ and no artificial variable appears in the optimum basis then we proceed to phase II.

Phase II.

In phase II start with the (optimal) solution contained in the final simplex table of the phase I. Assign the actual costs to the variables in the objective function and a zero cost to every surplus variable.

Eliminate the artificial which are non-basic at the and of the phase-I. Remove c_j row values of the optimum table and replace them by c_j values of the original problem. Now, apply simplex algorithm to the problem contained in the new table to obtain the optimal solution.

Disadvantages of Big-M Method Over Two Phase Method

(i) We can always use Big-M method to check the existence of a feasible solution but its computational procedure may be inconvenient because of the manipulation of the constant M.

Two phase method eliminates the artificial variables in the beginning.

(ii) When we solve a problem on a digital computer we have to assign some numerical value to M which must be larger than the values c_1, c_2, ... present in the objective function. But a computer has only a fixed number of digits.

SOLVED EXAMPLES

Example 1:

Max. $Z = 6x_1 - 2x_2$

subject to

$2x_1 - x_2 \le 2$

$x_1 \le 4$

$x_1, x_2 \ge 0.$

Solution:

The given problem is of maximization and all b_i's are positive.

To convert inequalities of constraints into equations introducing slack variables x_3 and x_4, given problem becomes

Max. $Z = 6x_1 - 2x_2 + 0x_3 + 0x_4$

subject to

$2x_1 - x_2 + x_3 = 2$

$x_1 + x_4 = 4.$

The starting B.F.S. is

$x_1 = 0, x_2 = 0,$

$x_3 = 2, x_4 = 4.$

The solution to the problem using simplex method is given below:

B	c_B	c_j / x_B	6 / Y_1	–2 / Y_2	0 / Y_3	0 / Y_4	Min. ratio x_B/Y_1
Y_3	0	2	(2)	–1	1	0	1 ←
Y_4	0	4	1	0	0	1	4
$Z=c_B$	$x_B=0$	Δ_j	6 ↑	–2	0 ↓	0	x_B/Y_2
Y_1	6	1	1	–1/2	1/2	0	Neg.
Y_4	0	3	0	(1/2)	–1/2	1	6 ←
Z=6	Δ_j	0	1 ↑	–3	0 ↓		
Y_1	6	4	1	0	0	1	
Y_2	–2	6	0	1	–1	2	
Z=12	Δ_j	0	0	–2	–2		

Since all Δ_j's are negative or zero therefore the solution obtained is optimal.

The optimal solution is

$x_1 = 4, x_2 = 6$ and

max $Z = 12$.

From the first simplex table we observe that the elements of column of Y_2 are either negative or zero which indicates that the feasible region is not bounded.

Hence a linear programming problem having unbounded feasible solution may have a bounded optimal solution.

Example 2:

If $x_1 = 1, x_2 = 0, x_3 = 1$ be a feasible solution of the L.P.P.

$$\text{Min. } Z = 2x_1 + 3x_2 + 4x_3$$

subject to $x_1 + x_2 + x_3 = 2$

$$x_1 - x_2 + x_3 = 0,\ x_1, x_2, x_3 \geq 0$$

then show that the given feasible solution is not basic.

Solution:

The given system of constraint equations can be written in matrix form $A\,x = b$

$$\Rightarrow \quad \begin{bmatrix} 1 & 1 & 1 \\ 1 & -1 & 1 \end{bmatrix} \begin{bmatrix} x_1 \\ x_2 \\ x_3 \end{bmatrix} = \begin{bmatrix} 2 \\ 0 \end{bmatrix}.$$

$$\therefore \quad \alpha_1 = \begin{bmatrix} 1 \\ 1 \end{bmatrix},\ \alpha_2 = \begin{bmatrix} 1 \\ -1 \end{bmatrix},\ \alpha_3 = \begin{bmatrix} 1 \\ 1 \end{bmatrix},\ b = \begin{bmatrix} 2 \\ 0 \end{bmatrix}.$$

The given feasible solution $x_1 = 1, x_2 = 0, x_3 = 1$ will not be basic if the vectors associated to non-zero variables are not linearly independent *i.e.*, if α_1 and α_3 are linearly dependent.

If we choose $\lambda_1 = -1$ and $\lambda_2 = 1$, we have

$$\lambda_1 \alpha_1 + \lambda_2 \alpha_2 = -1 \begin{bmatrix} 1 \\ 1 \end{bmatrix} + 1 \begin{bmatrix} 1 \\ 1 \end{bmatrix} = \begin{bmatrix} -1+1 \\ -1+1 \end{bmatrix} = \begin{bmatrix} 0 \\ 0 \end{bmatrix} = 0.$$

$\therefore$ the vectors α_1 and α_3 are linearly dependent.

Hence, the given feasible solution is not basic.

Example 3:

Maximize $Z = 2x_1 + 5x_2 + 7x_3$

subject to

$$3x_1 + 2x_2 + 4x_3 \le 100$$
$$x_1 + 4x_2 + 2x_3 \le 100$$
$$x_1 + x_2 + 3x_3 \le 100,$$
$$x_1, x_2, x_3 \ge 0.$$

Solution:

The given problem is of maximization and all b_i's are positive.

Introducing slack variables x_4, x_5, x_6 to convert constraint inequalities into equations, the given problem becomes

$$Z = 2x_1 + 5x_2 + 7x_3 + 0x_4 + 0x_5 + 0x_6$$

subject to $3x_1 + 2x_2 + 4x_3 + x_4 = 100$

$x_1 + 4x_2 + 2x_3 - x_5 = 100$, $x_1 + x_2 + 3x_3 + x_6 = 100$

		c_j	2	5	7	0	0	0	Min. ratio
B	c_B	x_B	Y_1	Y_2	Y_3	Y_4	Y_5	Y_6	x_B/Y_3
Y_4	0	100	3	2	(4)	1	0	0	25 ←
Y_5	0	100	1	4	2	0	1	0	50
Y_6	0	100	1	1	3	0	0	1	100/3
$Z=c_B$	$x_B=0$	Δ_j	2	5	7	0	0	0	
					↑	↓			
Y_3	0	25	3/4	1/2	1	1/4	0	0	50
Y_5	0	50	1/2	(3)	0	–1/2	1	0	50/3 ←
Y_6	0	25	–5/4	–1/2	0	–3/4	0	1	Neg.
$Z=c_B$	$x_B=175$	Δ_j	–13/4	3/2	0	–7/4	0	0	
				↑			↓		
Y_5	7	50/3	5/6	0	1	1/3	–1/6	0	
Y_2	5	50/3	–1/6	1	0	–1/6	1/3	0	
Y_6	0	100/3	–4/3	0	0	–5/6	1/6	1	
$Z=c_Bx_B$ = 200		Δ_j	–3	0	0	–3/2	–1/2	0	

The starting B.F.S. is

$$x_1 = 0,\ x_2 = 0,\ x_3 = 0,\ x_4 = 100,\ x_5 = 100,\ x_6 = 100.$$

The solution to the problem using simplex method is given below:

In the last all Δ_j's are zero or negative therefore the solution is optimal.

Hence the optimal solution is

$$x_1 = 0,\ x_2 = 50/3,\ x_3 = 50/3 \text{ and Max. } Z = 200.$$

Example 4:

Maximize $Z = 2x_1 + 4x_2$

subject to $2x_1 + x_2 \le 18$

$$3x_1 + 2x_2 \ge 30$$

$$x_1 + 2x_2 = 26;\ x_1,\ x_2 \ge 0.$$

Solution:

The problem is of maximization and all b_i's are positive.

Introducing the necessary slack, surplus and artificial variables, the problem reduces to the following form:

$$\text{Max. } Z = 2x_1 + 4x_2 + 0x_3 - 0x_4 - MA_1 + MA_2$$

subject to $2x_1 + x_2 + x_3 = 18$

$$3x_1 + 2x_2 + 0x_3 - x_4 + A_1 = 30$$

$$x_1 + 2x_2 + 0x_3 + 0x_4 + A_2 = 26$$

The starting B.F.S. is

$$x_1 = 0,\ x_2 = 0,\ x_3 = 18,\ x_4 = 0,$$

$$A_1 = 30,\ A_2 = 26.$$

The solution to the problem using simplex algorithm is given below:

First Simplex Table

B	c_B	c_j / x_B	2 / Y_1	4 / Y_2	0 / Y_3	0 / Y_4	–M / A_1	–M / A_2	Min. ratio x_B/Y_2
Y_3	0	18	2	1	1	0	0	0	18
A_1	–M	30	3	2	0	–1	1	0	15
A_2	–M	26	1	(2)	0	0	0	1	13 ←
$Z = c_B x_B = -56M$		Δ_j	2+4M	4+4M ↑	0	–M	0	0 ↓	

Computing Δ_j using the formula $\Delta_j = c_j - c_B Y_j$, we get

$$\Delta_1 = c_1 - c_B Y_1 = 2 - (0, -M, -M)(2, 3, 1) = 2 + 4M$$
$$\Delta_2 = c_2 - c_B Y_2 = 4 - (0, -M, -M)(1, 2, 2) = 4 + 4M$$
$$\Delta_4 = c_4 - c_B Y_4 = 0 - (0, -M, -M)(0, -1, 0) = -M.$$

Y_2 is the entering vector. Using min. ratio rule we find that 2 is the pivot element which indicates that A_2 is the outgoing vector.

Second Simplex Table

		c_j	2	4	0	0	–M	–M	Min. ratio
B	c_B	x_B	Y_1	Y_2	Y_3	Y_4	A_1	A_2	x_B/Y_1
Y_3	0	5	3/2	0	1	0	0	–1/2	10/3
A_1	–M	4	(2)	0	0	–1	0	–1	2 ←
Y_2	4	13	1/2	1	0	0	0	1/2	26
Z = 52 – 4M		Δ_j	2M ↑	0	0	–M	0 ↓	–2 – 2M	

Y_1 is the incoming vector and A_1 is the outgoing vector.

Third Simplex Table

		c_j	2	4	0	0	–M	–M
B	c_B	x_B	Y_1	Y_2	Y_3	Y_4	A_1	A_2
Y_3	0	2	0	0	1	3/4	–3/4	1/4
Y_1	2	2	1	0	0	–1/2	1/2	–1/2
Y_2	4	12	0	1	0	1/4	–1/4	3/4
Z=52	Δ_j	0	0	0	0	–M	–M	

Since all Δ_j are negative or zero therefore the solution obtained is optimal.

$\therefore$ the optimal solution is

$x_1 = 2$, $x_2 = 12$, $x_3 = 2$ and other variables = 0.

The objective function Z = 52.

Example 5:

Minimize $Z = x_1 + x_2 + x_3$

subject to

$$x_1 - 3x_2 + 4x_3 = 5$$
$$x_1 - 2x_2 \leq 3$$

$2x_2 - x_3 \geq 4,$

$x_1, x_2 \geq 0$ *and* x_3 *is unrestricted.*

Solution:

First we shall convert the minimization problem into maximization by substituting Z' = – Z.

The objective function changes to

Max. $Z' = -x_1 - x_1 - x_3$.

Since x_3 is unrestricted therefore replacing it by

$$x_3' - x_3'' \text{ where } x_3', x_3'' \geq 0.$$

Also introducing slack variables x_4, surplus variables x_5 and artificial variables A_1 and A_2, the given problem becomes

$$\text{Max } Z' = -x_1 - x_2 - x_3' + x_3'' + 0x_4 + 0x_4 + 0x_5 - MA_1 - MA_2$$

s.t. $x_1 - 3x_2 + 4x_3' - 4x_3'' + A_1 = 5$

$x_1 - 2x_2 + x_4 = 3$

$0x_1 + 2x_2 - x_3' + x_3'' - x_5 + A_2 = 4,$

$x_1, x_2, x_3', x_3'', x_4, x_5, A_1, A_2 \geq 0.$

Now solve the problem using simplex algorithm.

The optimal solution is

$\Rightarrow \quad x_1 = 0, x_2 = 21/5,$

$\Rightarrow \quad x_3 = 22/5$

and Min. Z = 43/5.

Example 6:

Maximize $Z = 40x_1 + 35x_2$

subject to $2x_1 + 3x_2 \leq 60$

$4x_1 + 2x_2 \leq 96,$

$x_1, x_2 \geq 0.$

For the clear understanding of the simplex method the solution to this problem is illustrated below in a step-wise manner.

Solution:

Step 1. The given problem is of maximization and all the b_i's are already positive.

Step 2. Converting the inequalities of constraints into equations by introducing slack variables x_3 and x_4, we get

$2x_1 + 3x_2 + x_3 = 60$ and $4x_1 + 3x_2 + x_4 = 96$.

The coefficients of slack variables are zero in the objective function. Therefore the given problem becomes

$$\text{Maximize } Z = 40x_1 + 35x_2 + 0x_3 + 0x_4$$

$$\text{subject to } 2x_1 + 3x_2 + x_3 + 0x_4 = 60$$

$$4x_1 + 3x_2 + 0x_3 + x_4 = 96$$

$$x_1, x_2, x_3, x_4 \geq 0.$$

This is the standardized form of the given problem.

Step 3. The simplex method begins with an initial basic feasible solution in which the values of basic variables are zero.

$\therefore$ $x_1 = 0$, $x_2 =$ which gives $x_3 = 60$, $x_4 = 96$.

Step 4. Constructing the initial simplex table.

First Simplex Table

		c_j	40	35	0	0	Min. ratio
B	c_B	x_B	Y_1	Y_2	Y_3	Y_4	x_B/Y_1
Y_3	0	60	2	3	1	0	60/2 = 30
Y_4	0	96	(4)	3	0	1	96/4 = 24 ←
$Z = c_B\ x_B = 0$		Δ_j	40 ↑	35	0	0 ↓	

Step 5. Computing Δ_j for all non-basic variables x_j, $j = 1, 2$, using the formula $\Delta_j = c_j - c_B Y_j$

$\Delta_1 = c_1 - c_B Y_1 = 40 - (0, 0)(2, 4) = 40$

$\Delta_2 = c_2 - c_B Y_2 = 35 - (0, 0)(3, 3) = 35.$

Since all Δ_j's are not less than or equal to zero, therefore the solution is not optimal. So we proceed to next step to improve the solution.

Step 6. Incoming and outgoing vectors.

Since $\Delta_1 = 40$ is the maximum value of Δ_j, $j = 1, 2$, therefore $\alpha_1 = Y_1$ is the incoming vector.

$$\text{Now } \frac{x_B}{Y_1} = \left(\frac{x_{B1}}{y_{11}}, \frac{x_{B2}}{y_{21}}\right) = \left(\frac{60}{2}, \frac{96}{4}\right) = (30, 24).$$

$$\frac{x_{Br}}{y_{r1}} = \min_i \left[\frac{x_{Bi}}{y_{i1}}, y_{i1} > 0\right] = \min_i \left(\frac{x_{B1}}{y_{11}}, \frac{x_{B2}}{y_{21}}\right) = 24$$

$$= \frac{x_{B2}}{y_{21}}$$

$\therefore$ r = 2 which gives $\beta_2 = Y_4$ as the outgoing vector.

$\therefore$ $y_{21} = \alpha_{21}$ is the key element which is equal to 4.

To bring Y_1 in place of Y_4 we proceed in the following manner.

Dividing the second row containing the key element $\alpha_{21} = 4$ by 4 to make if unity.

Now, we shall subtract appropriate multiples of this new row form the other remaining row so as to obtain zeros in the remaining positions of Y_1.

Subtitling 2 times of the second row from the first row and subtract 40 times of the second row from the row containing Δ_j's to obtain new values of Δ_j's.

Constructing the second simplex table in which β_2 is replaced by α_1.

Second Simplex Table

		c_j	10	35	0	0	Min ratio
B	c_B	x_B	Y_1	Y_2	Y_3	Y_4	x_B/Y_2
Y_3	0	12	0	(3/2)	1	–1/2	8 ←
Y_1	40	24	1	3/4	0	1/4	32
$Z = c_B\ x_B = 960$		Δ_j	0	5 ↑	0 ↓	–10	

Also computing Δ_j by using the formula $\Delta = c_j - c_B Y_1$ for x_2, x_4, we get

$$\Delta_2 = c_2 - c_B Y_2 = 35 - (0, 40)\left(\frac{3}{2}, \frac{3}{4}\right) = 5$$

$$\Delta_4 = c_4 - c_B Y_4 = 0 - (0, 40)\left(-\frac{1}{2}, \frac{1}{4}\right) = -10.$$

Δ_1 and Δ_3 are zero as they correspond to unit column vectors.

Since all Δ_j's are not less than or equal to zero therefore the solution obtained is not optimal.

$\Delta_2 = 5$ is the maximum value of Δ_j.

$\therefore$ $\alpha_2 = Y_2$ is the incoming vector.

$$\text{Now } \frac{x_{Br}}{y_{r2}} = \min_{i}\left[\frac{x_{Bi}}{y_{i2}}, y_{i2} > 0\right]$$

$$= \min\left[\frac{x_{B1}}{y_{12}}, \frac{x_{B2}}{y_{22}}\right] = \min\,[8, 32] = 8 = Y_3.$$

$$\alpha_{12} = y_{12} = \frac{3}{2} \text{ is the key element.}$$

To bring Y_2 in place of Y_3 we proceed in he following manner. Dividing the first row by 3/2 to make the key element unity. Subtracting 3/4 times of the first row from the second row and subtracting 5 times of the list row form the two containing Δ_j's to obtain new values of Δ_j's. Constructing the third simplex table in which Y_3 is replaced by Y_2.

Third Simplex Table

B	c_B	c_j / x_B	40 / Y_1	35 / Y_2	0 / Y_3	0 / Y_4	Min. ratio
Y_2	35	8	0	1	2/3	–1/3	
Y_1	40	18	1	0	–1/2	1/2	
$Z=c_B$	x_B=1000	Δ_j	0	0	–10/3	–25/3	

Since all the Δ_j's are less than or equal to zero therefore the above solution is optimal.

Hence the optimal solution is

B	c_B	c_j / x_B	40 / Y_1	35 / Y_2	0 / Y_3	0 / Y_4	Min. ratio / x_B/Y_1
Y_3	0	60	2	3	1	0	60/2 = 30
Y_4	0	96	(40)	3	0	1	96/4 = 24
$Z=c_B$	x_B=0	Δ_j	40 ↑	35	0	0 ↓	x_B/y_2
Y_3	0	12	0	(3/2)	1	–1/2	8
Y_1	40	24	1	3/4	0	1/4	32
$Z=c_B$	x_B=960	Δ_j	0	5 ↑	0 ↓	–10	
Y_2	35	8	1	1	2/3	–1/3	
Y_1	40	18	1	0	–1/2	1/2	
$Z=c_B$	x_B=1000	Δ_j	0	0	–10/3	–25/3	

$$x_1 = 18,\ x_2 \Rightarrow 8 \text{ and max. } Z = 1000.$$

The above solution with its different computational steps can be more conveniently represented by a single table as shown below:

Example 7:

Max. $Z = x_1 + 2x_2 + 3x_3 - x_4$

subject to $x_1 + 2x_2 + 3x_3 = 15,\ 2x_1 + x_2 + 5x_3 = 20$

$x_1 + 2x_2 + x_3 + x_4 = 10,\ x_1, x_2, x_3, x_4 \geq 0.$

Solution:

The given problem is of maximization and all b_i's are positive. Also the constraints are equations.

		c_j	1	2	3	–1	–M	–M	Min. ratio
B	c_B	x_B	Y_1	Y_2	Y_3	Y_4	A_1	A_2	x_B/Y^3
A^1	–M	15	1	2	3	0	1	0	5
A_2	–M	20	2	1	(5)	0	0	1	4 (Mini) ←
Y^4	–1	10	1	2	1	1	0	0	10
$Z=c_B$ = –35M – 10	x_B	Δ_j	3M+2	3M+4	8M+4 ↓	0	0	0 ↓	x_B/Y_2
A_1	–M	3	–1/5	(7/5)	0	0	1		15/7 (Mini) ←
Y_3	3	–4	2/5	1/5	1	0	0		20
Y_4	–1	6	3/5	9/5	0	1	0		10/3
$Z=c_B$ = –3M+6	x_B	Δ_j	$\frac{(-M+2)}{5}$	$\frac{7M+16}{5}$ ↑	0	0	0 ↓		x_B/Y_1
Y_2	2	15/7	–1/7	1	0	0			Neg.
Y_3	3	25/7	3/7	0	1	0			25/3
Y_4	–1	15/7	(6/7)	0	0	1			5/2 (Mini) ←
$Z=c_B$ = 90/7	x_B	Δ_j	6/7 ↑	0	0	0 ↓			
Y_2	2	5/2	0	1	0	1/6			
Y_3	3	5/2	0	0	1	–1/2			
Y_1	1	5/2	1	0	0	7/6			
$Z=c_B$ = 15	x_B	Δ_j	0	0	0	–1			

Examining the constraints we observe that in order to obtain a unit matrix of order 3 we need two more unit vectors as one unit vector is formed by the coefficients of x_4.

Therefore, introducing two artificial variables A_1 and A_2 in the first two constraints and assigning large negative penalty –M to the artificial variables, the given problem becomes

$$\text{Max. } Z = x_1 + 2x_2 + 3x_3 - x_4 - MA_1 - MA_2$$

subject to $x_1 + 2x_2 + 3x_3 + A_1 = 15$

$$2x_1 + x_2 + 5x_3 + A_2 = 20,\ x_1 + 2x_2 + x_3 + x_4 = 10.$$

The starting basic feasible solution is

$$x_1 = 0,\ x_2 = 0,\ A_1 = 15,\ A_2 = 20,\ x_4 = 10.$$

The solution to the problem using simplex method is given below:

Since all Δ_j's are negative or zero therefore the solution is optimal.

Hence the optimal solution is

$$x_1 = 5/2 = x_2 = x_3,\ x_4 = 0 \text{ and Max. } Z = 15.$$

Example 8:

If $x_1 = 2, x_2 = 3, x_3 = 1$ be a feasible solution of the linear programming problem

$$\textit{Max.}\quad Z = x_1 + 2x_2 + 4x_3$$

s.t. $2x_1 + x_2 + 4x_3 = 11$

$$3x_1 + x_2 + 5x_3 = 14$$

$$x_1, x_2, x_3 \geq 0.$$

then find a basic feasible solution from the given feasible solution.

Solution:

The given L.P.P. can be expressed as

$$\text{Max. } Z = x_1 + 2x_2 + 4x_3,$$

s.t. A x = b

$$\Rightarrow \quad \begin{bmatrix} 2 & 1 & 4 \\ 3 & 1 & 5 \end{bmatrix} \begin{bmatrix} x_1 \\ x_2 \\ x_3 \end{bmatrix} = \begin{bmatrix} 11 \\ 14 \end{bmatrix}$$

$$\Rightarrow \quad \alpha_1 x_1 + \alpha_2 x_2 + \alpha 3\ x_3 = b, \qquad \text{...(1)}$$

where $\alpha_1 = \begin{bmatrix} 2 \\ 3 \end{bmatrix},\ \alpha_2 = \begin{bmatrix} 1 \\ 1 \end{bmatrix},\ \alpha_3 = \begin{bmatrix} 4 \\ 5 \end{bmatrix},\ b = \begin{bmatrix} 11 \\ 14 \end{bmatrix}.$

Since x1 = 2, $x_2 = 3$, $x_3 = 1$ is a feasible solution to the given L.P.P. therefore from (1)

$$2\alpha_1 + 3\alpha_2 + \alpha_3 = b.$$

Now the vectors $\alpha_1, \alpha_2, \alpha_3$ associated with non-zero variables x_1, x_2, x_3 will be linearly dependent if one of these vectors can be expressed as the linear combination of the remaining two vectors.

Let $\lambda_1 \alpha_1 + \lambda_2 \alpha_2 = \alpha_3$ ...(2)

$$\Rightarrow \quad \lambda_1 \begin{bmatrix} 2 \\ 3 \end{bmatrix} + \lambda_2 \begin{bmatrix} 1 \\ 1 \end{bmatrix} = \begin{bmatrix} 4 \\ 5 \end{bmatrix}$$

$$\Rightarrow \quad \begin{bmatrix} 2\lambda_1 + \lambda_2 \\ 3\lambda_1 + \lambda_2 \end{bmatrix} = \begin{bmatrix} 4 \\ 5 \end{bmatrix}$$

$$\Rightarrow \quad 2\lambda_1 + \lambda_2 = 4, \; 3\lambda_1 + \lambda_2 = 5.$$

Solving these, we get

$$\lambda_1 = 1, \lambda_2 = 2.$$

Substituting the values of λ_1 and λ_2 in (2), we get

$$\alpha_1 + 2\alpha_2 = \alpha_3$$

$$\Rightarrow \quad \alpha_1 + 2\alpha_2 - \alpha_3 = 0$$

or $$\sum_{i=1}^{3} \lambda_i \alpha_i = 0$$

which gives $\lambda_1 = 1$,

$$\lambda_2 = 2, \lambda_3 = -1.$$

Now, we shall determine which of the three variables x_1, x_2, x_3 should be zero.

Using $v = \underset{1 \le i \le 3}{\max} \left(\frac{\lambda_i}{x_i} \right)$,

$$\Rightarrow \quad v = \max \left(\frac{\lambda_i}{x_1}, \frac{\lambda_2}{x_2}, \frac{\lambda_3}{x_3} \right),$$

$$\Rightarrow \quad v = \max \left(\frac{1}{2}, \frac{2}{3}, -\frac{1}{1} \right) = \frac{2}{3} = \frac{\lambda_2}{x_2}.$$

Since $x_i - \frac{\lambda_i}{v} \ge 0$, therefore

$$\left(x_i - \frac{\lambda_1}{v}, x_2 - \frac{\lambda_2}{v}, x_3 - \frac{\lambda_3}{v} \right)$$

is the reduced feasible solution. We have

$$x_1 - \frac{\lambda_1}{v} = 2 - \frac{1}{2} = \frac{1}{2},$$

$$x_2 - \frac{\lambda_2}{v} = 0,$$

$$\Rightarrow \qquad x_3 - \frac{\lambda_3}{v} = \frac{5}{2}.$$

$\therefore$ The new feasible solution is $x_1 = \frac{1}{2}$,

$$x_3 = 0, x_3 = \frac{5}{2}.$$

Now $\alpha_1 = \begin{bmatrix} 2 \\ 3 \end{bmatrix}$, and $\alpha_3 = \begin{bmatrix} 4 \\ 5 \end{bmatrix}$ are the vectors associated to non-zero variables x_1 and x_3.

Since α_1 and α_3 are linearly independent vectors therefore the new feasible solution

$$x_1 = \frac{1}{2}, x_2 = 0, x_3 = \frac{5}{2}$$

is the basic feasible solution.

Note: In order to find another basic feasible solution we proceed as follows:

Since $\alpha_1, \alpha_2, \alpha_3$ are L.D. therefore one of them can be expressed as the linear combination of the other two.

Let $\lambda_2 \alpha_2 + \lambda_3 \alpha_3 = \alpha_1$. ...(3)

Now proceed as in Example 9.

We have $\lambda_1 = -1, \lambda_2 = -2$,

$$\lambda_3 = 1, v = \frac{1}{1} = \frac{\lambda_3}{x_3}.$$

B.F.S. is $x_1 = 3, x_2 = 5, x_3 = 0$.

Example 9:

Consider the set of equations

$$5x_1 - 4x_2 + 3x_3 + x_4 = 3$$

$$2x_1 + x_2 + 5x_3 - 3x_4 = 0$$

$$x_1 + 6x_2 - 4x_3 + 2x_4 = 15,$$

$x_1, x_2, x_3, x_4 \geq 0.$

If $x_1 = 1, x_2 = 2, x_3 = 1, x_4 = 3$ *is a feasible solution then find a basic feasible solution.*

Solution:

The given set of equations can be expressed in the matrix form

$$A\,x = b$$

$$\Rightarrow \begin{bmatrix} 5 & -4 & 3 & 1 \\ 2 & 1 & 5 & -3 \\ 1 & 6 & -4 & 2 \end{bmatrix} \begin{bmatrix} x_1 \\ x_2 \\ x_3 \\ x_4 \end{bmatrix} = \begin{bmatrix} 3 \\ 0 \\ 15 \end{bmatrix}$$

$$\Rightarrow \alpha_1 x_1 + \alpha_2 x_2 + \alpha_3 x_3 + \alpha_4 x_4 = b \qquad ...(1)$$

$$\text{where } \alpha_1 = \begin{bmatrix} 5 \\ 2 \\ 1 \end{bmatrix}, \alpha_2 = \begin{bmatrix} -4 \\ 1 \\ 6 \end{bmatrix}, \alpha_3 = \begin{bmatrix} -3 \\ 5 \\ -4 \end{bmatrix}, \alpha_4 = \begin{bmatrix} 1 \\ -3 \\ 2 \end{bmatrix}, b = \begin{bmatrix} 3 \\ 0 \\ 15 \end{bmatrix}.$$

Since $x_1 = 1, x_2 = 2, x_3 = 1, x_4 = 3$ is a feasible solution to the given set of equations, therefore from (1)

$$\alpha_1 + 2\alpha_2 + \alpha_3 + 3\alpha_4 = b. \qquad ...(2)$$

Now the vectors $\alpha_1, \alpha_2, \alpha_3, \alpha_4$ associated with non-zero variables x_1, x_2, x_3, x_4 will be linearly dependent if one of these vectors can be expressed as the linear combination of the remaining three vectors.

$$\text{Let } \lambda_2 \alpha_2 + \lambda_3 \alpha_3 + \lambda_4 \alpha_4 = \alpha_1 \qquad ...(3)$$

$$\Rightarrow \lambda_2 \begin{bmatrix} -4 \\ 1 \\ 6 \end{bmatrix} + \lambda_3 \begin{bmatrix} 3 \\ 5 \\ -4 \end{bmatrix} + \lambda_4 \begin{bmatrix} 1 \\ -3 \\ 2 \end{bmatrix} = \begin{bmatrix} 5 \\ 2 \\ 1 \end{bmatrix}$$

$$\Rightarrow \begin{bmatrix} -4\lambda_2 + 3\lambda_3 + \lambda_4 \\ \lambda_2 + 5\lambda_3 - 3\lambda_4 \\ 6\lambda_2 - 4\lambda_3 + 2\lambda_4 \end{bmatrix} = \begin{bmatrix} 5 \\ 2 \\ 1 \end{bmatrix}$$

$$\Rightarrow -4\lambda_2 + 3\lambda_3 + \lambda_4 = 5$$

$$\lambda_2 + 5\lambda_3 - 3\lambda_4 = 2$$

$$6\lambda_2 - 4\lambda_3 + 2\lambda_4 = 1.$$

Solving these, we get

$$\lambda_2 = \frac{22}{43}, \lambda_3 = \frac{139}{86}, \lambda_4 = \frac{189}{86}.$$

Substituting these values in (3), we get

$$\frac{22}{43}\alpha_2 + \frac{139}{86}\alpha_3 + \frac{189}{86}\alpha_4 = \alpha_1$$

$$\Rightarrow \quad 86\alpha_1 - 44\alpha_2 - 139\alpha_3 - 189\alpha_4 = 0 \qquad \text{...(4)}$$

$$\Rightarrow \quad \sum_{i=1}^{4} \lambda_i \alpha_i = 0, \text{ which gives}$$

$$\lambda_1 = 86,\ \lambda_2 = -44,\ \lambda_3 = -139,\ \lambda_4 = -189.$$

Using $v = \max\limits_{1 \le i \le 4} \left(\frac{\lambda_i}{x_i}\right)$, we have

$$v = \max\left(\frac{\lambda_1}{x_1}, \frac{\lambda_2}{x_2}, \frac{\lambda_3}{x_3}, \frac{\lambda_4}{x_4}\right)$$

$$= \max\left(\frac{86}{1}, -\frac{44}{2}, -\frac{139}{1}, \frac{-189}{3}\right) = \frac{86}{1} = \frac{\lambda_1}{x_1}.$$

$\therefore$ the variable x_1 should be zero

i.e., the vector a1 should be eliminated.

Eliminating α_1 between (2) and (4), we get

$$\frac{44\alpha_2 + 139\alpha_3 + 189\alpha_4}{86} + 2\alpha_2 + \alpha_3 + 3\alpha_4 = b$$

$$\Rightarrow \quad 0.\alpha_1 + \frac{216}{86}\alpha_2 + \frac{225}{86}\alpha_3 + \frac{447}{86}\alpha_4 = b$$

$$\therefore \quad x_1 = 0,\ x_2 = \frac{216}{86},\ x_3 = \frac{225}{86},\ x_4 = \frac{447}{86}$$

is the new feasible solution.

Since the vectors

$$\alpha_2 = \begin{bmatrix} -4 \\ 1 \\ 6 \end{bmatrix},\ \alpha_3 = \begin{bmatrix} 3 \\ 5 \\ -4 \end{bmatrix},\ \alpha_4 = \begin{bmatrix} 1 \\ -3 \\ 2 \end{bmatrix}$$

associated to non-zero variables are L.I. therefore the new feasible solution is the basic feasible solution.

Note: Another feasible solution is

$$x_1 = \frac{25}{139},\ x_2 = \frac{234}{139},$$

$$x_3 = 0,\ x_4 = \frac{228}{139}.$$

Example 10:

Solve the following system of linear equations by using simplex method

$$x_1 - x_3 + 4x_4 = 3$$
$$2x_1 - x_2 = 3$$
$$3x_1 - 2x_2 - x_4 = 1$$
$$x_1, x_2, x_3, x_4 \geq 0.$$

Solution:

Introducing the dummy objective function Z with costs zero to each given variable and cost (–1) to each artificial variable the given equations can be written as a linear programming problem in the following form

$$\text{Max. } Z = 0x_1 + 0x_2 + 0x_3 + 0x_4 - A_1 - A_2 - A_3$$

subject to

$$x_1 - x_3 + 4x_4 + A_1 = 3$$
$$2x_1 - x_2 + A_2 = 3$$
$$3x_1 - 2x_2 - x_4 + A_3 = 1,$$
$$x_1, x_2, x_3, x_4, A_1, A_2, A_3 \geq 0.$$

The starting B.F.S. is

$$x_1 = 0, x_2 = 0, x_3 = 0,$$
$$x_4 = 0, A_1 = 3, A_2 = 3, A_3 = 1.$$

The solution to the problem using simplex algorithm is

B	c_B	c_j / x_B	0 / Y_1	0 / Y_2	0 / Y_3	0 / Y_4	–1 / A_1	–1 / A_2	–1 / A_3	Min. ratio x_B/Y_1
A_1	–1	3	1	0	–1	4	1	0	0	3
A_2	–1	3	2	–1	0	0	0	1	0	3/2
A_3	–1	1	(3)	–2	0	–1	0	0	1	1/3 ←
$Z = c_B x_B = -7$	Δ_j		6 ↑	–3	–1	3	0	0	0 ↓	X_B/Y_4
A_1	–1	8/3	0	2/3	–1	(13/3)	1	0		8/13
A_2	–1	7/3	0	1/3	0	2/3	0	1		7/2
Y_1	0	1/3	1	–2/3	0	–1/3	0	0		Neg.
$Z = c_B x_B = -5$	Δ_j		0	1	–1	5 ↑	0 ↓	0		

Y_4	0	8/13	0	(2/13)	–3/13	1	0	4 ←
A_2	–1	25/13	0	3/13	2/13	0	1	25/3
Y_1	0	7/13	1	–8/13	–1/13	0	0	Neg.
–25/13		Δ_j	1 ↑	3/13	2/13 ↓	0	0	x_B/Y_3
Y_2	0	4	0	1	–3/2	13/2	0	Net.
A_2	–1	1	0	0	(1/2)	–3/2	1	2 ←
Y_1	0	3	1	0	–1	4	0	Neg.
Z= –1		Δ_j	0	0	1/2 ↑	–3/2	0 ↓	
Y_2	0	7	0	1	0	2		
Y_3	0	2	0	0	1	–3		
Y_1	0	5	1	0	0	1		
Z=0	Δ_j	0	0	0	0			

Since all $\Delta_j \leq 0$ therefore the problem has optimal solution given by

$$x_1 = 5, x_2 = 7,$$
$$x_3 = 2, x_4 = 0.$$

Example 11:

Apply simplex method to find the inverse of the matrix $\begin{bmatrix} 4 & 3 \\ 3 & 2 \end{bmatrix}$.

Solution:

Let $A = \begin{bmatrix} 4 & 3 \\ 3 & 2 \end{bmatrix}$ and

$b = \begin{bmatrix} 4 \\ 6 \end{bmatrix}$ be a dummy real vector.

Consider the system of equations

$$A\,x = b \text{ given by } \begin{bmatrix} 4 & 3 \\ 3 & 2 \end{bmatrix}\begin{bmatrix} x_1 \\ x_2 \end{bmatrix} = \begin{bmatrix} 4 \\ 6 \end{bmatrix},$$

$x_1, x_2 \geq 0.$

Introducing the artificial variables x_3, x_4 and the dummy objective function Z, the linear programming problem becomes

$$\text{Max. } Z = 0x_1 + 0x_2 - x_3 - x_4$$

$$\text{s.t.} \quad 4x_1 + 3x_2 + x_3 = 4$$

$$3x_1 + 2x_2 + x_4 = 6,$$

$$x_1, x_2, x_3, x_4 \geq 0.$$

The starting B.F.S. is $x_3 = 4, x_4 = 6$.

B	c_B	c_j / x_B	0 / Y_1	0 / Y_2	–1 / A_1	–1 / A_2	Min. ratio x_B/Y_1
A_1	–1	4	(4)	3	1	0	4/4 = 1 ←
A_2	–1	6	3	2	0	1	6/3 = 2
$Z=c_B$	$x_B= -10$	Δ_j	7 ↑	5	0 ↓	0	
Y_1	0	1	1	3/4	1/4	0	
A_2	–1	3	0	(1/4)	–3/4	1	
$Z=c_B$	$x_B= -3$	Δ_j	0	–1/4 ↑	–7/4	0	

Since all Δ_j's are negative or zero therefore the solution is optimal. But the matrix A is still not converted into the unit matrix. For this introduce Y_2 into the basis and drop A_2. The new simplex table becomes

B	c_B	c_j / x_B	0 / Y_1	0 / Y_2	–1 / A_1	–1 / A_2
Y_1	0	10	1	0	–2	3
Y_2	0	–12	0	1	3	–4
$Z=c_B$	$x_B=0$	Δ_j	0	0	–1	–1

Since the columns of the given matrix A have become the columns of the unit matrix I therefore

$$A^{-1} = \begin{bmatrix} -2 & 3 \\ 3 & -4 \end{bmatrix}.$$

Example 12:

Find the inverse of the matrix

$$B_\alpha = (\beta_1, \beta_2, \alpha)$$

where $\quad B = (\beta_1, \beta_2, \beta_3),$

$$\alpha = \begin{bmatrix} 2 \\ 1 \\ 3 \end{bmatrix} \text{ and } B^{-1} = \begin{bmatrix} 7 & -3 & -3 \\ -1 & 1 & 0 \\ -1 & 0 & 1 \end{bmatrix}.$$

Solution:

We know that $Y = (y_1, y_2, y_3) = B^{-1}\alpha$

$$\therefore \quad Y = \begin{bmatrix} 7 & -3 & -3 \\ -1 & 1 & 0 \\ -1 & 0 & 1 \end{bmatrix} \begin{bmatrix} 2 \\ 1 \\ 3 \end{bmatrix} = \begin{bmatrix} 2 \\ -1 \\ 1 \end{bmatrix}$$

or $\quad y_1 = 2,\ y_2 = -1,\ y_3 = 1.$

$$\text{Now } A_3 = \left(-\frac{y_1}{y_3}, -\frac{y_2}{y_3}, \frac{1}{y_3} \right) = (-2, 1, 1)$$

$$\therefore \quad E = (e_1, e_2, A_3) = \begin{bmatrix} 1 & 0 & -2 \\ 0 & 1 & 1 \\ 0 & 0 & 1 \end{bmatrix}$$

$$\text{Now} \qquad B_\alpha^{-1} = EB^{-1} = \begin{bmatrix} 1 & 0 & -2 \\ 0 & 1 & 1 \\ 0 & 0 & 1 \end{bmatrix} \begin{bmatrix} 7 & -3 & -3 \\ -1 & 1 & 0 \\ -1 & 0 & 1 \end{bmatrix}$$

$$= \begin{bmatrix} 9 & -3 & -5 \\ -2 & 1 & 1 \\ -1 & 0 & 1 \end{bmatrix}.$$

Example 13:

Max. $Z = 2x_1 + 3x_2$

subject to $-x_1 + 2x_2 \leq 4$

$x_1 + x_2 \leq 6$

$x_1 + 3x_2 \leq 9$, x_1, x_2 *are unrestricted.*

Solution:

The given problem is of maximization and all b_i's are positive. We know that the simplex method is applicable if the variables are non-negative. In the given problem x_1 and x_2 are unrestricted (may be +, – or zero). *In such cases we replace all these variables by the difference of two non-negative variables and solve the problem in usual manner.*

$\therefore$ Making the transformation

$$x_1 = x_1' - x_1'' \text{ and } x_2 = x_2' - x_2'$$

such that $x_1', x_2'', x_2', x_2'' \geq 0$.

The given problem becomes

$$\text{Max. } Z = 2(x_1' - x_1'') + 3(x_2' - x_2'')$$

$$\text{s.t. } -(x_1' - x_1'') + 2(x_2' - x_2'') \le 4$$

$$(x_1' - x_1'') + (x_2' - x_2'') \le 6$$

$$(x_1' - x_1'') + 3(x_2' - x_2'') \le 9$$

$$x_1', x_2', x_1'', x_2'' \ge 0.$$

		c_j	2	–2	3	–3	0	0	0	Min. ratio
B	c_B	x_B	Y_1'	Y_1''	Y_2'	Y_2''	Y_3	Y_4	Y_5	x_B/Y_2'
Y_3	0	4	–1	1	(2)	–2	1	0	0	2 ←
Y^4	0	6	1	–1	1	–1	0	1	0	6
Y^5	0	9	1	–1	3	–3	0	0	1	3
$Z=c^B$ =0	x^B	Δ_j	2	–2	3 ↑	–3	0 ↓	0	0	
Y_2'	3	2	–1/2	1/2	1	–1	1/2	0	0	Neg.
y_4	0	4	3/2	–3/2	0	0	–1/2	1	0	8/3
Y_5	0	3	(5/2)	–5/2	0	0	–3/2	0	1	6/5 ←
$Z=c_B$ =6	x_B	Δ_j	7/2 ↑	–7/2	0	0	–3/2	0	0 ↓	xB/Y3
y_2'	3	13/5	0	0	1	–1	1/5	0	1/5	13
Y_4	0	11/5	0	0	0	0	(2/5)	1	–3/5	11/2 ←
Y_1'	2	6/5	1	–1	0	0	–3/5	0	2/5	Neg.
$Z=c_B$ =51/5	x_B	Δ_j	0	0	0	0	3/5 ↑	0 ↓	–7/5	
Y_2'	3	3/2	0	0	1	–1	0	–1/2	1/2	
Y_3	0	11/2	0	0	0	0	1	5/2	–3/2	
Y_1'	2	9/2	1	–1	0	0	0	3/2	–1/2	
$Z=c_B$ =27/2	x_B	Δ_j	0	0	0	0	–3/2	–1/2		

To change constraint inequalities into equations introducing slack variables x_3, x_4 and x_5, the given L.P.P. becomes

$$\text{Max. } Z = 2x_1' - 2x_1'' + 3x_2' - 3x_2'' + 0.x_3 + 0.x_4 + 0.x_5$$

$$-x_1' + x_1'' + 2x_2' - 2x_2'' + x_3 = 4$$
$$x_1' - x_1'' + x_2' - x_2'' + x_4 = 6$$
$$x_1' - x_1'' + 3x_2' - 3x_2'' + x_5 = 9.$$

The starting B.F.S. is $x_3 = 4, x_4 = 6, x_5 = 9$.

The solution to the problem using simplex algorithm is given below:

Since all Δ_j's are negative or zero therefore the solution is optimal.

∴ The optimal solution is

$x_1' = 9/2, x_1'' = 0, x_2' = 3/2, x_2'' = 0,$

Max. Z = 27/2

$\Rightarrow x_1 = x_1' - x_1'' = 9/2,$

$x_2 = x_2' - x_2'' = 3/2,$

Max. Z = 27/2.

Example 14:

Apply Big-M method to solve the problem

$$Max\ Z = -x_1 - x_2$$

subject to

$$3x_1 + 2x_2 \geq 30$$
$$-2x_1 + 3x_2 \leq -30$$
$$x_1 + x_2 \leq 5,$$
$$x_1, x_2 \geq 0.$$

Solution:

The given problem is of maximization.

Since bi in second constraint is negative therefore multiplying both sides by – 1, we et

$$2x_1 - 3x_2 \geq 30.$$

To convert inequalities of constraints into equations, introducing slack, surplus and artificial variables wherever necessary the given problem becomes

$$\text{Max. } Z = -x_1 - x_2 + 0x_3 + 0x_4 + 0x_5 - MA_1 - MA_2$$

subject to

$$3x_1 + 2x_2 - x_3 + A_1 = 30$$
$$2x_1 - 3x_2 - x_4 + A_2 = 30$$
$$x_1 + x_2 + x_5 = 5$$

where $x_1, x_2, x_3, x_4, x_5,$

$A_1, A_2 \geq 0$.

The initial B.F.S. is $x_1 = 0, x_2 = 0, x_3 = 0,$

$x_4 = 0, x_5 = 5, A_1 = 30, A_2 = 30.$

The solution to the problem using simplex method is given below:

B	c_B	c_j / x_B	−1 / Y_1	−1 / Y_2	0 / Y_3	0 / Y_4	0 / Y_5	−M / A_1	−M / A_2	Min. ratio x_B/Y_1
A_1	−M	30	3	2	−1	0	0	1	0	10
A_2	−M	30	2	−3	0	−1	0	0	1	15
Y_5	0	5	(1)	1	0	0	1	0	0	5 ←
$Z=c_B x_B = -60M$		Δ_j	5M−1 ↑	−M	−M	−M	0 ↓	0	0	
A_1	−M	15	0	−1	−1	0	−3	1	0	
A_2	−M	20	0	−5	0	−1	−2	0	1	
Y_1	−1	5	1	1	0	0	1	0	0	
Z=−35 M−5		Δ_j	0	−6M	−M	−M	−5M	0	0	

Since all $\Delta_j \leq 0$ therefore the solution obtained is optimal. But the artificial variables A_1, A_2 appear in the basis at a positive level which implies that *the given L.P.P. has no feasible solution.*

Note: Sometimes the constraints may be inconsistent so that there is no feasible solution to the problem. Such a situation is called ***infeasibility**. In the case of infeasibility one or more artificial variables appear in the final simplex table.*

Two Phase Method. As an alternative to the Big-M method, there is another method for dealing with linear programming problems involving artificial variables. This is called the two-dealing with linear and as its name suggests it separates the solution procedure into two phases. In phase-I, all the he artificial variables are eliminated from the basis. In phase II, we use the solution from phase I as the initial basic feasible solution and use the simplex method to determine the optimal solution.

Example 15:

Solve the following problem by using the two-phase method.

Min. $Z = 40x_1 + 24x_2$

subject to $20x_1 + 50x_2 \geq 4800$

$80x_1 + 50x_2 \geq 7200,\ x_1,\ x_2 \geq 0.$

Solution:

The given problem is of minimization. Converting it to maximization by taking the objective function as

$$Z' = -Z.$$

The objective function becomes

$$\text{Max } Z' = -Z = -40x_1 - 24x_2.$$

To change the inequalities of constraint into equations introducing surplus and artificial variables, we get

$$20x_1 + 50x_2 - x_3 + A_1 = 4800$$
$$80x_1 + 50x_1 - x_4 + A_2 = 7200$$
$$x_1, x_2, x_3, x_4, A_1, A_2 \geq 0,$$

x_3, x_4 are surplus variables and A_1, A_2 are artificial variables.

Phase I. Assigning cost 0 to all other variables and cost –1 to artificial variables, the new objective function of auxiliary problem becomes

$$\text{Max } Z' = 0x_1 + 0x_2 + 0x_3 + 0x_4 - A_1 - A_2$$

subject to the constraints given above.

Now applying the simplex method in the usual manner, we have the following table:

B	c_B	c_j / x_B	0 / Y_1	0 / Y_2	0 / Y_3	0 / Y_4	–1 / A_1	–1 / A_2	Min. ratio x_B/Y_1
A_1	–1	4800	20	50	–1	0	1	0	240
A_2	–1	7200	(80)	50	0	–1	0	1	90 ←
$Z = c_B x_B = -12000$		Δ_j	100 ↑	100	–1	–1	0	0 ↓	
A_1	–1	3000	0	(75/2)	–1	1/4	1	–1/4	80 ←
Y_1	0	90	1	5/8	0	–1/80	0	1/80	144
Z= –2910		Δ_j	0	75/2 ↑	0	1/4	0 ↓	–5/4	
Y_2	0	80	0	1	–2/75	1/50	2/75	–1/50	
Y_1	0	40	1	0	1/60	–1/60	–1/60	–1/60	
Z=0	Δ_j	0	0	0	0	–1	–1		

Since all $\Delta_j \leq 0$ and no artificial variable appears in the basis therefore an optimum solution to the auxiliary problem has been attained.

Phase II. Now assign the actual costs to the original variables and cost zero to the surplus variables, the objective function becomes

$$\text{Max } Z' = -40x_1 - 24x_2 + 0x_3 + 0x_4.$$

Replace the c_j row values in the final simplex table of phase I by the c_j values of the original objective function.

Also delete the artificial variables from the final simplex table of phase I. Now apply the simplex method in the usual manner to this table.

		c_j	–40	–24	0	0	**Min. ratio**
B	c_B	x_B	Y_1	Y_2	Y_3	Y_4	x_B/Y_3
x_2	–24	80	0	1	–2/75	1/50	neg.
x_1	–40	40	1	0	(1/60)	–1/60	2400 ←
$Z'=c_B\ x_B = -3520$		Δ_j	0 ↓	0	2/75 ↑	–38/75	
x_2	–24	144	8/5	1	0	–1/50	
x_3	0	2400	60	0	1	–1	
$Z' = -3456$ Δ_j		–8/5	0	0	–12/25		

Since all Δ_j's are negative or zero therefore the solution obtained is optimal.

Hence the optimal solution is $x_1 = 0$, $x_2 = 144$ and max $Z = -Z' = 3456$.

Example 16:

Apply two phase simplex method to solve

$$\text{Min. } Z = x_1 - 2x_2 - 3x_3$$

subject to $-2x_1 + x_2 + 3x_3 = 2$

$$2x_1 + 3x_2 + 4x_3 = 1,$$

$$x_1, x_2, x_3 \geq 0.$$

Solution:

Converting the objective function to maximization form by substituting $Z = -Z'$, we get

$$\text{Max. } Z' = -x_1 + 2x_2 + 3x_3.$$

Introducing the artificial variables A_1 and A_2, the constraint equations become

$$-2x_1 + x_2 + 3x_3 + A_1 = 2$$
$$2x_1 + 3x_2 + 4x_3 + A_2 = 1$$

where $x_1, x_2, x_3, A_1, A_2 \geq 0$.

The new objective function of auxiliary problem is

$$\text{Max } Z' = 0x_1 + 0x_2 + 0x_3 - A_1 - A_2,$$

subject to the constraints mentioned above.

Now apply simplex method in the usual manner to remove artificial variables.

B	c_B	c_j / x_B	0 / Y_1	0 / Y_2	0 / Y_3	–1 / A_1	–1 / A_2	Min. ratio / x_B/Y_3
A_1	–1	2	–2	1	3	1	0	2/3
A_2	–1	1	2	3	(4)	0	1	1/4 ←
Z'= –3	Δ_j	0	4	7 ↑	0	0 ↓		
A_1	–1	5/4	–7/2	–5/4	0	1	–3/4	
Y_3	0	1/4	1/2	3/4	1	0	1/4	
Z'= –5/4	Δ_j	–7/4	–5/4	0	0	–3/4		

Since all Δ_j's are negative or zero, an optimum basic feasible solution to the auxiliary problem has been attained. But *max Z' is negative and artificial variable A_1 appears in the basic solution at a positive level therefore the original L.P.P. does not possess any feasible solution.*

Example 17(a):

Max. $Z = 10x_1 + 20x_2$

subject to $2x_1 + 4x_2$

$x_1 + 5x_2 \geq 15,$

$x_1, x_2 \geq 0.$

Solution:

The given problem is of maximization and all b_i's are positive.

Introducing surplus variables x_3, x_4 and artificial variables A_1, A_2, the given problem becomes

Max. $Z = 10x_1 + 20x_2 + 0x_3 + 0x_4 - MA_1 - MA_2$

subject to $2x_1 + 4x_2 - x_3 + A_1 = 16$

$x_1 + 5x_2 - x_4 + A_2 = 15,$

$x_1, x_2, x_3, x_4, A_1, A_2, \geq 0.$

The starting B.F.S. is

$x_1 = 0, x_2 = 0, x_3 = 0, x_4 = 0, A_1 = 16, A_2 = 15.$

The final simplex table in respect of this problem is

		c_j	10	20	0	0	–M	–M	Min. ratio
B	c_B	x_B	Y_1	Y_2	Y_3	Y_4	A_1	A_2	
Y_1	10	15	1	5	0	–1	0	1	
Y_3	0	14	0	6	1	–2	–1	2	
Z=150	Δ_j	0	–30	0	10 ↑	–M	–M – 10		

From the table we observe that Y_4 is the incoming vector but we can not find outgoing vector because all min. ratios are negative. Therefore the solution is unbounded.

Note: If in a situation there is at least one Δ_j greater than zero but there is no non-negative ratios or min. ratios $\rightarrow \infty$ then we have unbounded solution.

L.P.P. having more than one optimum solution.

Example 17(b):

Max. $Z = 6x_1 + 4x_2$

subject to $2x_1 + 3x_2 \leq 30$

$3x_1 + 2x_2 \leq 30$

$x_1 + x_2 \geq 3,\ x_1, x_2, \geq 0.$

Solution:

To convert inequalities into equations, introducing slack, surplus and artificial variables, the problem becomes

Max. $Z = 6x_1 + 4x_2 + 0x_3 + 0x_4 + 0x_5 - MA_1$

subject to $2x_1 + 3x_2 + x_3 = 30$

$3x_1 + 2x_2 + x_4 = 24$

$x_1 + x_2 - x_5 + A_1 = 3,$

$x_1, x_2, x_3, x_4, x_5, A_1 \geq 0.$

The starting B.F.S. is $x_1 = 0, x_2 = 0, x_3 = 30, x_4 = 24, x_5 = 0, A_1 = 3$.

The solution to the problem using simplex method is given below:

B	c_B	c_j / x_B	6 / Y_1	4 / Y_2	0 / Y_3	0 / Y_4	0 / Y_5	–M / A_1	Min. ratio x_B/Y_1
Y_3	0	30	2	3	1	0	0	0	15
Y_4	0	24	3	2	0	1	0	0	8
A_1	–M	3	(1)	1	0	0	–1	1	3 ←
$Z = c_B x_B = -3M$		Δ_j	6+M □↑	4+M	0	0	–M	0 ↓	x_B/Y_5
Y_3	0	24	0	1	1	0	2		12
Y_4	0	15	0	–1	0	1	(3)		5 ←
Y_1	6	3	1	1	0	0	–1		–
Z=18		Δ_j	0	–2	0	0 □↓	6 ↑		
Y_3	0	14	0	(5/3)	1	–2/3	0		
Y_5	0	5	0	–1/3	0	1/3	1		
Y_1	6	8	1	2/3	0	1/3	0		
Z=48		Δ_j	0	0	0	–2	0		

Since all $\Delta_j \leq 0$ therefore the solution is optimal. The optimal solution is $x_1 = 8, x_2 = 0$, max $Z = 48$. Again $\Delta_2 = 0$ and Y_2 is not in the basis B therefore an alternative solution also exists. Thus the problem does not have unique solution.

Taking Y_2 as incoming and Y_3 as outgoing vector we obtain the following simplex table:

B	c_B	c_j / x_B	6 / Y_1	4 / Y_2	0 / Y_3	0 / Y_4	0 / Y_5	Min. ratio
Y_2	4	42/5	0	1	3/5	–2/5	0	
Y_5	0	39/5	0	0	1/5	1/5	1	
Y_1	6	12/5	1	0	–2/5	3/5	0	
$Z = c_B x_B \Delta_j$ =48		0	0	0	–2	0		

All $\Delta_j \leq 0$ therefore this solution is also optimal having the same maximum value of Z.

Second optimal solution is

$x_1 = 12/5$, $x_2 = 42/5$ and

max Z = 48.

We know that the convex combination of B.F.S. is also an optimal solution.

Thus if we obtain two alternative optimum solution then we can obtain any number of optimum solutions.

For any arbitrary value of λ the following table gives different optimum solution:

Variables	I Sol.	II Sol.	Gen. Sol.
x_1	8	12/5	$8\lambda + (12/5)(1 - \lambda)$
x_2	0	42/5	$0\lambda + (42/5)(1 - \lambda)$
x_3	14	0	$14\lambda + 0(1 - \lambda)$
x_4	0	0	$0\lambda + (1 - \lambda)$
x_5	5	39/5	$5\lambda + (39/5)(1 - \lambda)$
A_1	0	0	$0\lambda + 0(1 - \lambda)$

Taking a particular value of λ, $\lambda = \frac{1}{2}$ (say),

the third optimal solution is

$x_1 = 26/5$, $x_2 = 21/5$ and Max. Z = 48.

Example 17(c):

maximize $Z = 3x_1 + 5x_2 + 4x_3$

subject to $2x_1 + 3x_2 \leq 8$

$2x_2 + 5x_3 \leq 10$

$3x_1 + 2x_2 + 4x_3 \leq 15,$

$x_1, x_2, x_3 \geq 0.$

Solution:

The given problem is of maximization and all the b_i's are non-negative.

Converting the inequalities of constraints into equations by introducing slack variables x_4, x_5, x_6. Also the coefficients of slack variables are zero in the objective function. Thus the given problem becomes

$$Z = 3x_1 + 5x_2 + 4x_3 + 0x_4 + 0x_5 + 0x_6$$

subject to $2x_1 + 3x_2 + 0x_3 + x_4 = 8$

$0x_1 + 2x_2 + 5x_3 + x_5 = 10$

$3x_1 + 2x_2 + 4x_3 + x_6 = 15.$

The starting basic feasible solution is

$x_1 = 0, x_2 = 0, x_3 = 0, x_4 = 8, x_5 = 10, x_6 = 15$. The solution to the problem using simplex method is given in the following table.

B	c_B	c_j / x_B	3 / Y_1	5 / Y_2	4 / Y_3	0 / Y_4	0 / Y_5	0 / Y_6	Min. ratio / x_B/Y_2
Y_4	0	8	2	(3)	0	1	0	0	8/3
Y_5	0	10	0	2	5	0	1	0	10/2 = 5
									←
Y_6	0	15	3	2	4	0	0	1	15/2
$Z=x_B$	$x_B=0$	Δ_j	3	5	4	0	0	0	x_B/Y_3
				↑			↓		
Y_2	5	8/3	2/3	1	0	1/3	0	0	–
Y_5	0	4/3	–4/3	0	(5)	–2/3	1	0	14/15
								←	
Y_6	0	2/3	5/3	0	4	–2/3	0	1	29/12
$Z=c_B$ =40/3	x_B	Δ_j	–1/3	0	4	–5/3	0	0	x_B/Y_1
				↑		↓			
Y_2	5	8/3	2/3	1	0	1/3	0	0	4
Y_3	4	14/15	–4/15	0	1	–2/15	1/5	0	–
Y_6	1	89/15	(41/15)	0	0	–2/15	–4/5	1	89/41
									←
$Z = c_B\ x_B$ = 256/45		Δ_j	11/15	0	0	–17/15	–4/5	0	
			↑					↓	
Y_2	5	50/41	0	1	0	15/41	8/41	–10/41	
Y_3	4	62/41	0	0	1	–6/41	5/41	4/41	
Y_1	3	89/41	1	0	0	–2/41	–12/41	15/41	
$Z = c_B\ x_B$ = 765/41		Δ_j	0	0	0	–45/41	–24/41	–11/41	

In the last table all Δ_j's for non-basic variables are negative therefore it gives optimal solution.

∴ Optimal solution is

$$x_1 = \frac{89}{41},\ x_2 = \frac{50}{41},\ x_3 = \frac{62}{41}$$

and Max. $Z = \frac{765}{41}$.

Example 18:

Maximize $Z = 3x_1 + 2x_2 + 5x_3$

subject to $x_1 + 2x_2 + x_3 \leq 430$

$$3x_1 + 2x_3 \leq 460$$

$$x_1 + 4x_2 \leq 420,$$

$$x_1, x_2, x_3 \geq 0.$$

olution:

The given problem is of maximization and all the b_i's are non-negative.

Convert the inequalities of constraints into equations by introducing slack ıriables x_4, x_5, x_6.

The given problem becomes

$$Z = 3x_1 + 2x_2 + 5x_3 + 0x_4 + 0x_5 + 0x_6$$

subject to

$$x_1 + 2x_2 + x_3 + x_4 = 430$$

$$3x_1 + 0x_2 + 2x_3 + x_5 = 460$$

$$x_1 + 4x_2 + 0x_3 + x_6 = 420.$$

The initial basic feasible solution is

$$x_1 = 0, x_2 = 0,$$

$$x_3 = 0, x_4 = 430,$$

$$x_5 = 460, x_6 = 420.$$

The solution to the problem using simplex algorithm is given in the ɔwing table:

Since all Δ_j's are negative or zero therefore the solution is optimal.

Hence the optimal solution is

$$x_1 = 0,\ x_2 = 100,\ x_3 = 230 \text{ and max } Z = 1350.$$

B	c_B	c_j / x_B	3 / Y_1	2 / Y_2	5 / Y_3	0 / Y_4	0 / Y_5	0 / Y_6	Min. ratio / x_B/Y_3
Y_4	0	430	1	2	1	1	0	0	430
Y_5	0	460	3	0	(2)	0	1	0	230
									←
Y_6	0	420	1	4	0	0	0	1	–
$Z=c_B$	$x_B=0$	Δ_j	3	2	5	0	0	0	x_B/Y_2
					↑		↓		
Y_4	0	200	–1/2	(2)	0	1	–1/2	0	100
									←
Y_3	5	230	3/2	0	1	0	1/2	0	–
Y_6	0	420	1	4	0	0	0	1	420/4
Z=1150		Δ_j	–9/2	2	0	0	–5/2	0	
				↑		↓			
Y_1	2	100	–1/4	1	0	1/2	–1/4	0	
Y_3	5	230	3/2	0	1	0	1/2	0	
Y_6	0	20	2	0	0	–2	1	1	
Z=1350	Δ_j	–4	0	0	–1	–2	0		

Example 19:

Minimize $Z = x_2 - 3x_3 + 2x_5$

subject to

$$3x_2 - x_3 + 2x_5 \leq 7$$

$$-2x_2 + 4x_3 \leq 12$$

$$-4x_2 + 3x_3 + 8x_5 \leq 10,$$

$$x_2, x_3, x_5 \geq 0.$$

Solution:

The given problem is of minimization. Convert it to maximization problem by taking the objective function as Z' = – Z.

The objective function becomes

$$\text{Max. } Z' = -Z = -x_2 + 3x_3 - 2x_5.$$

To convert the inequalities of constraints into equations introducing slack variables x_1, x_4 and x_6, we get

$$x_1 + 3x_2 - x_3 + 0x_4 + 2x_5 + 0x_6 = 7$$

$$0x_1 - 2x_2 + 4x_3 + x_4 + 0x_5 + 0x_6 = 12$$
$$0x_1 - 4x_2 + 3x_3 + 0x_4 + 8x_5 + x_6 = 10$$

and the objective function becomes

$$\text{Max. } Z' = 0x_1 - x_2 + 3x_3 + 0x_4 - 2x_5 + 0x_6.$$

The starting basic feasible solution is

$x_1 = 7, x_2 = 0,$

$x_3 = 0,$

$x_4 = 12,$

$x_5 = 0, x_6 = 10.$

The solution to the problem using simplex algorithm is given below:

B	c_B	c_j / x_B	0 / Y_1	–1 / Y_2	3 / Y_3	0 / Y_4	–2 / Y_5	0 / Y_6	Min. ratio / x_B/Y_3
Y_1	0	7	1	3	–1	0	2	0	–ive
Y_4	0	12	0	–2	(4)	1	0	0	3 ←
Y_6	0	10	0	–4	3	0	8	1	10/3
$Z'=c_B$	$x_B=0$	Δ_j	0	–1	3 ↑	0 ↓	–2	0	x_B/Y_2
Y_1	0	10	1	(5/2)	0	1/4	2	0	4 ←
Y_3	3	3	0	–1/2	1	1/4	0	0	–ive
Y_6	0	1	0	–5/2	0	–3/4	8	1	–ive
$Z'=9$	Δ_j	0 ↑	1/2 ↓	0	–3/4	--2	0		
Y_2	–1	4	2/5	1	0	1/10	4/5	0	
Y_3	3	5	1/5	0	1	3/10	2/5	0	
Y_6	0	11	1	0	0	–1/2	10	1	
$Z' = 11$	Δ_j	–1/5	0 ↑	0 ↓	–4/5	–12/5	0		

Since all Δ_j's ≤ 0 therefore the solution given by last table is optimal.

Hence the optimal solution is

$$x_2 = 4, x_3 = 5, x_5 = 0$$

and min. $Z = -Z' = -11.$

EXERCISES

Solve the following problems using basic simplex method:

1. State and prove the fundamental theorem of linear programming.
2. Food A contains 20 units of vitamin X and 40 units of vitamin Y per gram. Food B contains 30 units each of vitamin X and Y. The daily minimum human requirements of vitamins X and Y are 900 units and 1200 units respectively. How many grams of each type of food should be consumed so as to minimize the cost if food A costs 60 praise per gram and food B costs 80 praise per gram.

Solve the following L.P.P. using two phase method:

3. Min. $Z = x_1 + x_2$

   subject to

   $2x_1 + x_2 \geq 4$

   $x_1 + 7x_2 \geq 7$

   $x_1, x_2 \geq 0.$

4. Max. $Z = 3x_1 + 2x_2 + x_3 + 4x_4$

   subject to

   $4x_1 + 5x_2 + x_3 + 5x_4 = 5$

   $2x_1 - 3x_2 - 4x_3 + 5x_4 = 7$

   $x_1 + 4x_2 + 5x_3 - 4x_4 = 6$

   $x_1, x_2, x_3, x_4 \geq 0.$

Apply Big-M method to solve the following problems:

5. Min. $Z = 4x_1 + 8x_2 + 3x_3$

   subject to

   $x_1 + x_2 \geq 2$

   $2x_1 + x_3 \geq 5$

   $x_1, x_2, x_3 \geq 0.$

6. Max. $Z = -2x_1 - x_2$

   subject to

   $3x_1 + x_2 = 3$

   $4x_1 + 3x_2 \geq 6$

   $x_1 + 2x_2 \leq 4$

   $x_1, x_2 \geq 0.$

7. *Solve the following problems using basic simplex method:*

(a) Maximize $Z = 3x_1 + 2x_2$

subject to

$x_1 + x_2 \leq 4$

$x_1 - x_2 \leq 2,$

$x_1, x_2 \geq 0.$

(b) Min. $Z = x_1 - 3x_2 + 2x_3$

subject to

$3x_1 - x_2 + 2x_3 \leq 7$

$-2x_1 + 4x_2 \leq 12$

$-4x_1 + 3x_2 + 8x_3 \leq 10$

$x_1, x_2, x_3 \geq 0.$

(c) Max. $Z = 5x_1 + 10x_2 + 8x_3$

subject to

$3x_1 + 5x_2 + 2x_3 \leq 60$

$4x_1 + 4x_2 + 4x_3 \leq 72$

$2x_1 + 4x_2 + 5x_3 \leq 100$

$x_1, x_2, x_3 \geq 0.$

(d) Max. $Z = 2x_1 + 4x_2 + x_3 + x_4$

subject to

$x_1 + 3x_2 + x_4 \leq 4$

$2x_1 + x_2 \leq 3$

$x_2 + 4x_3 + x_4 \leq 3$

$x_1, x_2, x_3, x_4 \geq 0.$

(e) Max. $Z = 5x_1 + 3x_2$

subject to

$3x_1 + 5x_2 \leq 15$

$5x_1 + 2x_2 \leq 10$

$x_1, x_2 \geq 0.$

8. *Solve the following problems using basic simplex method:*

(a) Max. $Z = 7x_1 + 5x_2$

subject to

$-x_1 - 7x_2 \geq -6$

$4x_1 + 3x_2 \leq 12$

$x_1, x_2 \geq 0.$

(b) Max. $Z = 3x_1 + 2x_2$

subject to

$2x_1 + x_2 \leq 40$

$x_1 + x_2 \leq 24$

$2x_1 + 3x_2 \leq 60$

$x_1, x_2 \geq 0.$

(c) Max. $Z = 3x_1 + 5x_2$

subject to

$3x_1 + 2x_2 \leq 18$

$x_1 \leq 4$

$x_2 \leq 6,$

$x_1, x_2 \geq 0.$

(d) Max. $Z = 5x_1 + 3x_2$

subject to

$x_1 + x_2 \leq 2$

$5x_1 + 2x_2 \leq 10$

$3x_1 + 8x_2 \leq 12$

$x_1, x_2 \geq 0.$

9. Max. $Z = 5x_1 + 7x_2$

subject to the constraints

$x_1 + x_2 \leq 4$

$3x_1 - 8x_2 \leq 24$

$10x_1 + 7x_2 \leq 35$

$x_1, x_2 \geq 0.$

10. Max. $Z = 4x_1 + 2x_2$

subject to

$3x_1 + x_2 \leq 27$

$x_1 + x_2 \geq 21$

$x_1, x_2 \geq 0.$

11. Min. $Z = 2y_1 + 3y_2$

    subject to

    $y_1 + y_2 \geq 5$

    $y_1 + 2y_2 \geq 6$

    $y_1, y_2 \geq 0.$

12. Min. $Z = 4x_1 + 8x_2 + 3x_3$

    subject to

    $x_1 + x_2 \geq 2$

    $2x_1 + x_3 \geq 5$

    $x_1, x_2, x_3 \geq 0.$

13. $3x_1 + 2x_2 = 4, 4x_1 - y_2 = 6.$
14. $x_1 + x_2 = 1, 2x_1 + x_2 = 3.$
15. Prove that if the system A x = b of m linear equation in n unknowns (m ≤ n) with rank A = m has a feasible solution, then it has a basic feasible solution also.
16. Max. $Z = x_1 - x_2 + 3x_3$

    subject to

    $x_1 + x_2 + x_3 \leq 10$

    $2x_1 - x_3 \leq 2$

    $2x_1 - 2x_2 + 3x_3 \leq 0$

    $x_1, x_2, x_3 \geq 0.$

17. Max. $Z = 4x_1 + 10x_2$

    subject to

    $2x_1 + x_2 \leq 50$

    $2x_1 + 5x_2 \leq 100$

    $2x_1 + 3x_2 \leq 90$

    $x_1, x_2 \geq 0.$

18. Max. $Z = x_1 - 2 + 3x_3$

    subject to

    $x_1 + x_2 + x_3 \leq 10$

    $2x_1 - x_3 \leq 2$

    $2x_1 - 2x_2 + 3x_3 \leq 0$

$x_1, x_2, x_3 \geq 0.$

19. If $x_1 = 2$, $x_2 = 4$ and $x_3 = 1$ be a F.S. to the system of equations

$$2x_1 - x_2 + 2x_3 = 2,$$
$$x_2 + 4x_2 = 18,$$

then find two basic feasible solutions.

20. The company produces two types of products say type A and B. Product B is of superior quality and product A is of a lower quality. Profits on the two types of products are Rs. 30 and 40 respectively. The data on resources required and capacity available is given below:

	Requirements		
	Product A	*Product B*	*Capacity available per method*
Raw materials (kg)	60	120	12000
Machining (hours per piece)	8	5	600
Assembly (man hour)	3	4	500

How should the company manufacture the two type of product in order to have a maximum overall profit ?

21. Max. $Z = 3x_1 + 4x_2$

subject to

$$x_1 - x_2 \leq 1$$
$$-x_1 + x_2 \leq 2$$
$$x_1, x_2 \geq 0.$$

22. Max. $Z = 2x_1 + 4x_2$

subject to

$$2x_1 + 3x_2 \leq 48$$
$$x_1 + 3x_2 \leq 42$$
$$x_1 + x_2 \leq 21$$
$$x_1, x_2 \geq 0.$$

23. Max. $Z = 2x_1 + x_2$

subject to

$$x_1 + 2x_2 \leq 10$$
$$x_1 + x_2 \leq 6$$
$$x_1 - x_2 \leq 2$$

1

$x_1 - 2x_2 \leq 1$

$x_1, x_2 \geq 0.$

24. Max. $Z = 4x_1 + 5x_2 + 9x_3 + 11x_4$

subject to the constraints

$x_1 + x_2 + x_3 + x_4 \leq 15$

$7x_1 + 5x_2 + 3x_3 + 2x_4 \leq 120$

$3x_1 + 5x_2 + 10x_3 + 15x_4 \leq 100$

$x_1, x_2, x_3, x_4 \geq 0.$

25. Max. $Z = 8x_1 + 11x_2$

subject to

$3x_1 + x_2 \leq 7$

$x_1 + 3x_2 \leq 8$

$x_1, x_2 \geq 0.$

26. (2, 1, 3) is a feasible solution of the set of equations

$4x_1 + 2x_2 - 3x_3 = 1,$

$6x_1 + 4x_2 - 5x_3 = 1.$

Reduce the feasible solution to a b.f.s. of the set.

27. $x_1 = 1, x_2 = 1, x_3 = 1, x_4 = 0$ is a feasible solution to the system of equations

$x_1 + 2x_2 + 4x_3 + x_4 = 7,$

$2x_1 - x_2 + 3x_3 - 2x_4 = 4.$

Reduce the feasible solution to two different basic feasible solutions.

28. If $x_3 = 4, x_4 = 8$ is the non-degenerate basic feasible solution to the L.P.P.

Max. $Z = x_1 + 2x_2,$

s.t. $x_1 + 2x_2 + x_3 = 4,$

$x_1 + 4x_2 + x_4 = 8,$

$x_1, x_2, x_3, x_4 \geq 0$

then obtain the new b.f.s.

29. Show that $x_1 = 4, x_2 = 0, x_3 = 0, x_4 = 4$ is optimal basic feasible solution to the L.P.P.

Max. $Z = x_1 + 2x_2$

s.t. $x_1 + 2x_2 + x_3 = 4,$

$x_1 + 4x_2 + x_4 = 8,$

$x_1, x_2, x_3, x_4 \geq 0.$

30. Show that if a linear programming problem has a feasible solution, it also has a basic feasible solution.

31. Minimize $Z = x_1 + x_2 + 3x_3$

subject to

$3x_1 + 2x_2 + x_3 \leq 3$

$2x_1 + x_2 + 2x_3 \leq 2$

$x_1, x_2, x_3 \geq 0.$

32. Max. $Z = 2x_1 + 4x_2 + 3x_3$

subject to

$3x_1 + 4x_2 + 2x_3 \leq 60$

$2x_1 + x_2 + 2x_3 \leq 40$

$x_1 + 3x_2 + 2x_3 \leq 80$

$x_1, x_2, x_3 \geq 0.$

33. Max. $Z = 5x_1 + 2x_2 + 3x_3 - x_4 + x_5$

subject to the constraints

$x_1 + 2x_2 + 2x_3 + x_4 = 8$, $3x_1 + 4x_2 + x_3 + x_5 = 7$, $x_1, x_2, x_3, x_4, x_5 \geq 0.$

34. Max. $Z = 3x_1 - x_2$

subject to

$2x_2 + x_2 \geq 2$

$x_1 + 3x_2 \leq 3$

$x_2 \leq 4$

$x_1, x_2 \geq 0.$

35. Max. $Z = 8x_2$

subject to

$x_1 - x_2 \geq 0$

$2x_1 + 3x_2 \leq -6$

x_1, x_2 are unrestricted.

36. Max. $Z = 4x_1 + 5x_2 - 2x_3$

subject to

$x_1 + x_2 + x_3 = 10$
$x_1 - x_2 \geq 11$
$2x_1 + 3x_2 + x_3 \leq 40$
$x_1, x_2, x_3 \geq 0.$

37. Max. $Z = 3x_1 - x_2$

subject to

$2x_1 + x_2 \geq 2$
$x_1 + 3x_2 \leq 2$
$x_2 \leq 4$
$x_1, x_2 \geq 0.$

38. Max. $Z = 5x_1 + 8x_2$

subject to

$3x_1 + 2x_2 \geq 3$
$x_1 + 4x_2 \geq 4$
$x_1 + x_2 \leq 5$
$x_1, x_2 \geq 0.$

39. Max. $Z = 5x_1 - 2x_2 + 3x_3$

subject to

$2x_1 + 2x_2 - x_3 \geq 2$
$3x_1 - 4x_2 \leq 3$
$x_2 + 3x_3 \leq 5$
$x_1, x_2, x_3 \geq 0.$

40. Min. $Z = 5x_1 + 6x_2$

subject to

$2x_1 + 5x_2 \geq 1500$
$3x_1 + x_2 \geq 1200$
$x_1, x_2 \geq 0.$

41. Min. $Z = x_1 + x_2 + 3x_3$

subject to

$3x_1 + 2x_2 + x_3 \leq 3$
$2x_1 + x_2 + 2x_3 \geq 3$
$x_1, x_2, x_3 \geq 0.$

42. Max. $Z = 2x_1 + 4x_2 + x_3 + x_4$

subject to

$x_1 + 3x_2 + x_4 \leq 4$

$2x_1 + x_2 \leq 3$

$x_2 + 4x_3 + x_4 \leq 3$

$x_1, x_2, x_3, x_4 \geq 0.$

43. Max. $Z = 3x_1 + 2x_2 - 2x_3$

subject to

$x_1 + 2x_2 + 2x_3 \leq 10$

$2x_1 + 4x_2 + 3x_3 \leq 15$

$x_1, x_2, x_3 \geq 0.$

44. Max. $Z = 7x_1 + x_2 + 2x_3$

subject to

$x_1 + x_2 - 7x_3 \leq 10$

$4x_1 + x_2 + x_3 \leq 20$

$x_1, x_2, x_3 \geq 0.$

45. A finished product must weigh exactly 150 gms. The two raw materials used in manufacturing the product are : A with cost of Rs. 2 per unit and B with a cost of Rs. 8 per unit. At least 14 units of B and not moire than 20 units of A must be used. Each unit of A and B weighs 5 and 10 grams respectively. How much of each type of raw material should be used for each unit of the final product in order to minimize the cost ?